THE TRUTH ABOUT CHINA

'A compelling, clear-eyed yet colourful tale of a changing China and the rise and fall of Australia's relationship with this newly assertive superpower. A riveting read of modern China from a young Australian living on the inside.'—**Fran Kelly**

Bill Birtles was the ABC's China correspondent in Beijing from 2015 to 2020, his posting coming to a sudden end when he was rushed out of the country by Australian diplomats in an unprecedented diplomatic standoff. Reporting from both major cities and remote provinces throughout the mainland, Hong Kong and Taiwan, he covered an era-defining period of change, upheaval and diplomatic tension as China asserted itself on the world stage. Originally from Sydney, Birtles first studied Mandarin in the Chinese capital and later worked inside the government's most important state media and propaganda organ, the Xinhua newsagency, before returning to Beijing for the ABC. He is now covering South-East Asia as the ABC's Indonesia Bureau Chief, based in Jakarta.

THE TRUTH
ABOUT CHINA

PROPAGANDA, PATRIOTISM
AND THE SEARCH FOR ANSWERS

BILL BIRTLES

ALLEN&UNWIN
SYDNEY•MELBOURNE•AUCKLAND•LONDON

First published in 2021

Allen & Unwin
83 Alexander Street
Crows Nest NSW 2065
Australia
Phone: (61 2) 8425 0100
Email: info@allenandunwin.com
Web: www.allenandunwin.com

A catalogue record for this
book is available from the
National Library of Australia

ISBN 978 1 76087 986 0

Set in 12.75/17 pt Adobe Garamond by Midland Typesetters, Australia
Printed and bound in Australia by Griffin Press, part of Ovato

10 9 8 7 6 5 4 3 2

The paper in this book is FSC® certified.
FSC® promotes environmentally responsible,
socially beneficial and economically viable
management of the world's forests.

For Casper
I hope you live a big life

CONTENTS

1

AN UNEXPECTED PHONE CALL

At about half past five in the afternoon on 31 August 2020, I received the call that changed everything. I was in my office, furiously tapping out a big story that would erupt across the screens of Australian news outlets, when my phone rang.

It was one of the managers from International News back in Sydney. His tone serious, he told me that DFAT—the Department of Foreign Affairs and Trade—had just called the ABC.

And two other media outlets.

'Fuck, fuck, fuck!'

I banged the phone on my desk, my two colleagues outside my office wondering what on earth was going on.

'I'm just about to file this and they must be ringing up all the media to leak it,' I exclaimed down the phone. It was a major scoop exposing just how dire the situation had become in China, and I'd had it on my own.

The manager was confused. He wasn't ringing about that or any other story. 'I'm calling to tell you the Australian government wants to get you out of China,' he said.

We were talking about the same topic and didn't even realise it.

———

Hours before, I'd stumbled upon what appeared to be a massive escalation in China's aggression towards Australia. Although I felt like the last person in Beijing to know about it, the story somehow hadn't been reported.

On a quiet street surrounded by embassies, I met a contact who for two weeks had fended off questions and rumours about someone close to him being in trouble. He confirmed that Cheng Lei, a Chinese-Australian TV anchor well known to Australians in Beijing, had been taken from her apartment and detained by state security police.

Lei, a mother of a ten-year-old girl and eight-year-old boy, was sociable, down to earth and irreverently funny. Well-liked and respected, she didn't feel the need to defend the more egregious propaganda editorial lines of her employer, CGTN, China's government mouthpiece television network. As an anchor and business reporter, she was a step removed from CGTN's more political roles, and she had no problem taking the piss out of her situation as an Australian fronting China's highly nationalistic voice.

I knew her personally but not particularly well. A few years earlier we'd jointly hosted a gala event for the Australian business chamber, and more recently I'd spoken to her at a few social events, but I wasn't aware that her close friends and colleagues had been harbouring increasing concerns for her welfare.

My first inkling of a major diplomatic crisis had come from an unlikely source. Zoe Daniel, the former ABC Washington bureau chief and a colleague I hadn't had much to do with, messaged me out of the blue to ask if I knew Cheng Lei.

'Yes, why?'

Journalists from CGTN's Washington bureau had told Zoe that they couldn't reach Cheng Lei, and her WeChat moments feed had gone silent—a stark contrast to the regular work-related updates and pictures of her kids. Her last post from 13 August was about the opening of Shake Shack in Beijing—about two weeks earlier. I didn't look at WeChat posts much, but her friends who did knew the silence online was uncharacteristic. Zoe wanted to know if I knew anything.

Her inquiry surprised me. 'I doubt Cheng Lei's in trouble,' I said. Everyone always assumed the worst in China when often there was an innocuous explanation. I remembered a joke message I'd sent to Lei on WeChat almost two weeks earlier that went unanswered, but I didn't think much of it at the time.

But it was very weird, so I went straight to a close friend of Cheng Lei's who would know if anything was wrong. The friend, known for being direct and honest, told me that Cheng Lei had gone back to Australia due to 'a pretty serious personal crisis', which explained why her employer was hushing up her sudden departure.

In one of my poorer moments of journalistic judgement, I bought the story. In hindsight it had some pretty big holes in it. Suddenly flying from China to Australia during the Covid pandemic wasn't easy—there weren't even direct flights from Beijing. But my contact was known for not bullshitting, and would know better than anyone else if anything was happening.

I messaged Zoe to tell her what I'd been told, joking, 'Glad she hasn't been taken by the Chinese cops.'

Those nonchalant words were still on my message screen five days later when Zoe texted again. Her contacts at CGTN in Washington had noticed what I failed to check. Not only had Cheng Lei gone mute, but also her presence on CGTN's website and social-media accounts had been meticulously purged. Page by page, video after video, anyone looking for this star of the network received a 404 error message.

I went back to my contact, who, face to face over a flat white, confessed that the concerns about Cheng Lei were real, and the window for her arrest to be quietly worked out behind closed doors had closed.

Cheng Lei, he said, had been taken from her apartment, her computer and devices had been seized, and Australian diplomats had already held their first consular visit with her over video chat. She was being held in Beijing under the dreaded 'residential surveillance at a designated location', an Orwellian legal procedure unique to China that seeks to mask enforced disappearance as something akin to house arrest. It means you've been physically arrested and detained by police, usually at a prison-like facility, and denied access to lawyers and family. Officially you haven't even been formally arrested, let alone charged. Investigators can shut off detained suspects from the outside world and interrogate them for six months while they build a case. It's an unimaginably powerful legal tool for authorities to use and abuse.

Being held in 'RSDL' could only mean one thing: Cheng Lei was being investigated for national security crimes. My contact told me Lei had given permission during that once-a-month

4

virtual visit for the Foreign Affairs Minister Marise Payne to issue a statement publicising the case and asked me if I would hold off breaking the news until then.

No one could imagine Cheng Lei doing anything that would genuinely harm China's national security. Politics was at play.

———

Back at the office, I had my story ready to go. I'd asked the ABC cameraman Steve Wang to stay back and prepare for a late night of broadcast coverage.

Cheng Lei wasn't known to audiences in Australia, but she was an unusually high-profile Australian for China to target. It wasn't just her presence as a face of a Chinese government news channel, but also her close ties to the Australian community in Beijing. She was a regular emcee at embassy and business chamber events. She was a promotional 'ambassador' for Australian education. She spoke at International Women's Day events. Few visiting politicians or international business bigwigs would get through a China visit without sitting down to be interviewed by her. There really wasn't anyone I could think of who better epitomised the idea of Australia–China engagement than Cheng Lei.

Australia's relations with China were worsening by the week as Beijing slapped bans on various Australian exports in apparent retaliation for Australia's hardening stance towards its biggest trading partner. Cheng Lei's arrest would send a shock-wave through Australia's political and business community.

I was waiting on a response from the Foreign Minister's office when the manager from ABC International, back at home, told me DFAT had rung him instead.

'They want you to prepare to leave China as soon as possible.'

His words made no sense. I had a big story ready to break, and whatever it was about, Cheng Lei's detention had absolutely nothing to do with me.

In typical DFAT style, the officials hadn't given my bosses in Australia any clear reason for the warning, but they'd also called the *Australian Financial Review* to warn their correspondent Mike Smith to get out too.

The manager had no idea about the Cheng case and, after hearing me explain it, he told me I should have immediately notified HQ when I learnt the details hours earlier.

'It hadn't occurred to me that the sudden detention of an Australian Chinese state-media employee would have any bearing on my safety,' I said. No foreign journalist had been detained by state security police before and Cheng's case didn't change that.

He maintained that DFAT's advice had been delivered as a matter of urgency.

Perplexed, I was thinking someone had overreacted, and it would quickly be sorted out. For five years I'd watched the relationship between Australia and China unravel little by little, but surely it hadn't reached a point where Australian journalists needed to flee the country. I felt safe, as did my partner and my colleagues.

And yet the wheels for my departure were already in motion.

———

The next morning I rode a bike to a cafe for a hastily arranged meeting. It was a brilliant late summer's day and the streets around the Workers' Stadium area were buzzing with young office workers carrying little plastic bags of egg pancakes and milk tea, DiDi hire car drivers jostling for road space and a constant flow of people on share bikes.

I had slept relatively well despite breaking the news to my partner, Yinan, that the Australian government wanted us to pack up our lives and evacuate from her country with immediate effect.

'What's the actual reason?' she asked me.

I couldn't tell her. The ABC bosses couldn't tell me. DFAT wouldn't tell them.

We'd spent the evening talking in circles about what was likely going on, punctuated by calls to close friends. The most likely speculation was that the Australian authorities were planning to take some sort of investigative action against Chinese state-media journalists in Australia and they wanted me and Mike Smith out before they started.

Perversely, Yinan and I took some comfort from how sudden and unexplained it was. Before we went to sleep, we convinced ourselves that it must be a misunderstanding that could be untangled on a new day.

By coincidence, Mike Smith was also in Beijing that morning. As the one Australian media correspondent lucky enough to be based in far more cosmopolitan Shanghai, his visits to the capital were few and far between. I'd first met Mike at the headquarters of Huawei in Shenzhen during a reporting trip and we'd later crossed paths in Hong Kong and Shanghai. I'd seen him in Beijing for work, but usually those living in the capital would head to Shanghai for weekend breaks rather than the other way around. Shanghai lacked Beijing's excessively dry air, political conservatism and brutalist Soviet architecture; it was the sort of metropolis you actually wanted to live in.

Mike too had received an unexpected call from his bosses the afternoon before, prompting him to cancel a reporting assignment in the city of Tianjin not long after he'd landed. Tianjin is about 30 minutes from Beijing via high-speed rail, so he came to the capital and teed up a meeting at the embassy to discuss what the heck was going on.

As I rode a share bike towards the cafe where we'd arranged to meet, he messaged to say he was hopelessly lost. While he was only a block away, in Beijing that could mean kilometres. The city's Soviet-style layout meant huge roads and massive blocks with much smaller roads connecting compounds within. Mike was near the embassy of Canada, the country most similar to Australia in feeling the diplomatic wrath of China in recent years.

Once I found him, we walked towards Lily's American Diner, a cafe that would be outdated by Australian standards but was one of the few places where you could guarantee a decent Western breakfast in central Beijing.

We'd also invited Stephen McDonnell, a good friend and a man with a longer lens on China than most reporters. He'd been there for fifteen years, initially with the ABC and then with the BBC. If you were going to bounce speculation off anyone about strange happenings in Chinese diplomacy, Stephen was a good sounding board.

We left our phones in a bag inside the cafe in case they were bugged, and sat on a terrace outside. In a slightly comical touch, a waiter appeared with an iPad-style menu that constantly foiled our efforts to order. In China's race to become a technological superpower, everyone latched on to 'smart' devices, but this meant the waiter was unable to take our coffee orders verbally and insisted that we keep tapping on the 'complete order' button until it worked.

Order finally placed, we bounced a few ideas around. Stephen had requested to come along for the embassy briefing, figuring any safety warnings must surely apply to all Australians working in the media there. But the embassy had shut him out, telling him this briefing was only for Mike and me. This made us all the more curious.

———

By the time Mike and I arrived at the embassy, we had talked ourselves into thinking it was probably a precautionary warning. They clearly thought we were in danger, but I wasn't sure how much. Only a month or so before, the Australian government had updated its travel warnings to China to advise that foreigners may be at an increased risk of arbitrary detention. To friends and family, it sounded quite alarming, but on the ground, life went on as normal.

I felt more hopeful as we entered the building, in a prime position on a major road in Dongzhimen, a diplomatic quarter just north of the city's premier night-life district Sanlitun.

The embassy was a relatively stylish understated 1990s building, reminding me of Australia's Parliament House, far nicer than the brown brick bunkers of the neighbouring Canadian and German embassies. We'd been there many times over the years for events and dinners, and even to cast ballots in Australian elections. But as we scanned our coronavirus tracking health codes and went through the security arrangements at the gates, our usual lighthearted banter wasn't going down well with the staffer sent to meet us.

'We're still having that dinner event later this week, right?' I asked.

'We'll see,' she tersely deflected.

It was most abnormal.

We were taken to the ambassador's office—a first for us—and the solemn tone of the briefing sapped my optimism immediately. Everyone present was dead serious. We were told in no uncertain terms that we were in danger of being detained by the Chinese police, and we should make arrangements to get on a flight out of China as soon as possible.

We weren't told exactly why, but it appeared to be linked to Cheng Lei's case.

'How do you know this?' we asked.

They wouldn't say.

'How long do we have?' Mike Smith asked.

A senior diplomat looked at his watch. 'Well, it's 11 am now . . .'

A chill went through me.

They were talking hours, not days.

Once we flew out, they told us, 'You will not be coming back.'

'Shit, it's over,' I thought, tears starting to well in my eyes as the reality dawned. It wasn't that I was worried—I still thought it highly unlikely a journalist for foreign media would be detained—it was the drilled-in certainty of the message. Just like that, my time in China was to finish.

With the briefing nearly wrapped up and having received assurances that Yinan would very likely be granted an exemption to enter Australia, I told them what was really rattling me.

'My partner's pregnant,' I blurted out.

One of the embassy employees broke into a tight smile, exclaiming 'Congratulations', the most bittersweet of expressions glinting in her eyes.

———

Yinan was at work, standing by for my call.

'It's bad news,' I started off.

I told her the embassy was steadfast in wanting us out but had resolutely declined to tell us why.

She took it pretty stoically. She'd called Beijing home for twenty years after a childhood spent between Tibet, eastern Zhejiang province and the southern central city of Changsha. She had studied in the United Kingdom, then returned to China and built a career in media; she was well aware of the precarious fortunes of foreign journalists in China.

While we planned to leave China together at the end of my posting, it was always somewhere in the future. The end date of my assignment was always being pushed out. Originally I'd arrived in China intending to work for three years, but it had turned into four, then four and a half, then five. Once coronavirus sowed disruption deep into 2020, the countdown was reset again. Vague extensions of six months turned into nine, and recently we'd been thinking I would be there until at least mid-2021.

Having met in Beijing, partly as the result of a mutual friend's efforts to set us up, our relationship blossomed, and Yinan and I had begun to talk of moving to Jakarta for my next posting. We'd discussed trying for a baby there, continuing a recent tradition of ABC correspondents with young children rotating through the Indonesian capital. But circumstances brought those plans forward. Never waste a crisis, they say; Beijing was a far better place for a Chinese mother to have a child than the expat hospitals of Jakarta.

We'd only found out a few weeks earlier. Things had moved fast that summer, and we'd found a good private hospital and an obstetrician Yinan trusted. But as the walls moved in on our departure, we were still digesting the news that she was pregnant. Upping stumps at ten weeks and moving to Australia with a few days' notice was not in our plan.

Amid calls to HQ and long discussions with my shell-shocked Chinese colleagues, we still thought it was inconceivable that China would pick a massive diplomatic fight with another country by arbitrarily detaining a journalist. Businesspeople, sure. Analysts and think tankers, okay. But nothing blows up an international media storm like targeting one of the media's own. It seemed like a step too far to me, perhaps based on rising paranoia in Australia about the safety of foreigners in China. People abroad always thought things were much scarier in China than they really were. What threw me, though, was the urgency of the diplomats in Beijing. They live it, they get it. And they wanted me out.

I continued to ponder all of this as I rushed to the Foreign Ministry that afternoon to continue covering the Cheng Lei story, which I'd broken the night before. It was dominating political news and I was still up to my neck in covering it. The Foreign Ministry spokeswoman, Hua Chunying, gave the sort of answer I'd come to expect.

'I don't have any specific information, China is a country of rule of law,' she read in answer to a Dorothy Dixer question from a Beijing-controlled Hong Kong media outlet. 'If you want more information I can ask competent authorities. I have nothing to offer here.'

It's the sort of answer that would be extraordinarily secretive by Australian standards, but reflected the Foreign Ministry's lowly position in the Chinese power structure. Investigations instigated by the secretive and powerful Ministry of State Security usually elicited these sorts of Foreign Ministry responses. Outsiders commonly assume that China's government operates with one voice, but the spokesperson's vague answers reflected that the Foreign Ministry quite often had no idea what was going on.

2

A RUSHED FAREWELL

Twenty-four hours after the briefing at the embassy, I still refused to believe we would be forced to go.

The earliest flight from China to Australia we could find was on Friday, two days away. Covid-related quarantines and border bans were complicating flights and transfer options. I hoped the few days we would wait might help clarify what was going on and lead to us staying. The warnings we would be arrested were jump-starting my managers into action back in Australia, but they were also becoming aware of the long-term impact on the ABC.

The implications for news coverage were serious. If I left China in the middle of the pandemic, neither I nor anyone from the ABC would be back anytime soon. As I explained to head office, Beijing would interpret the flight of the Australian media based on government safety advice as a highly political act.

Vague regulations governing foreign media stipulated that a bureau's registration would be cancelled if an organisation went more than ten months without an accredited foreign journalist. Given that the incoming *Sydney Morning Herald/The Age* correspondent Eryk Bagshaw had already been left waiting almost a year for a visa, it looked pretty unlikely the ABC would be granted any fast-tracking favours after I left. DFAT was effectively telling the ABC and other organisations that they had to shut down their operations in China, for an indefinite period, after 46 years. Without explaining why we were at such dire risk.

It seemed a bit rich that the journalists sent to pick through the Chinese government's opaqueness were expected to comply unquestioningly with opaque decisions made by our own. But that was the feeling of a phone call I received that morning from a very senior diplomat.

I said that the ABC was still waiting on more information back in Australia before making any moves to rush us out.

'I would have expected you to have booked flights already,' he said.

Again the urgency and certainty in his voice hit me.

The diplomat told me there was a China Eastern flight from the eastern city of Hangzhou to Sydney the next evening. If we booked a connecting ticket out of Beijing, we could fly out mid-morning. The embassy would make arrangements to ensure we were placed on a 'do not bump' list. They also gave me clear instructions on how to apply for Yinan's entry exemption.

'What did he say?' Yinan asked me, an anxious look on her face.

Sitting at the dining table with her in our small apartment, it all proved too much. I broke down in tears and told her we had to go.

The posting was over . . . for both of us . . . and we didn't even know why exactly.

We booked the flights for the next day, looked around at all the stuff in the apartment—including an elaborate tank of tropical fish and two cats we'd adopted—and snapped into action. We had a day to pack up our lives and get out.

———

I'd been to many farewells during my posting for ABC staff, but none like this. I was packing up my office, having a scotch on the balcony, and saying rushed goodbyes, all at once.

The local staff—two producers, one cameraman, an office manager and a driver—weren't sharing the sudden safety concerns that had gripped the ABC. They were more worried about their jobs. They could see the writing on the wall in a country where 'news assistants' are not legally allowed to do any reporting without an accompanying foreign journalist. And even though in reality all 'assistants' do plenty of journalism themselves, it wouldn't work for television to send them out to film and interview people independently, with ever-present security guards and police pouncing on anyone with a camera to check their credentials.

We'd spent five years working closely together, travelling for epic assignments in far-flung parts of the country and even abroad. We should have been having a proper farewell, but there was just disbelief at how rapidly things were moving.

I wanted to linger but the afternoon involved bank runs and going back and forth to our apartment to tie up loose ends. Yinan had hastily gathered together a small group of friends and colleagues and called her parents, who were on holiday in a beachside town three hours away, to ask them to rush back to Beijing. She didn't want to say why on the phone, given that the call might be monitored, but her tone made it clear that the vague unease her parents had always held about my job was warranted.

As evening approached, the apartment looked like a halfway house. Clothes and documents were scattered everywhere, while more than a dozen people squeezed in. With the late afternoon sun retreating through the window over the mountains to the west, emotion sat heavy in the air.

For me, the situation wasn't completely unexpected. Sudden change was part of my job. Two Australian correspondents for US media, both of whom I knew well, had been run out of China earlier in the year due to politics. I'd been to farewells for both. One, Phil Wen, was a good mate who had gone from Australian newspapers to securing a dream job at the apex of serious journalism, *The Wall Street Journal*. His first story was a scoop revealing the cousin of Communist Party leader Xi Jinping had gambled around 100 million dollars through Melbourne's Crown casino. The other, Chris Buckley of *The New York Times*, had somehow obtained 400 pages of internal Chinese government documents revealing the detailed inner workings of a mass incarceration program of ethnic minority Uighurs in China's far west. Both men knew why they were getting kicked out. Watching those other expulsions earlier in the year had taught me not to take anything for granted. Journalism in China always carried the risk of a sudden departure.

But for Yinan it was devastating. Her colleagues from a theatre company she had set up after quitting the foreign media were all there. They were far more than colleagues, they were

Yinan's tight-knit circle of friends, some with young children, who had built a small creative start-up around an unusual passion for teaching Western children's theatre in China. They worked together, went on family outings together, and shared a bond with Yinan forged through long days and nights on the stage. They looked devastated.

Yinan's close friends and former colleagues from her days working as a journalist for the German media were also there, as were my closest friends in Beijing.

We ordered a food delivery in a distinctively Chinese style. Haidilao, a massively popular hotpot chain, delivered the full experience to the door: two massive pots, an electric hotplate to boil them on, plus huge amounts of sliced beef, seafood, vegetables and all the accompaniments you would normally get in the restaurant. Cardboard bowls and disposable chopsticks mimicked the dine-in feeling.

As the pots began to bubble with their mixture of spice and oil, our guests dunked their fishballs and slices of beef. The aroma of boiling meat and chilli oil added another layer to the drama. Young children belonging to Yinan's friends made a beeline for the hot pots, oblivious to why the adults all looked shocked. Drinks were flowing freely as I tried to get rid of whatever wine or whiskey was left in the cupboard.

But I wasn't partaking much. Each time another friend arrived, I had to explain the whole situation again. The unanswered questions. The urgency. The doubts. The upheaval.

When Yinan's parents arrived, dressed in holiday hiking gear, I had to go through it all again . . . in Mandarin.

It probably would have been pretty hard in English, but it was particularly daunting using Chinese to tell your future in-laws that you're taking their only child, pregnant with their first grandchild, away from them to a far-away country in the middle of a global pandemic due to concerns harboured by a foreign government that I was about to be arrested for reasons that were political and nothing to with me personally.

All things considered, they took it pretty well.

'It's to do with China–Australia relations,' Yinan's mum nodded.

'Because Australia's been doing things to upset the relationship,' she surmised, well versed in the news from the Chinese perspective.

'So I'm glad it doesn't sound personal,' she said.

More than anything they looked exhausted and overwhelmed.

Complicating matters were the constant calls back and forth to my bosses. Even though we'd arranged a flight out the next morning, we still weren't 100 per cent certain we'd be getting on the plane. DFAT's unwillingness to spell out the reasons for its safety advice was rubbing everyone up the wrong way. The ABC's management was asking questions back in Australia too and wasn't getting any clear answers, even from the highest levels.

As the hotpot boiled and drinks flowed, I took a call from David Anderson, the ABC's managing director. He asked for my assessment.

'I feel safe, Yinan feels safe and if it's up to us, we don't want to leave,' I told him. He congratulated me on the pregnancy news, passing on ABC Chair Ita Buttrose's best wishes too. I'd never met the legendary Ita, but she was now one of the first to know we were expecting. That idea of not telling anyone until twelve weeks had gone out the window. Most likely the Foreign Minister now knew. Surreal.

The Australian authorities were due to give a fresh briefing the next morning to the ABC, hopefully one that shed some light.

Management felt some solid justifications were needed before shutting down the bureau and fleeing the country.

So now we were having a farewell party and didn't even know if we were leaving.

3

A MIDNIGHT KNOCK

As midnight approached, I wanted everyone out.

No one was helping pack anymore and discussions had long moved on to Trump, politics and whatever else was in the news. I was dreading having to wake up at 5 am to pack because I'd done such a poor job of it the night before, or to unpack, depending on the latest. So I was encouraging our guests to say their farewells. We organised a hotel nearby for Yinan's weary parents, and some friends promised to come to the airport the next morning if it turned out we were leaving. I craved sleep.

And then someone knocked on the door.

Two police officers stood outside in their standard light blue uniform. After hours of wine-fuelled banter, I suspected they were responding to a noise complaint.

'They're asking for you, Bill,' someone said.

I poked my head into the corridor. Behind the two cops were five people in plain clothes. It definitely wasn't about the noise.

'Shit, the diplomats were right,' I thought, having spent so much mental energy doubting them.

Our remaining guests gathered around the door and started to panic. Some were trying to argue with the uniformed officers. Yinan's 70-year-old mother, barely five foot tall, stood in the middle struggling to make sense of what was happening.

'We just want to talk to Bill, not anyone else,' a policeman said as some of our friends valiantly argued they should accompany me. It still wasn't clear if he wanted me to go somewhere else or to chat at the door.

I suspected they'd had the home under surveillance, but opening the apartment door to a crowd probably wasn't part of their plan. The policeman told our friends to calm down and assured them they would talk with me in the alcove.

'It's okay, I'll step out and have a chat,' I told my friends.

I didn't have much choice. In case I was taken away, Stephen McDonnell stood at the door with his phone primed, an Australian embassy contact ready to dial. Others held their phones ready to film. Yinan gripped her mother's arm.

The policeman, in a thick Beijing accent, again told everyone to calm down. Then he closed the door, sealing my friends inside and me outside with seven strangers.

The policeman, who never gave his name, pulled out a badge. The familiar crest of China's public security bureau glinted, with the words 'Beijing National Security Bureau' underneath.

Seeing that, I pushed open the door.

'Ring the embassy, it's national security!'

The policeman pulled the door shut.

'We're here to inform you you're involved in a case.'

A chill went through me.

'Don't worry, your freedom of movement is guaranteed, but you're not allowed to leave China,' the policeman continued, a young interpreter beside him repeating every word, in an English monotone.

'Sorry, what?'

I was somewhat reassured that a dozen people had their ears pressed to the other side of the door to catch anything I missed.

'So if you attempt to leave, you will not be permitted,' the officer said.

'In other words, there's an exit ban on me?' I clarified.

He said yes, and asked for my mobile number (which I assumed they already had).

'We will ring you tomorrow afternoon to organise a chat,' he said. With a smile, speaking in his thick Beijing accent, he repeated, 'A nice slow chat.' He seemed to think that this might reassure me.

And then the seven walked off, leaving me bewildered.

———

Back inside, we absorbed what had just happened.

Seven state security police had turned up in the middle of the night, but not to arrest me. In a perverse way, it almost felt like a courtesy call to advise me not to bother packing for the next morning's flight.

Relief was mixed with confusion.

And then my phone rang.

'Hey, about that flight tomorrow,' Mike Smith said with the guarded tone of someone who's just been reminded he's under surveillance. 'There's now a problem.'

'Let me guess,' I said.

Poor Mike had just received the same type of visit at his home in Shanghai. He'd had to face seven officers alone, with one of them thrusting a TV-style camera in his face.

Whatever was happening, the language from the cops made it sound like we weren't the focus of their investigation, but rather persons of interest in an existing case. Otherwise why not arrest us then and there? And telling us they would ring us the following afternoon was downright bizarre.

But at least it solved one problem.

The packing could wait.

4

HOTEL AUSTRALIA

I awoke to the repetitive buzz of my phone on silent, vibrating defiantly as I fought a semi-conscious battle to stay asleep.

The phone won.

While it was still 6 am in Beijing, it was already 8 am in Sydney, and ABC management was in a flurry of talks about how to proceed.

The warm sun of another clear Beijing day was pouring through the cracks in the curtain. As plans were falling into place, I emerged into the main room of the apartment where a theatre colleague of Yinan's, Gao Xuan, and Stephen McDonnell were asleep on the sofa and the floor. The duo of unlikely bouncers had stayed the night in case the fuzz made a return visit. In the early hours of the morning, Stephen had still been holding court, a glass of Japanese sake in hand, kicking the air and assuring us, 'If the cops come back, I'll use my kung fu skills on them!' Call it moral support.

The events of the night before had put us in an unprecedented situation.

Foreign journalists hadn't been embroiled in national security cases before, so Yinan and I agreed to head over to the embassy to talk it through. The diplomats organised a car to pick us up.

I packed a backpack with little more than I would normally take to a briefing at work. Our cats and the fish tank were still in the apartment, along with all our possessions, and I expected to sort it all out later, freed from the madness of the night before.

When I shut the door on my home of more than four years, I had no idea I would never see it again.

As Yinan and I walked out of the front entrance of the building to a waiting car, I waved to the ever-friendly security guard—a small, grey-haired, middle-aged man who I'd chewed the fat with many times over the years.

'Zao,' I called out to him. 'Morning.'

He just stared back silently. Word must have travelled fast about the national security suspect living on Floor 25.

The drive to the Australian embassy only took about fifteen minutes but it was like heading home without the eleven-hour flight. Everything from the accents to the power sockets is familiar, but when you've been living in China for five years it's a shock to the system. For Yinan it was overwhelming, to be battling the nausea and fatigue of early pregnancy while being rushed to a foreign embassy by diplomats, all because of your partner's job.

She was stoic. It was all happening too fast to sink in for either of us.

Inside the embassy, a briefing made it clear we were in uncharted territory. There was relief that neither Mike in Shanghai nor I in Beijing had been detained as feared, but midnight visits and requests for meetings over national security cases left more questions than answers. No one was sure what the Chinese wanted.

Eventually, one of the diplomats raised the idea that Yinan and I stay in the embassy for our safety, a possible 'big step' that would normally only be used in exceptional circumstances. It needed high-level approval, but soon a consensus formed that our situation fitted the bill. This wasn't ideal, as I knew it meant we wouldn't be able to pack up our own apartment. It seemed like an escalation tactic to turn an issue between the police and me into a diplomatic negotiation.

'We're going to be staying here tonight, and then maybe a little longer,' I told Yinan, who had been waiting in another room.

We were checking in to 'Hotel Australia'—for how long, nobody knew.

Around 2.30 that afternoon, while we were still in the embassy, my phone rang. I'd been anticipating a call from the National Security Police. My employers, the diplomats and, of course, Yinan were eagerly waiting too, at the very least to see what extra light could be shed.

So when it rang, displaying an unknown mobile number from the nearby industrial city of Shijiazhuang, I put it on speaker phone. A small group gathered around the table.

A woman with a deadpan Americanised accent was on the other end. 'I am calling from the Beijing National Security Bureau. As we informed you last night at your home, you are involved in a case and we need to speak to you.' It sounded like she was reading from a script. 'Can we meet at three o'clock?'

It sounded like an invitation rather than a summons, lacking the urgency you might expect from national security investigators.

I told her I wouldn't be able to meet. 'I'm at the embassy and not convinced my safety will be assured.'

'Why?' she asked.

'Because you've detained another Australian journalist, Cheng Lei.' More than a year earlier, they had also detained another Australian citizen, Yang Hengjun. Nobody wanted to risk a third.

'Your freedom of movement is guaranteed,' she said. 'Are you refusing to meet?'

I wasn't budging. Trust was in short supply and, although I was incredibly curious to find out what they wanted, we needed some safeguards.

The woman ended the call with the same steady monotone. 'Okay, we will ring you later. Bye.'

———

The next days unfolded at an excruciatingly slow pace. Yinan and I were assigned a spare apartment overlooking Dongzhimen Outer Street, a busy thoroughfare facing the 'Australia–Canada Hotel', a third-rate business hotel with a dubious-looking karaoke joint in the basement. 'Hotel Australia' was far nicer, but the presence of an ABC correspondent and a Chinese national was awkward to say the least.

For the first day we were largely confined to the apartment, as few diplomats knew of the crisis and wouldn't want to explain why a journalist might be poking around on the embassy grounds. By day two of our 'hostage diplomacy' stay, we were somewhat let off the leash. More diplomats and their families had been briefed about our presence and we even received a rare invitation to the embassy bar for Friday-night drinks, at which Australian journalists had once been a fixture, but not since I'd been in China.

These shifts reflected the unique sensitivities of the posting, especially during the early 2010s when journalists such as John Garnaut and Phillip Wen started investigating the more trouble-some aspects of the Australia–China relationship.

It almost felt like my invitation to the bar meant things had gone full circle—that I was only there because the rela-tionship had hit a new low. Either way, Australians are awfully helpful in a crisis and you couldn't ask for a better bunch of people to be stuck in a jam with. Yinan's friends and my ABC colleagues were also incredibly helpful, even though we couldn't give them the full picture of what was going on. As our stay lengthened, they would go to the apartment to gather up clothes and essentials to bring over, and feed the cats and fish.

After a few days, our fridge was full of food and you could have been mistaken for thinking we were settling in for months. Prior to the upheaval we'd started looking for a bigger apart-ment in Beijing; we laughed how we'd now found it in a good central location.

Great security too.

But the days passed slowly; we could do little but wait.

———

As the weekend rolled around, things became quiet. I saw some friends in WeChat groups online organising a lunch. Others asked me about playing a game of squash. The city and the normal life of bustling Beijing seemed so close. You could hear it, smell it, see it out the window.

I couldn't let on to acquaintances and colleagues in Australia that anything was amiss.

There was a belief among the diplomats that they could quietly negotiate with the Chinese side to lift the exit ban on Mike and me.

Then we could safely leave China.

'It's the least worst option,' they repeatedly told me.

But if the media found out that I was taking shelter in the Beijing embassy and that Mike and his partner were cooped up in the house of the Shanghai consul-general, it would blow up.

And given the highly nationalistic sensitivities of the Chinese government, it might make things a lot worse, backing the government into a corner where it can't look publicly weak by letting the foreigners leave.

So the lack of media coverage was seen as a factor in the delicate negotiations underway. It was a perverse situation for a journalist to be in. For years I'd chipped away from the outside on national security cases in China involving others, trying to put together a jigsaw puzzle through snippets of information from cautious lawyers and even more cautious families. Rarely did Chinese authorities give much away, while Australian diplomats had long taken the view that media coverage was a hindrance rather than a help, at least in the initial stages.

Yet here I was in an unprecedented, sensitive national security case that triggered a diplomatic stand-off and I was helping to keep a lid on it. I was more worried about Yinan than anyone else. It was one thing for the Australians to be sheltering me, but they wouldn't have much choice if the Chinese demanded that Yinan leave the embassy. It was better to go along with the low-profile approach.

———

Late on the Saturday, I received an update which made it clear that talks had been going on at high levels. 'We've learnt the Chinese don't sleep,' one diplomat joked.

The key sticking point was the police request to interview me and Mike Smith. The Chinese authorities regarded this as essential and had even sought to portray it as procedural, likely to take only twenty minutes. In exchange, they would allow us to leave China, the 'least-worst option'.

They had also agreed to certain safeguards. Our diplomats couldn't 100 per cent guarantee that these promises weren't a ruse to detain me, but to deceive us would involve going back on some concrete promises made to the Australian side, so this wasn't considered likely, and the consensus was that the Chinese were acting in good faith. It was up to me to decide if I wanted to proceed. If I didn't, there was no Plan B. A prolonged stay at the embassy and the story breaking in the media were the only certainties.

'I really don't feel comfortable about this,' Yinan told me.

Not being privy to the briefings, she was left to rely on my versions of the meetings, and she perhaps thought I was putting a gung-ho spin on it: a journalist seeing a story opportunity, when things were actually much more serious for us.

I conferred with Mike Smith, who was on day four of a surreal stay at the Shanghai consul-general's house with his partner. He'd decided to accept the interview with police, seeing no other way out of our predicament.

Yinan and I decided to sleep on it.

—

The next morning Beijing's weather took a turn for the worse. The crisp sunlight of late summer made way for a monotone overcast sky. Autumn knocked a few degrees off the temperature. This weather seemed better suited to our predicament, and we agreed to accept the police interview that day.

An end to our Hotel Australia stay was in sight and a move to the real Australia increasingly near, but the Chinese police were in no hurry. Morning came and went, then afternoon, and I'd still heard no word.

I'd agreed to be interviewed in a Beijing hotel, with Mike Smith to leave the Shanghai Consulate residence and accept his interview only once I'd safely returned to the embassy in Beijing. But it was evening before the Chinese side gave the green light. Perhaps it was a tactic to let our paranoia build throughout the day. Or perhaps they only worked night shifts.

By the time we finally set off, it was nearing 8 pm and I'd downed a few cans of sugary convenience-store coffee on the off chance that it would be a long night. I didn't want to be signing anything or speaking to interrogators when tired.

As the diplomatic car drove away from the embassy, the Australian flag fluttering on the bonnet, I looked out at the familiar streets of Sanlitun district: the wide motorways, the Bentley dealership on Xindong Road, the neon projections on the Sanlitun Intercontinental, the kids—well, teenagers and young adults really, so many of them as usual—walking around in front of the bright lights of Sanlitun's main shopping mall Taikoo Li with fruit tea in one hand, a smartphone in the other.

Under different circumstances it would have been like any other night.

The shopfronts and buildings continued to change so fast, but they all felt so familiar.

It was like driving through your home neighbourhood for the last time.

———

The Zhaolong Hotel was barely fifteen minutes' drive from the embassy. I'd passed it countless times and never given it a second look. It was an old government-owned hotel that had well and truly been upstaged by flashier international rivals.

Hearing that I would meet the police there, I had pictured it as a real dump, like many state-owned hotels: pleather sofas, worn carpet and the smell of cigarettes embedded into the wallpaper and curtains.

But when we arrived it didn't fit the description I'd created. The Zhaolong had undergone renovations and looked like a mid-range Holiday Inn. I arrived with a diplomatic entourage and went through the usual scanning procedures to confirm I hadn't recently been near a coronavirus hotspot. A sudden thought hit me: not bringing my phone and thus being unable to scan the QR code may derail the interview! But I was far too curious by this point and I knew we were in far too deep to pull out.

As those accompanying me went to wait in the lobby bar, a man and a woman, both relatively young, ushered me over to the lifts. The woman was the interpreter who was at my door five nights earlier. They were both wearing coronavirus masks and plain clothes.

We hopped in the lift and they pressed the button. Level 22. It was a small, crowded lift and a long ride up. I wanted to make small talk, but what do you say? The interpreter seemed like so many of the women I'd worked with or met in media circles, fluent in English and seemingly well-versed in understanding Western culture. Had she ended up working for the national security branch of police through some devotion to duty? Or was it just a job she landed to utilise her language skills?

Asking her how she ended up working for state security didn't quite seem appropriate. So we went up in an awkward silence.

On Level 22, another two men in plain clothes were outside the lifts. You got the sense the Zhaolong Hotel wasn't doing brisk business. I wondered if the police could just commandeer a floor at short notice or if they had to pay for the room. So many questions would go unasked.

The men ushered me to a hotel room with a partially opened door. Inside I could make out a setting I'd seen in countless news reports: several police in uniform at a desk, with a camera pointed at a chair. I'd assumed during the negotiations that it would be more a 'cup of tea' type set-up, but this was a proper police interview and didn't look like it would be brief.

The police waved me to the chair, a very comfortable hotel lounger. They told me to put on my mask and informed me that I was there due to section 9 of China's national security law.

The policeman asking the questions was the same 'old Beijing' cop who'd done all the talking outside my apartment. He was flanked by two younger officers, a woman who acted as interpreter and a young man who seemed to be his lackey. The other interpreter who'd met me downstairs had the job of typing notes.

The room otherwise looked like a typical hotel room, with crackers and a bottle of wine sitting in the corner above a mini fridge. The curtains were closed but I guessed it had a pretty decent view of Sanlitun. I wondered if you could see my apartment building.

'What is your full name? What is your passport number? Where do you live?' asked the officer.

I understood but waited for the interpreter to render it into English.

My biggest fear was that they would use something I said to incriminate Cheng Lei or help to build a case against her. I was aware that my words could be deliberately misconstrued to claim collusion or espionage, and there wasn't going to be a fair court trial to hear it. So I went in with the approach of listening and answering in English as slowly as possible.

Once we passed the initial basic questions, the officer asked me if I'd ever written stories related to China. It was a simple question, but it threw me off.

'I'm the China correspondent, every story I write is related to China,' I said, and I swear I heard the interpreter suppress a laugh as she typed the notes. It did seem like a ridiculous question.

'But what "important" stories have you covered?' the officer followed up.

I'd had similar questions in the past during 'cups of tea' with Foreign Ministry officials and I never knew what the right answer was. The Hong Kong protests? The trade war? The general disintegration of Australia–China ties?

I always assumed the interlocutor had the answer themselves, so I played a straight bat and said the annual National People's Congress political meeting and the pandemic, which were recent big stories. Well, at least the pandemic was.

He wanted more details, so I told him we'd recently been to the Qingdao beer festival to do a story about China's tourism industry opening up post-pandemic. It was an assignment fresh in my mind and seemed far removed from the seriousness of Cheng Lei's detention.

'Do you like Tsingtao beer?' he asked me with enthusiasm. 'It has a very fresh taste, doesn't it?'

I felt like I was chatting to a random man on the street making small talk with a curious foreigner, but then he asked me if I'd reported on the new Hong Kong national security law, which was sweeping and powerful and had been imposed without consultation upon the people of Hong Kong.

A chill went through me.

This wasn't what the interview was supposed to be about.

'When you did your reports, what channels did you go through to get your information?' he asked me.

I was worried now, thinking about all the local researchers we'd hired during six months of coverage in 2019. I thought about the protestors we'd interviewed and others I'd stayed in touch with, including some who held jobs inside the Hong Kong government. Is this what they're getting at, I wondered? Could benign off-the-record chats with Hong Kong public servants be breaching state secrets? Could something I say in the Beijing hotel room end up incriminating people in Hong Kong?

I played it straight, telling him I got my information from both official channels and people I interviewed in Hong Kong. I didn't say who, and he didn't ask me.

He wrote down some notes, the translator tapped away, and silence hung in the air.

And that was it. On to the next topic.

Relief.

'Do you know China Central Television journalist Cheng Lei?' the policeman asked.

'Yes, I do,' I said, glad that the topic of discussion had moved on to something more predictable.

He asked if I knew her situation, and I said, 'I'm aware state security has arbitrarily detained her,' to which he corrected me on 'arbitrary', telling me China 'is a rule of law country'. He went into a little spiel about Cheng Lei being investigated in accordance with the rules and regulations; he seemed to relish the chance to methodically lecture a foreign journalist. It must have been quite a novelty.

I wondered how much thought had gone into choosing this officer to conduct my interview. The authorities would have known that foreign journalists would write about anything that happened in the interrogation room, and inviting media coverage must have been part of the Chinese side's calculation.

He asked me when I'd first met Cheng Lei, who introduced me to her, the last time I spoke to her and whether I'd used any digital methods to communicate with her.

I gave honest but not particularly useful answers, because I wasn't close to Cheng Lei. She was a media acquaintance who I saw intermittently at events. I'd once co-hosted a Business Chamber gala with her and we'd tried to arrange a doubles tennis match with some other friends. That was the extent of it. Neither myself nor Mike Smith—who had met her once in his life—were the two best candidates if the police were genuinely seeking useful information.

The questions along these lines continued and my frustration built. The interrogation seemed more like a performance. It certainly wasn't a good reason why I should have to suddenly flee the country, and I said as much in Chinese, throwing caution to the wind. Unaware that the Australian security agencies had earlier raided the homes of four Chinese state-media journalists back in Australia and confiscated their devices, I told him I'd be appalled if the Australian government treated Chinese journalists the way I was being treated.

It was the sort of comment that would have made good fodder for Chinese state TV: 'Aussie Journalist Condemns Australian Gov't Raids on Chinese Media'.

But I had been kept in the dark from the Australian side about the real reasons we were being targeted. The idea that it was all just retaliation for something the Australians had done was just a theory at the time. All I knew was the Chinese side had singled out the two remaining Australian media journalists for midnight visits, exit bans and dubious interrogations.

The interview continued, the officer continuously rebuffing my protests that it was all a political game by repeatedly telling me that the investigation was being conducted in accordance with relevant laws and regulations. He almost smiled as he slowly repeated those lines, clearly enjoying toying with me.

At the end, the translator printed out a transcript of the interview for me to check. It was in Chinese and I scanned the pages line by line, making sure of its accuracy before signing off on it.

With the interview at an end, I sat on the lounger feeling absolutely deflated. My years in China were at an end, and for what? A farcical police interview that had spooked the Australian government into rushing me out of the country.

As I got up to leave, I joked about taking home the bottle of wine on the mini-bar cabinet. The officer jovially tried to foist it into my hands.

'Take it,' he laughed. 'The hotel has a lot of it, it's cheap, no problem!' He ushered me out the door, where others took me down in the lift and back out, ever so briefly, into Beijing street life for one last glimpse before the trip back to the embassy.

I'd first seen these streets in 2008 as a beginner Chinese language student. Back then, the city was in a frenzy of change to prepare for the Olympic Games. It inspired me to quit my job and move to Beijing in 2010 to seek a better understanding of what China was all about.

But now I was seeing these streets for a final time under circumstances I never could have imagined. A bewildering farewell to a city that had become my second home.

We left China the following day.

5

THE GOOD OLD DAYS

The four-year gap between the 2008 Beijing Olympics and the beginning of Xi Jinping's reign as Communist Party Secretary General in 2012 looks in hindsight like a golden period for China and the world.

I've heard older people, both Chinese and foreigners, attach similar nostalgia to earlier periods, particularly the 1980s or '90s, but those four years have particular resonance for Australians. It wasn't just that Beijing had invited the world in for the Olympics and triggered an upsurge of interest in China. Those years were also when Australia had elected Kevin Rudd as prime minister, a Mandarin-speaking ex-diplomat who seemed to symbolise the future opportunity of China. Rudd wowed the electorate with polished-sounding Chinese soundbites and, when prime minister, an entire Mandarin speech to university students in Beijing. He was present in the 'bird's nest' national stadium on 8 August 2008 to witness the masterful display of power, scale and discipline in the Olympics opening ceremony.

Only weeks before, I'd been in Beijing taking my first proper dive into serious Chinese language study. By the time the Olympics commenced amid a national frenzy, I'd travelled south and was watching the opening ceremony on a massive projector screen next to Hong Kong harbour. Seeing the camera cut to Kevin Rudd in the crowd waving a little flag as the Australian athletes marched summed up what seemed to be the inevitable force of history.

The future was China and the winners would be those who engaged.

Two years later, the buzz of the games was gone but the excitement about China hadn't worn off. Its annual Gross Domestic Product was still growing at near double-digit rates. Other countries had been smashed by the Global Financial Crisis but China was continuing to vacuum up Australian iron ore and coal. Mining tycoons were catapulted up the rich lists. Talk of 'the Asian century' was dogma in Australian national politics. And I was back in Beijing getting among it.

Kevin Rudd's fortunes were waning. He was deposed as prime minister that year for domestic political reasons, but the rough edges of his China engagement had been exposed. The real glue binding Australia and China together—iron ore exports—had started to weaken as Chinese attempts to buy up a big stake of Australia's second-largest miner, Rio Tinto, came unstuck. An Australian Rio executive, Stern Hu, was jailed in Shanghai on commercial secrets and bribery charges that had more than a whiff of revenge about them, no matter the merits of the prosecution case. But in China, the sky still seemed to be the limit.

I'd just wrapped up months of study at a language school that symbolised the contradiction in China's open-yet-closed state. Technically I was among a cohort of foreigners studying Chinese at Beijing's University of International Relations, an institution known for educating future diplomats and even spies. But the language school, more a money-making offshoot of the university than anything else, was nowhere near the campus and the one brief time we were bussed there to play local students in soccer, we weren't given much chance to get to know any of them.

Still, jumping into Beijing's bustling life, even as a complete outsider, was addictive and when an Australian friend helped line up a job interview at China's government news agency, I took the chance. State media was a common path for foreign journalists to work their way into China careers, before China's outward relations unravelled and the state-media content became (even) more politicised.

But back in 2010 there was a great deal more optimism. The Xinhua News Agency, which started life as the Red China News Agency in the 1930s, was one of a handful of government media outlets hiring 'foreign experts'. The impressive title disguised the fact that they were all overpaid English-polishing roles and the expertise needed extended little beyond a fluent command of one's mother tongue and an understanding of news cycles. But as a way to secure a twelve-month work visa without having to teach children, such jobs were valuable and I landed a contract at Xinhua's much-hyped new 24-hour English television channel, CNC.

The rough edges of a new TV channel in a traditional news-wire agency made for interesting work. The staff, nearly all in their twenties and thirties, routinely complained to me about their official salaries. Yet many of them seemed to be swimming in money. Several drove new BMWs or Mercedes. Others spent their holidays travelling around Europe. One colleague, a vague and not particularly well-adjusted young man called Gaoshan, told me he'd been sent to a prestigious Texas military college for high school. Rumours abounded that this stoner in his mid-twenties was from an extremely rich family. It dawned on me after a while that nearly everyone I worked with had ended up in this division of Xinhua through family or personal connections, and although the salaries were low, the benefits, security and prestige of working for the state's pre-eminent news outlet outweighed anything else.

These were the great beneficiaries of China's rise, the well-off children with overseas educations able to land cushy prestigious state jobs through family connections. That's not to say it's dissimilar in other countries, but the newsroom environment certainly struck me as odd. Aside from a handful, most staff had little enthusiasm for the work itself.

The network was fledgling and hampered by the fact that China's government already ran a 24-hour English news network that was established and run by experienced television staff. China Central Television, known as CCTV, was dominant in China and expanding rapidly online as the government pumped billions of new dollars into bolstering its major media outlets. Xinhua too had received a cash injection but curiously decided to spend some of it on trying to muscle in on the global TV market just as television was beginning its slow decline.

From my humble vantage point on the newsroom floor, most of the cash appeared to have gone towards new studios and young producers, and not enough towards poaching people who knew how to make TV. The result was an eye-opener into the strengths and weaknesses of the Chinese state-led model.

One day while discussing the lack of overseas content we had access to, a manager named 'Teacher' Peng bemoaned that Westerners use lawyers to negotiate international broadcast contracts whereas 'We Chinese' prefer to directly talk to our counterparts. That didn't explain how CCTV had managed to sort out so many agreements. I was summoned to a high floor in Xinhua's pencil-like headquarters for a meeting with higher-ups who wanted to see if I could help get their channel on air in Australia, preferably on an ABC free-to-air digital channel. It was an ambitious request but symbolic of the fast-moving pursuit of opportunities driving China. Xinhua also launched a search engine to try to rival the domestic search giant Baidu. The best I could offer was to help make an approach to a senior manager at the ABC, but the Xinhua bosses who summoned me to request it never followed up.

Another time a young colleague had been tasked by her manager to research the news style of Al Jazeera, the state-owned Qatari television network that was viewed by many inside Xinhua as a respectable model of a government-run news channel. Al Jazeera seemed to prove that government ownership of a news outlet didn't turn off viewers, even though Qatar was a very different owner from China. But the colleague tasked to report back on Al Jazeera's website was in a bit of a bind. China's Cyberspace administration had recently blocked access to Al Jazeera's website. She couldn't get on to the homepage because her team at Xinhua had not provided any appropriate virtual private network (VPN) software to help her circumvent the censorship. She spent a few hours trying to download free but buggy VPN software and ultimately gave up.

These were small but telling signs of whether or not CNC would succeed.

Coinciding with those twelve months at Xinhua was a period of information opening-up that by today's standards looks like a high point of transparency.

It wasn't that the deeply conservative men running China chose to have a Chairman Mao-style 'Hundred Flowers' moment. (Mao had for a brief period in the 1950s encouraged intellectuals to express blunt and even critical opinions about the nation's governance before later punishing many who spoke up.) It was more that the new technology got ahead of the regulators and, as the country's burgeoning internet companies exploded with new social-media services, the leadership was unsure how much it needed to rein them in.

Already I'd seen the beginnings of China's decoupling of the internet in action. In 2008 when I first studied in Beijing, YouTube, Facebook and Google were all available to use. Buses used to rumble around the student district of Haidian with Google China ads on them. Then-Premier Wen Jiabao even opened an official Facebook account. You could watch the Tiananmen Square crackdown Tank Man video on streaming services if you wanted to, even though a long list of websites with content deemed unacceptable to the ruling Communist Party were already blocked.

By 2010 when I returned, the Olympics had passed and so had promises of openness. The Chinese government's deeply embedded distrust of anything it couldn't control proved too strong and through its vast censorship apparatus, known informally as the 'Great Firewall', it started blocking the world's biggest websites.

By accident or design, the censorship proved to be one of the most astute acts of protectionism in the history of global trade and services. By blocking the fast-growing American social-media sites and cutting dead their ability to monopolise the market, or at least take major stakes, China's government was fencing in 1.4 billion people for its own companies to fight over.

And fight they did, with colleagues in the Xinhua newsroom trying to sign me up to Facebook knock-offs KaixinWang (Happy Net), RenRen (Everybody) and the biggest cheese of all, the Twitter-like Weibo (Micro-blog).

The ultimate winner of China's social-media wars, WeChat, hadn't even been developed yet. It was Weibo that initially generated the most excitement. It quickly became a platform for ordinary people to publicly vent grievances, and perhaps most usefully, for public institutions such as courts to provide a direct channel of information to the masses.

It was instrumental in a major scandal erupting, engulfing China's Red Cross over alleged misappropriation of charity funds by an employee of a linked company. She'd been seen on Weibo driving luxury cars and flaunting her wealth. Most famously, investigative reporters utilised the platform to expose an egregious cover-up by local officials of a high-speed train crash in the eastern city of Wenzhou, in which 40 people died. Officials ordered carriages to be buried in the sort of hasty cover-up that might have worked in the pre-internet days.

All this gave me great hope sitting in the Xinhua newsroom that more and more steps were being taken towards greater transparency. My colleagues took a great interest in these scandals and there was a bit of a 'civic public square' feeling, even though Xinhua itself was still pumping out stodgy state-media articles that looked increasingly irrelevant. The state propaganda and esoteric Party language that still filled the headlines of government media news sites was largely ignored and there was little ideological discipline on show. At one of the many Xinhua banquets, one manager raised a glass and jokingly made a toast to 'socialism'. Things appeared to be opening up and it was hard to believe that such a dynamic country could remain shackled to such an outdated form of authoritarianism.

There were signs, however, of what was to come.

On my first day on the job, a manager took me on a tour through the newsroom, introducing me to my new colleagues. One of them shook my hand and told me she had a question.

'Why is the Western media so negative towards China?'

It seemed a bit blunt for an initial meet and greet, but a second new colleague asked me the exact same question a few minutes later. It clearly was front of mind among Xinhua journalists, but several non-media types would later ask me that same question in social settings.

Feelings were still very raw over the international media coverage of the Beijing Olympics torch relay two years earlier, where images of protests overseas and media questions about China's human rights record jarred with the patriotic message at home. Errors in some Western media reports, such as the mislabelling of photos depicting protests in India and Nepal as being in Tibet, fuelled the anger.

Perhaps surprisingly for a newsroom, discussions of politics were rare. There was a reason, as a British colleague, Lewis, had found out. Lewis, while only 31, was such a veteran of the newsroom that he had the nickname 'Lao Lu', or 'Old Lew'. One day back in 2010, Lewis had been there when the jailed Chinese democracy activist Liu Xiaobo was awarded the Nobel Peace Prize. Xinhua refused to cover it, waiting on instructions from above that didn't come for three days. When pressed on why this news channel promising to give 'a new perspective on China' to audiences wouldn't report this massive story, the director of CNC, Mi Ligong, normally a calm man, showed a rare flash of indignant anger. There were still very much lines not to be crossed. Eventually the channel reported a three-line statement from China's Foreign Ministry condemning Norway for allowing the independent Peace Prize Committee to give the award, and that was that.

Not long after I began work there, I was slogging through a slow afternoon shift in the Xinhua newsroom, reading a repetitive churn of lifeless wire stories about bilateral political meetings and updates on natural disasters. All of a sudden, one of the TVs hanging above the desks started playing the 1989 Tiananmen Tank Man vision. It was tuned to CNN, a channel subject to occasional blackouts. On this afternoon, the functionary in the censorship department responsible for flicking the 'off' switch must have been asleep at the wheel.

I sat staring at the report, waiting for the screen to go dark. But it continued, and I turned to Gaoshan, my Texas-educated colleague coasting through a shift nearby, to ask him if he recognised the scene.

Despite being a lazy colleague and a stoner, Gaoshan was no fool. He once asked me to bring him a copy of Zhao Ziyang's journal that had been published abroad. Zhao was a former Communist Party Secretary-General who was ousted by hard-liners in the lead-up to the Tiananmen Square crackdown and later purged from the history books. Gaoshan clearly took more of an interest in politics and history than most of his colleagues.

He squinted at the CNN screen through his glasses. 'That's Beijing,' he deduced, but didn't recognise the vision of the man with the plastic shopping bags stalling a column of tanks.

'That's the vision from Tiananmen in 1989,' I said.

Gaoshan had never seen vision of the Tank Man or even a still photograph, despite it being the defining image from the protests abroad. He watched for a little longer and without looking away from the screen exclaimed, 'I bet this was filmed by foreigners.'

He was right, of course. Multiple TV crews including the ABC caught the Tank Man moment from the balcony of the Beijing Hotel. But his tone was dismissive, delegitimising the meaning of the vision because of who the messenger was.

It would be a good six years before Donald Trump would begin telling Americans not to trust the media, but in China it was already a familiar message.

As long as it was foreign media.

6

CANTONESE CULTURE

It was October 2015 and a good four years since I'd worked alongside the children of the Party loyalists at Xinhua in Beijing. But those two years in China—one studying, one working—had only reeled me in deeper. I'd gone back to Sydney to the ABC with a clear goal in mind—to get back to China. And that's why I was standing on the docks of a little-known southern city called Zhanjiang. The ABC had decided to post me to China as a correspondent, and the visit of an Australian Royal Navy frigate for joint exercises with the Chinese Navy was my first assignment out of Beijing. Under dense tropical clouds HMAS *Arunta* slowly manoeuvred into position as a sizeable welcoming party watched from the dock. Two straight lines of around 100 Chinese sailors in immaculate white naval uniforms waited for what seemed like an eternity. They chatted casually with the air of men who did these ceremonial welcomes regularly. A commanding officer stood ready to snap them into the disciplined uniform line they're known for. Two primary-school students bearing bouquets stood on the red carpet, constantly looking around for adult reassurance.

Then, after another lengthy wait, a second Australian warship docked, and the ceremony finally began. Officials from the Australian consulate in Guangzhou and the local branch of China's Foreign Ministry, known as the 'waiban', lined up in rank order. A small media pack of local journalists along with the ABC came in close to get the handshakes as the Commander of HMAS *Arunta* moved up the dignitary line. In his early forties, he looked more at home steering a warship through troubled waters than gladhanding local officials and military top brass.

'Thank you for inviting us!' he nervously exclaimed with each handshake as cameras hovered just over his shoulder. A Chinese officer interpreted the brief greeting for each dignitary.

Finally the Commander neared the official from China's Foreign Ministry, who, despite this being a military visit, was deemed the key person of importance on the red carpet. This was the culmination of all the talking points—the key moment to say something simple and memorable to make a smooth diplomatic impression.

He had been sailing into Guangdong province, so a nod to the region's traditional Cantonese culture was viewed as a safe and friendly thing to say. 'Cantonese culture, Cantonese culture,' the Commander repeated to himself that morning, according to an aide onboard the ship.

Finally he reached the official at the end of the red carpet, hand outstretched, media and advisers huddling in.

'Thank you for inviting us,' he said, growing more confident with the end of the formalities in sight. 'And we're very keen to learn about your Japanese culture.'

The naval media officer in the scrum winces at me.

The Chinese interpreter pauses.

The official from the Foreign Ministry looks at the interpreter, the silence hanging heavy in the lush tropical air.

And in Mandarin the interpreter simply tells the official, 'Thank you for inviting us and we're keen to learn about your culture.'

This is a time when faux pas were glossed over, warships made regular visits and the future belonged to China. Those who engaged would be the winners.

—

In 2015 China's relations with Australia and the West were still fairly rosy but serious strains were starting to show. The warship visit in Zhanjiang involved joint live-fire manoeuvres, a trust-building exercise that Australia had started to semi-regularly engage in with the Chinese Navy.

But the trip was overshadowed by China's growing aggressiveness in the South China Sea and US military efforts to counter it. It was the biggest story in Asia at the time.

Having landed my dream job, I'd returned to Beijing as spring turned to winter, but expectations that I'd be flat out with work were quickly dashed. Over in the United States, Donald Trump had announced plans to contest the Republican Party primaries and was whipping up a media storm. In Europe, terrorist attacks in France were putting everyone on edge.

In China, the big story was inaccessible by anything other than satellite imagery. As the days went by, I started to wonder if I was doing something wrong. Every former correspondent had warned me I would struggle to find a spare moment once on the job, but instead I was struggling to find stories that my editors wanted. Feeling frustrated and insecure, I tried to find ways into the South China Sea story.

All five countries bordering the contested waterway, plus Taiwan, had longstanding territorial claims while Indonesia's northernmost Natuna islands sit right at the southern base of China's famous nine-dash line. China, Vietnam, the Philippines and Taiwan had built up military outposts on their reefs and shoals. When Xi Jinping came to power in late 2012, things changed dramatically. China's military, coast guard, fisherman militia and state-owned enterprises had been deployed to radically transform small outposts into sophisticated military bases equipped with missiles, runways and advanced radar equipment.

In three short years Beijing had altered the 'facts on the ground', deploying a little-by-little strategy known as 'salami slicing' that involved incremental steps to deter neighbouring countries and the United States from any substantial response. The satellite images exposed the huge scale of the dredging in reef after reef. Runways and then missiles were photographed. The US administration under Barack Obama sent American warships near these fast-growing Chinese bases to assert 'freedom of navigation', but if anything it confirmed to Beijing how little the Americans would or could do. Completely outmatched in military might, the neighbouring countries could do even less, with incremental upgrades to Vietnamese and Philippines bases attracting Chinese diplomatic protests.

From a Chinese government perspective, this longstanding, complicated, six-way border dispute is simple. 'All the islands of the South China Sea have belonged to China since ancient times,' reads the official government position.

'China discovered them first, China named them first, China administered them first, China had jurisdiction over them first, this is beyond doubt,' Hou Yi, a government academic specialising in China's maritime borders said in a widely circulated state-media article released as tensions soared.

The evidence cited by Chinese scholars include a book dating back to the Han dynasty (AD 206–220) that described the rock and reef features in the South China Sea, apparently as a guide for Chinese fishermen. It proved, according to Hou Yi, that during the Han period 'at the very least Chinese fishermen had a deep understanding of the reef and rock features'.

During the Tang and Song dynasties (AD 618–1279), the Chinese established 'governance management' or a structure representing governance, Hou said, based on the title of another ancient book. 'This book was, of course, published by the authorities and it described the reefs and rocks in the east, west, middle and south of the South China Sea as all being under the jurisdiction of Hainan province.'

But it isn't just these maps that China uses to claim 'indisputable' sovereignty over such a large swathe of water. Chinese historians also claim fishermen from Hainan island planted coconut trees on the South China Sea islands. They also point to excavated wells, tombs and even small temples left on some of the rock features, although they claim Vietnamese and Filipino fisherman destroyed many of them during 'illegal incursions'.

More recent evidence cited by Chinese government historians involves Western and Japanese navigation maps. One British naval book refers to the presence of fishermen from Hainan and claims the name first attributed on Western maps to a key island, 'Itu Aba', came from a dialect of Hainan.

Two Second World War–era international agreements are also used by China to bolster its claims. The 1943 Cairo declaration between President Franklin D. Roosevelt, British Prime Minister Winston Churchill and the Republic of China's Generalissimo Chiang Kai-shek declared 'all the territories Japan has stolen from the Chinese, such as Manchuria, Formosa, and the Pescadores, shall be restored to the Republic of China'.

Given China's claim of ancient sovereignty, this is interpreted by Beijing to assume the South China Sea islands Japan occupied during the Second World War were to be 'returned' to China's sovereignty, even though the declaration doesn't explicitly say so.

Even a 1952 peace treaty signed in Taiwan between the defeated Japanese and the Republic of China government, which had itself been defeated by the Communists in China's civil war, is cited by Beijing to bolster its claims.

It was rare (and later became illegal) to see maps or globes being displayed that didn't include China's nine-dash line. From an early age, the idea that the South China Sea belonged to China was drilled into children through education, rather than the more complicated truth of the long-running, ongoing and highly contentious dispute.

Other claimant nations have, of course, put forward their own 'ancient' evidence to bolster their positions, although the Vietnamese claim a more recent continuous occupation from the fifteenth century onwards. These counterclaims may be glossed over in China's teaching of history but they're not ignored altogether. The widely circulated state-media interview with government scholar Hou Yi cites 60 maps presented by Filipino historians in 2014 used to refute Chinese claims to the Spratly Islands.

'Maps are very important evidence for a country's sovereignty claims but we must be clear about what types of maps can become evidence,' he's reported as saying. 'Officially published maps [from China] can be used as evidence, but privately published maps or those only mapping a region rather than a country are not eligible as evidence.'

With explanations like this dominating domestic discussion, it's little wonder China's government and its populace seemed taken aback by an international arbitration ruling in mid-2016 that decimated the legal basis for China's expansive nine-dash line. The case, brought by the Philippines, ruled on the legality of China's nine-dash line and the legal classification of rock and reef features under the United Nation's Convention on the Law of the Sea. China boycotted the hearings but had the judges ruled in Beijing's favour, it would have been enthusiastically added to the list of international agreements and judgments cited by China as evidence for such an expansive claim.

Instead, the judges came down heavily on the side of the Philippines, rejecting not only the notion that China could claim all maritime territory within the nine dashes but also picking apart China's claims that various reefs and rock features were big enough to grant it exclusive economic zones.

The decision didn't take sides on the competing claims but it dealt such a major blow to China's position that the government ordered state media to begin a huge campaign to delegitimise the ruling. 'Null and void' was the slogan circulating around the Chinese internet as Beijing disputed any adverse evidence to its claims, whether they be ancient maps from other countries or international tribunal decisions.

On the afternoon of the decision, I walked to the Philippines embassy near the ABC office. It was a balmy summer's day and police were erecting a tennis-style net above the gate to prevent angry Chinese nationalists throwing things at the building.

But there were none. Just dozens of police steering us away from the entrance.

Over the coming days, as China's government shaped a domestic narrative on the ruling that existed in a parallel world to that outside, it focused anger on the United States for supposedly 'manipulating' the tribunal, while sparing the Philippines from blame.

There was a reason for this: Beijing had already won the political battle. In the years between initiating the legal case and the judgment, the Philippines had changed government and the new strongman-style leader Rodrigo Duterte vowed to put aside the tribunal's ruling and seek closer economic ties with China.

Watching from Beijing, it was an extraordinary victory over international law. China had managed to ignore the ruling and coax the much weaker victor with the carrot of investment and the stick of military might.

China is certainly not the first great power to pick and choose international agreements to suit its interests, but such a complete rejection of the ruling played a major role in widening the trust deficit between China and the West.

And while Australian warships still navigated through the South China Sea on the way to joint exercises with the Chinese Navy, the controversy of the territorial dispute increasingly hung over such gatherings like a storm cloud.

Beijing treated the issue like a domestic affair that Australia had no right to voice an opinion on (unless, of course, it supported China's position).

But China's government seemed dismissive of how much concern its actions were creating even in countries it regarded as far removed from the dispute.

The South China Sea was the question that kept coming up when I reported on that 2015 visit, the elephant in the room.

Within a few years, those Australia–China goodwill military exercises would be put on hold.

7

BEIJING

When I first stayed prior to the 2008 Olympics, Beijing was a city of construction dust and drilling. China's capital was in a sprint towards the finish line, a makeover fit for the world to come and see. And although the Games had long passed when I returned in 2013 for a month of intensive language study, the construction was still going. The constant sound of hammering floated from a site in central Sanlitun in through the window of the Zhongyu Plaza opposite where my classes were held. An Intercontinental Hotel was going up; years later I would stay there with Yinan and her parents for a 'staycation'.

Beijing is a city of renewal, a place where restaurants you've just discovered can disappear, shops can pop up in the strangest of places and new towers rise in groups. Major developments were still rising, typified by SOHO, a developer known for creative architecture, making a statement with each new building.

To the north, futuristic glass dome-like towers were rising in the Wangjing district. In the inner east just opposite the Soviet-style colossus of China's Foreign Ministry, an ultra-modern building known as 'Galaxy' struck a bold contrast. A beautiful, flowing Phoenix Media building was going up in the east, near an ominous-looking dark tower called Central Park Plaza that at night looked like a bricks-and-mortar incarnation of Darth Vader.

Closest to home was the new Intercontinental development in Sanlitun, the district of restaurants and bars. The developer SOHO had taken a parcel of land that old timers told me used to host Beijing's original gritty bar street, with live music and an anything-goes culture unbefitting of the capital.

By 2015 when I returned to live in Beijing, the SOHO project was finished and aside from the hotel adorned in neon light projections, another series of towers hosted a hodgepodge of businesses—small noodle vendors, pet shops, plastic surgeons and even the offices of *The New York Times*. It had seemed soulless and sterile initially but was soon bustling with energy. It was the sort of place I should have moved to when my ABC posting began, but instead I took an apartment that the previous correspondent Huey Fern Tay had lived in, just a stone's throw from the bureau.

It was in the Qijiayuan Diplomatic Residency Compound, one of the very first built for diplomats and foreigners in the 1960s, a sprawling compound of twelve buildings along the east end of Beijing's main street, Chang'an Avenue.

But it was a cold and lonely place to move to. Paramilitary guards manned every gate, opening and closing them if you looked foreign but demanding ID from Chinese. It rightly irritated the Chinese-Australians working there. The guards were all young men, poker faced and often unresponsive if I offered a *Ni hao* upon coming in. They were trained to stand rigidly straight, their heads moving side to side monitoring the empty, quiet streets. They would rotate in shifts but I'd see the same young men multiple times a week and after a few months, the lack of warmth or small talk each time I'd greet them began to get to me. It felt very cold and very unfriendly, the sort of posture suited to a military base, not a home.

Over the frigid winter months, I started to adopt their practices, not bothering with a greeting, just sliding through the gates they opened for me in silence. I can't imagine how sociable extroverts would handle it.

Inside the compound, I was in a top-floor apartment facing the noisy twelve-lane road below with a small balcony covered in such a thick layer of dust that I could never use it. My neighbour was the military attaché for Pakistan, a middle-aged very serious man who lived with his wife and three young daughters. He was never particularly friendly and the rest of the floor was vacant. I'd only ever see him go out, climb into a chauffeured car from the embassy and disappear into the city.

The rest of the building was largely empty, as it was slated for demolition, with plans to build a newer and bigger version of it. I'd moved in knowing I'd have to move out.

Qijiayuan was in a diplomatic pocket of the city full of leafy embassies but little life. An unprofitable coffee shop run by some rich kid with no desperation to make a profit sat across the road next to the Friendship Store—once upon a time the only place foreigners could buy overpriced imported goods using foreign currency certificates. The Friendship Store had long ceased to have a purpose and now hosted a foreign goods supermarket and a Domino's pizza outlet.

When I moved into the compound, I thought the cafe opposite could be my 'local', an alternative to the many Starbucks outlets colonising the city. But the young man looked genuinely nervous when I turned up the morning after I moved in to order one of his eight-dollar coffees.

He faffed around with the shiny Italian coffee machine, seemingly unsure how to use it, before serving me what can best be described as a warm cup of potting mix. It summed up the diplomatic quarter—a part of Beijing that looked good but was lacking flavour and life.

When the management group running the diplomatic compound gave final orders to vacate the building nine months later, it was the push I needed. I found a building closer to the Sanlitun area through an American girl I was dating. HuaYuanZhiXing was a modern tower amid an older Beijing neighbourhood of six-floor brick walk-up buildings. The landlord was a middle-aged woman who seemingly made her living from owning property. She lived in Canada, posted a lot of updates about cats on her WeChat moments and was charging me more than she should have for a nice, renovated apartment that was still pretty small. But it had a view over the Workers' Stadium, one of the few places where you could still have a genuinely rowdy night in a large crowd.

Over the years I spent many nights at 'Gongti', as the stadium was called, watching the local team Beijing Guoan. The standard of soccer wasn't high but the atmosphere was solid: warm beers in big plastic cups, riot police and paramilitary soldiers guarding the pitch.

Foul-mouthed fans would launch the most obscene verbal tirades at the opponents, the away fans and the referees. I could see into the stadium from my window and hear 40,000 people roaring, a second before the goal made it to the TV screen in my living room.

My building was about a 25-minute walk to work but I used to tear an electric scooter down a main road to get there, crossing a massive intersection at Dongdaqiao and trying to go door to door within six minutes. In winter the ride became a war of attrition against the elements. The locals would affix blanket-like covers to their scooters and ride through the bitterly cold depths of winter. I tried, but by November the piercing winds from the north stung my eyes too much, making a ride to work a horribly uncomfortable endurance sprint.

It was during one of these winters that Beijing's government stepped up a drive to force out thousands of migrant workers. With more than 20 million inhabitants, city authorities understandably wanted to limit population growth. The household registration system aims to tie people to the schools and services of their home town or city, but China's modern economy has largely been powered by those who left home to work in factories, as couriers, construction workers, security guards, cooks and cleaners.

Every now and then, Beijing's government sought to put the brakes on population growth by targeting those who didn't have a valid work reason to be there. It was the same in Shanghai, Chongqing and other megacities—municipal governments grappling with a nation's worth of people. It was the sort of urban planning challenge that people in Sydney or Melbourne couldn't even comprehend.

In my time in Beijing, there were some radical changes. In 2016, Beijing's government started moving all of its offices and department buildings out of the centre of the city to a far eastern district called Tongzhou. Then Xi Jinping announced the creation of an entire new city from scratch 100 kilometres south-west of Beijing.

Xiong'an New District was announced with much fanfare in 2017 as a place where Beijing's state-owned enterprises would one day relocate their non-core operations. It was literally just farm fields and villages but not long after the announcement, the heavy machinery moved in and buildings started sprouting. A major new airport halfway between Xiong'an and Beijing was also built and opened. As a Sydneysider who watched state and federal governments stop and start for more than two decades about building a second airport at Badgerys Creek, it was a humbling lesson in getting things done.

With all this development still happening, Beijing remained a magnet for labourers and low-skilled workers from other provinces. But the late 2017 clear-out used a blunt instrument. A fire at a migrant workers' dorm prompted the demolition of an entire urban village in the city's south. Police and security guards went door to door evicting those living there with great haste before sending in the bulldozers. The fire prompted a 40-day safety audit across the capital, and local district governments didn't want to be seen to be sitting on their hands. So in dozens of workers' villages tucked into pockets of the capital, police and security guards went around checking credentials, forcing non-residents without proper accommodation or work documents to hastily pack their bags and go.

Driving through the demolished village in Daxing district, as the winter winds pierced through the twisted metal and crumbling debris, we caught a few stragglers—mainly young men carrying sacks of possessions on their backs, one of them telling us he was going to get a long-distance bus to southern Zhejiang province, where his boss had another factory.

He told us the evictions were less about safety and more because Beijing residents nearby didn't want an urban village of poor people living near them.

There was probably some truth to this. Beijingers are proud of their city, their culture, their history and their guttural accent, the sort of civic pride you would get in a place that so many others were desperate to move to. The property prices per square metre were among the highest in the world, the universities the best in China. Politically, any mover and shaker would seek to go there.

This created resentment towards the millions of outsiders who flocked to the city for work, pushing up the property prices and increasing congestion. In some ways, the attitudes towards migrant workers domestically in China could resemble attitudes towards migrants in more multicultural countries.

A close friend of mine, a native Beijinger, described his feelings as we watched busload after busload of teenage students from other provinces arrive at a museum. 'They're all *waidiren* [outsiders], and they'll all want to move to Beijing in the future, because that's where all the good jobs are,' he told me, as hundreds of students formed lines. 'What about my city? How can it absorb so many people always wanting to come here? This must be how you Australians feel when you see immigrants coming over.'

I'd also detected a nastier streak to it. We had an 'old Beijing' driver named Yao who wore his Beijingness on his sleeve, but he had a condescending and often spiteful attitude to one Chinese colleague who was not from Beijing, a young woman from China's south who, unlike Yao, was diligent, polite and a real asset to our office.

When she left to pursue greener pastures, we hired another female producer, also not from Beijing. Once again, Yao didn't like her, belittling her with comments in front of others. We sent him packing, replacing him with a much nicer, harder-working driver who was himself a migrant worker.

Despite these simmering attitudes, people across the capital were feeling the pinch from the abrupt eviction of thousands of outsiders. The manager of a swanky Sanlitun cafe apologised to me in advance about slow service, saying half his staff had suddenly been evicted. The baristas of Beijing weren't coffee-loving hipsters, but people who had travelled hundreds of kilometres for the job because it was better than whatever work they had back home. A gleaming capital run on the sweat of its second-class citizens was coming to grips with how much it needed them, and there was genuine sympathy and concern.

Another related change was taking place. Beijing was in the middle of a clean-up drive, dismantling illegal structures one by one. It sounds logical enough, but in reality, the 'illegal structures' and the people inside them gave a vibrancy to the city that thousands of Starbucks outlets could never match. Hole-in-the-wall pancake peddlers, street noodle restaurants, cheap speakeasies and family-run local stores were suddenly closed down. Many little shops that I'd bought vegetables from near my building vanished overnight, along with their owners. These sorts of places were so embedded in the capital's streets that I assumed they were permanent spaces, not ad-hoc add-ons that defied local planning laws.

The 'great brickening' became a saying as builders backed by black-uniformed 'teqin' special security guards constructed brick walls across doorways, leaving defiant shopkeepers to put ladders under windows so customers could still get in.

The result of all this was a cleaner, streamlined city that looked more beautiful but felt less lively. Beijing's city government seemed to think the future lay in shopping malls and new developments where high rent kept all the small-timers away. Chain cafes and restaurants, backed often by private equity firms, proliferated across not just Beijing but all the major cities.

As Beijing's odd shops and venues closed up, a favourite of the foreign journalist community also shut its doors. The Bookworm was a little intellectual haven perched on the second floor of a corner building in Sanlitun. For years it had hosted international writers' festivals, talks by both Chinese and foreign authors and, during my first stint in Beijing, a rowdy and wildly popular pub trivia night.

Although it catered to many Chinese customers, it was unmistakenly a 'foreign' venue, part-owned by an Irishman. The public talks were almost all in English, particularly if they touched on politics. It was its 'foreignness' that likely protected it for so long.

I'd filmed interviews with African community leaders there, moderated a talk by a visiting Australian author about ancient Constantinople and even went on an awkward coffee date there with a woman who had grand designs on a relationship before we'd even met. The Foreign Correspondents' Club used to hold informal drinks there, sometimes with a Chinese spook or two mingling among the crowd, awkwardly handing out business cards and turning small talk towards political topics far too abruptly.

In those years when Beijing was bricking up so many shops and restaurants while simultaneously tightening political control, the Bookworm's symbolism grew. I used to say that we'd know authorities had really cracked down when the Bookworm shut its doors.

And then, one day in late 2019, it did.

After fourteen years, the owners announced the business had fallen victim to the campaign against illegal structures. It was one of many, but for the small community of foreigners in Beijing, it left a deeper footprint than most.

———

As Beijing continued its modernisation drive, venues continued to close and change, with the pandemic adding a new element in 2020. Many small restaurants run by out-of-towners went bust as they weren't able to get back to Beijing in the initial months of the outbreak, and, when they did, the economy was suffering a rare sharp downturn. Other businesses were more agile, shutting down only to reopen with bigger venues.

Jing-A, the craft beer bar where Yinan and I first met, was one such establishment. A mutual media friend had originally suggested setting us up but never got around to it. Then one night, only weeks after plans for a set-up date fell apart, Yinan went out with girlfriends and wound up sitting next to me by chance at the long U-shaped bar that Jing-A was famous for. It was a haven for foreign media types and even though the bar later closed down, its model of pricey craft beer and high-end burgers reeled in investors who helped turn it into a chain success story.

After initially meeting, we then had our first proper date at a Vietnamese noodle restaurant; it too was later shut after being deemed an illegal structure. So it went in a city of constant change where, for better or worse, you could never quite feel sure of what could happen tomorrow. By contrast, when she eventually came to Sydney, Yinan described it as a place where 'everything feels settled', a city devoid of the constant 'struggle' to redefine itself.

Our relationship allowed me to occasionally peek into the minutiae of this struggle in Beijing. Yinan's parents' apartment had a balcony, on which a steel fence divided it from their neighbours' outdoor space. The fence was not positioned halfway, but rather more towards the neighbours' side, giving Yinan's parents the lion's share of the outdoor space. A younger couple moved in next door, saw the disparity, and offered to pay them a few thousand dollars to reposition the fence. Yinan's parents politely knocked them back. As they tell it, they had bought the apartment originally because it had such a nice large balcony space.

One week, when Yinan's parents were away, the neighbours brought in some handymen to reposition the fence. After arriving back in Beijing to find the fence moved, Yinan's parents went to the building committee that ran the compound. Unlike, say, an owners' corporation as Australians know it, this was a private company put in place by the property developer and it had no interest in interfering in this dispute. Nor did the police.

On her parents' behalf, Yinan called two different lawyers for advice. Both said the law couldn't help and gave her a suggestion on how to proceed. Yinan organised a work gang to put the fence back by force, saying that, sadly, this was the only way in China to safeguard your rights.

Her motley crew of foreign media researchers, theatre performers and university classmates were not the most intimidating group I'd ever seen. But one friend, Eva, brought along an 'old Beijing' flatmate of hers to lead the charge. Lei was a mid-thirties, solidly built, no-nonsense Beijinger who had a knack for standing her ground and convincing others to back down. Yinan described her as having 'gangster' connections but it appears that was just an impression Lei gave off. Either way, she was an enforcer who could intellectually disarm adversaries and give them hell if they resisted: the perfect person to lead this mob seeking 'justice' in this small-scale version of the South China Sea dispute.

Yinan's parents couldn't bear to be there while the confrontation took place, so they left their apartment early in the morning before the group of ten arrived in a convoy of cars to meet a couple of hired workers out the front. Yinan thought having a token foreigner would help her crew appear more intimidating, like a territorial claimant backed by the international community, so I stood around on the balcony while the workers fired up the axe grinder and started loudly sawing off the base of the fence.

A couple of compound security guards came by, watched from below and did absolutely nothing. Other residents stopped and stared, seemingly aware this was no business-as-usual job. Initially, the neighbours were nowhere to be seen.

The workers were able to successfully extricate the fence from the brick base while we stood waiting. Finally a woman in her thirties suddenly opened the glass door of the neighbouring apartment and rushed out onto the balcony in her pyjamas, hair askew, eyes still puffy. She recognised immediately what was happening. In the absence of her husband, she was left to take on the mob solo, arguing, yelling, pointing and, when all else failed, wailing.

With Lei at the fence throwing every rhetorical point back in her face, the neighbour was struggling to cope. In a moment of high drama, she threatened to throw herself off the balcony—which was only one floor up from ground level.

As she neared the edge, Lei grabbed her, held her in a bear hug and urged her not to hurt herself while continuing to remind her she never should have moved the fence in the first place.

As this drama unfolded, the two workers carried on, bit by bit dislodging the fence, dismantling the bricks at the base and barely batting an eyelid at the theatrics going on around them. One of Yinan's friends told me, 'They see this all the time.'

After a few hours of this, the neighbours rang the police, who turned up, had a chat separately to both sides and told them to go to the local station to give statements. The police later rang to say it wasn't their dispute to solve.

The whole episode seemed like a microcosm of China's disputes with its neighbours. The adjudicators were powerless to enforce order and all sides felt they had no choice but to take matters into their own hands. Those with the most numbers, connections and persistence prevailed. It was the law of the jungle that, reluctantly, they saw no option but to embrace.

The workers that day didn't reposition the fence back to its original position; they left it sitting on its side while the dispute raged. Yinan's parents never commissioned a follow-up job to weld it back into its former place. The neighbours never organised a countermove to again try to claim more space.

It just sat there on an undivided balcony, a symbol of a truce as the bad blood silently simmered.

———

Lei's day job wasn't shaking down errant neighbours on behalf of others, it was just a favour she was doing. But it wasn't clear what her job actually was. Like quite a few of Yinan's friends, she didn't seem to have one.

The explanation given to me was that she was a 'Beijinger', and as such, owned property that had exploded in value, which she rented out. She was also supposedly a part-owner of a hipster cafe popular with Beijing's European expats.

Then there was Yinan's decadently fun friend Eva, who seemed to spend her time kitesurfing at tropical Hainan or off the west coast of Australia. When she wasn't doing that, she was travelling to Thailand for holidays, where she bought an apartment, and occasionally filling in for a freelance month or two as a producer at German media. Yinan's explanation was that Eva had bought stocks in China's burgeoning market early, but Eva herself later told me she'd only dabbled and hadn't made any real money.

Then there were Yinan's theatre friends, who had gone all-in on a creative arts start-up—not traditionally the most lucrative of economic sectors. Two of them, a couple, were dividing their time between Beijing and a family holiday unit in Hainan.

It was all a bit perplexing and I'm sure I didn't have the full picture, but among the Beijing middle class there were quite a few people without obvious employment. I could only guess that family money from property explained it.

Beijing's real estate prices were a citywide obsession. The fervour reminded me very much of Sydney, minus the harbour views. Whenever I travelled out to the suburbs with colleagues for work, they would strike up small talk with the taxi drivers about the price per square metre in the area. In the more central areas of Beijing, it was around 70,000 yuan, valuing a 100-square metre apartment at 7 million yuan, or close to 1.4 million Australian dollars. Apartments big enough to house families stretched beyond the 2 million dollar mark, while in the outlying suburbs they cost half as much.

The property boom had made multimillionaires out of people who had apartments in the central areas of big cities, while leaving others scrambling for the lowest rungs on the property ladder. The staggering prices for prime apartments in the middle of congested, dense cities made it obvious why many Chinese investors sought to get their money out to more afford-able markets such as Australia.

Yinan had multiple university classmates who had made the move, introduced to off-the-plan apartments by Chinese real estate peddlers who promised an all-in-one lending and property management scheme to secure a slice of the Sydney or Melbourne market. Fresh air, good food and less pressure for kids were the big selling points. It wasn't a particularly deep impression of Australian society or culture, but it was none-theless an overwhelmingly positive picture they painted of an easier, healthier lifestyle, and it was not uncommon to meet people across Chinese cities who had a sister, son, cousin or friend who called an Australian city home.

———

If they weren't moving to Australia, they were coming back.

When the pandemic hit, hundreds of thousands of Chinese students who had swelled the enrolments of Australian universities in recent decades and enriched the campus coffers mostly returned to China. The stories they brought back were not always positive.

Long before I took an active interest in China, I had a taste of the international student experience in my tutorials at the University of New South Wales. The Chinese students in my media studies classes mostly kept quiet, stuck together and struggled with the theoretical academic language that tortured even native English speakers. I struggled to churn through Foucault and Derrida and apply their complex ideas in class presentations, so I can only imagine how perplexing it must have been as a nineteen-year-old student doing it in your second language.

But when I was an undergraduate, I didn't consider this; I merely grumbled with other Australians about how the international students brought down the overall standards with their English.

Back in the early 2000s the international student market from China was beginning to boom, but by the time I was back in China in 2015, Australia's universities were absolutely hooked on the rivers of gold these students brought in. A visiting representative from The University of Sydney sought a coffee with me in Beijing, perhaps to offset growing concerns in the media about the reliance on international students. At its pre-pandemic peak, two out of every three international students at The University of Sydney were from China.

When I put to the representative that this was a dangerous over-reliance, she told me the Vice Chancellor saw it as an endorsement for the university's 'international appeal'. Other Australian universities had similar numbers, propelling international education to Australia's most lucrative export after resources.

The reality, though, was that China's best and brightest didn't go to Australia. They sought admission to the best universities in Beijing and Shanghai or in the United States. Failing that, they'd try Oxford or Cambridge, and if the United Kingdom wasn't possible, then Australia, Canada and New Zealand. Australian education had a good reputation, but it was several rungs down the ladder.

And there were some worrying signs. Yinan introduced me to a friend who'd studied for three years at Macquarie University in Sydney and obtained a degree. I was stunned at the dinner to realise she couldn't string an English sentence together. It was fifteen years ago, she reasoned, and she'd forgotten all her English. She also lived inside a Chinese bubble while in Australia, she told me. It reinforced a perception that the Australian institutions, in a competitive rush to bring in full-fee paying students from abroad, were sometimes looking the other way on academic standards.

Another graduate I interviewed who was setting up a business in the southern boom city of Shenzhen bemoaned that there were too many Chinese students in Australia, denying him the opportunity to experience a foreign country. He couldn't get through our television interview in English, but he too had obtained a degree from an Australian university. He had made little effort to pierce the Chinese language and culture bubble while in Sydney, although Chinese international students often say it's tricky to make meaningful friendships with local students. This was one of the most common refrains I heard when seeking feedback on the student experience in Australia: 'Too many Chinese—it's like living in China.' Not too dissimilar to Australians complaining about fellow Australians in Bali, but I wondered how much the universities had really done to provide for a better experience.

The perception that Chinese students were seen as cash cows was strong, and when the Chinese government started issuing symbolic safety warnings about travel to and study in Australia during the pandemic, it spooked many in the tertiary sector. China's government would leap on Australian domestic reports of racism, issuing official safety warnings to Chinese students at times of diplomatic tension.

After years of growing rapidly, the Chinese student boom may have finally peaked. The fall from this peak, exacerbated by the pandemic, was an economic kick in the guts for the unis that had allowed themselves to get hooked, but the change will likely improve the experience for those Chinese students who continue to come to Australia.

The lure of overseas education in general, though, is unlikely to wane. My Chinese circle of friends and colleagues in Beijing had mostly done some years abroad. My two producer colleagues at ABC Beijing had both studied in Australia. A former colleague had left the ABC to take up the British Chevening scholarship in London, while others I knew had done time abroad in Germany and France. Most in the media circles had done their initial degrees at Chinese universities before going on to postgraduate courses abroad. Some initially managed to stay, but jobs were hard to come by and inevitably the career path led back to China.

Yinan had studied in a hard-to-pronounce Welsh university town that was so devoid of people that she felt scared on her first night. She studied television production but after graduating worked in a furniture shop in London, unable to use her professional qualifications until she returned to Beijing and ended up working for the Olympics broadcasting team.

The colleague who went to London on a scholarship tried different avenues in Europe to stay but reluctantly found herself back in Beijing, before getting out of the media altogether and taking a business-related job in Hong Kong.

These were common stories, as were the creative efforts to leave the media behind. Under Chinese government regulations, Chinese citizens can't work as reporters for the overseas media outlets. They are legally constrained to working as 'assistants' to foreign journalists, meaning in many cases they do much of the work for little credit and less pay.

But as Xi Jinping's government tightened the broader media environment, it became increasingly risky for Chinese nationals to work in foreign media. Some of the most accomplished operators who helped produce investigative reports were forced out of their jobs by the department of the Foreign Ministry that manages Chinese staff.

While you can hire anyone you choose, technically Chinese staff aren't allowed to directly work for a foreign media company, but instead are employed on behalf of the company by the Diplomatic Services Bureau—an arm of the Foreign Ministry. It means the staff member signs a contract with the DSB, which then 'manages' and employs them on behalf of the media outlet.

It's a layer of control that allows easier monitoring of their activities but also reserves the option to oust Chinese staff from a foreign company if the government deems them too troublesome.

It rarely used to happen, but in 2019 as the media became a diplomatic pawn between the United States and China, several Chinese staff for American media were made to leave their jobs in Beijing. Wider use of this power beyond the direct China–United States spat was foreshadowed when a producer for British media was targeted.

When a well-regarded senior producer for US outlet Bloomberg Haze Fan was later detained under national security laws, it sent a deep chill through the foreign media community. The risks of doing the job were rising. Local staff were routinely requested to attend meetings with state security agents or police. Those working for high-profile media outlets were the most likely to be targeted. I heard stories of agents asking Chinese staff for office wi-fi passwords and snooping on what their foreign reporters were looking to cover.

It's an annoyance for some, genuinely intimidating for others. Some local staff play dumb, while others play along, writing reports on what's going on in the office. There was no real way for a foreigner to understand this type of pressure, and I told colleagues they should always do what's best to protect themselves from trouble.

With work conditions like this, it's little wonder many Chinese journalists became disillusioned and sought to leave. Others had their optimism about the foreign media crushed. One former ABC producer left in part because she realised the overseas media wasn't the force for constructive criticism she'd hoped it would be. 'You have to beat everything up to get an audience,' she told me, realising after toiling away for years that Australian viewers respond more enthusiastically to simple narratives about China rather than nuanced, complex takes. It must have been beyond frustrating to have correspondent after correspondent rolling up, each with a preconceived idea of your country, asking for help to do the same stories over and over again.

An ever-changing procession of journalists was the one constant for those locals who forged long careers in the overseas media in Beijing. I was just the latest, rotating through a city of constant change, hoping to do justice to the slice of time I was lucky enough to experience.

8

THE REAL CHINA

Foreign correspondents in any country face the constant pull between covering the news agenda and getting off the beaten track. While the daily political and economic stories justify the need for bureaus in key hubs, it's the features far removed from those worlds that the reporter and the audiences remember.

Before moving to Beijing I'd devoured countless articles and reports from journalists about everything from Tibetan monks to nouveau riche millennials to endangered Siberian tigers on the Russian border. But in the 2010s, as the stakes got higher, 'hard news' increasingly became the mainstay of correspondents. China was no longer the 'rising giant' of the region, it had arrived. 'Curiosity' stories about its ancient cultures or modern manufacturing marvels no longer cut it; there were more imminent tales of territorial disputes, foreign interference and technological conflicts to deal with.

In many ways the shift in focus for China coverage reflected a growing maturity. Reporters and audiences were no longer treating China as a mysterious culture wrapped in a jargon-laden Soviet political shell worthy of occasional interest. The military build-up in the South China Sea was confronting, as was the belated realisation that Australia's major political parties were hooked on donations from Chinese property billionaires. Stories about the Shaolin monks could wait.

But the constant focus on politics and strategic rivalry painted a very narrow picture, far removed from the daily lives of people around me. It meant when awful things happened to people in China, audiences struggled to feel empathy towards citizens of a country so often seen through a political and economic lens.

One morning in the massive city of Shenyang in north-eastern China, I stumbled across the sort of story that would be hard to imagine back home. Sixty-year-old retiree Wang Jie invited me and cameraman Steve Wang into her apartment to tell her story of pure pain and suffering.

Ms Wang had been scammed by fraudsters peddling a get-rich-quick scheme from offshore. Such pyramid schemes and scams were widespread in China but Wang Jie's plight high-lighted the quiet cruelty the scammers inflicted.

She had lung cancer, now deeply embedded in her bones. She was slight and frail but warmly welcomed us in along with members of a local support group that had formed online. They'd all fallen victim to the same scam and were united by the sadness, embarrassment and anger of losing family savings to the fraudsters. Some had lost their marriages. Others' relationships with their adult children were ruined.

But Wang Jie's situation was worse than most. She'd led a comfortable middle-class life in the Shenyang suburbs, with three apartments and an adult son who'd gone abroad for study. With him far away, she'd turned to friends old and new for assurance and support when her cancer began. One of those friends, unfortunately, introduced her to the get-rich-quick scheme.

'This "friend" was very familiar with my situation,' Wang Jie told me. 'She said if you re-mortgage your house you will get back all the money and more.'

She recounted the story in minute detail as we sat in a sparsely furnished apartment, the only one she had left.

'This is an overseas investment project, foreigners are involved, you definitely won't lose your money,' she'd been told.

She noted how the friend would turn up with new handbags and a new iPhone, tangible proof, it seemed, of the scheme's value. Wang Jie also had medical costs to contend with and her son's overseas university fees were hefty. She was asset rich but cash poor, so she took out loans and started to tip small amounts in.

But month after month her friend continued to push the investment, presenting brochures and a marketing documentary showing a flashy headquarters for the investment company in London.

'All the marketing materials she gave me had Westerners in them,' she told me. 'I thought in Western countries the people had good morals. The scale of the operation was very impressive, it couldn't be fake.'

Determined to get her story out accurately, she showed me the brochures. It's easy for those with more financial nous to spot something too good to be true, less so for someone with Wang Jie's background and anxieties. Promises of guaranteed 15 per cent annual returns on investments would normally ring alarm bells but Wang Jie, like most of the scam's thousands of victims, never had much in the way of financial education. She'd been born in Chairman Mao's Communist China, came of age during the chaos of the Cultural Revolution and like much of the middle class became rich off the back of skyrocketing apartment prices when China's real estate market was finally unlocked in the 1990s.

In a country where everyone was on guard against scammers and questioning who to trust, it's no surprise she put her faith in a friend close to her. Often that's how the scammers worked, pushing those they'd already sucked in to go and market it to others, broadening the pot supposedly to fatten the overall returns.

Over six years, Wang Jie ended up investing the equivalent of 350,000 Australian dollars, most of it borrowed. When it went belly-up, the banks took her other two apartments and she was left with no money to pay for cancer treatment.

'Luckily the national health scheme gave me some free medicines but there were some I needed that I couldn't afford, so I didn't take them,' she said.

In desperation, Wang Jie went online and did her own research, eventually following the lead of others in her predicament and buying the raw chemical ingredients for chemotherapy medicines, mixing them herself at home. It was the cheapest way to seek treatment and we filmed her as her frail fingers slowly measured doses from unmarked containers and carefully tapped them into pill capsules she'd bought online. To the best of her knowledge, the proportions were right, but she was going off information from blogs.

My mother died of cancer two years before my posting to China. Like Wang Jie's, it had started elsewhere and slowly spread to her bones, but their treatment access was worlds apart.

During our long interview that morning in her cold apartment, Wang Jie came close to tears but never broke down, even when she told me the only reason she hadn't killed herself was because of her son. She told her story with a resolute stoicism, hopeful that publicising the case could bring the perpetrators, one of them allegedly an Australian businessman, to justice.

It was utterly heartbreaking. Other members of the support group quietly sobbed off to the side.

We parted ways, and I interviewed others who had fallen victim to the same pyramid scheme. Marriages ruined, lives upended in cities all across China and Taiwan. The scam company, known as EuroFX, roped in as much as 1 billion dollars before coming unstuck. Victims told me how the account logins that allowed them to watch their growing fortunes suddenly started having problems. A British businessman alleged to have masterminded the scheme sent fake credit cards that he said would allow investors to access their money after the websites shut down.

When another investor, Li Shanbao, discovered she'd been had, she embarked on a cross-border crusade to find and warn other victims and get to the bottom of the scam. Known to her followers as *Chao Ma*, 'Mother Chao', she made multiple trips to the United Kingdom to visit the EuroFX company and see for herself if the buildings in the advertising brochures were real.

Some linked with the scam threatened her, but she persisted. 'What I found was all negative. I was told the company didn't have any staff, that the bank cards were fake—I just crumbled. I couldn't sleep,' she told me. 'That's when I told my daughter our family is broke.'

Chao Ma was in her sixties, had short hair and reading glasses and was much like the other investors I met, except she was an absolute force of nature. She'd organised for us to meet the victims in Shenyang, then more in a steel town called Anshan, and then even more in the coastal city of Dalian. She took us across China's north-east in both high-speed trains and old rattlers, funnelling us to meetings where middle-aged victims sat around wearing shirts printed with the face of the alleged Australian scam master with big characters that read 'Criminal'.

At every stop along the way there were tears and tales of financial ruin, medical bills and family breakdown. People were jostling to tell their story on camera, perhaps as catharsis more than anything. We filmed far more than we'd ever need but we couldn't say no in the face of such desperation. The people who had lost everything putting their faith in the EuroFX scam were now pinning their hopes of justice and compensation on Chao Ma. She was a rock star to these communities. Our assignment took on a degree of expectation I wasn't used to when her followers applauded as Steve Wang and I walked into one of the victims' meetings.

The Australian media, she'd told them, were here to help bring the mastermind to justice.

———

We later went to Taiwan to interview more victims and a lawyer involved in the case. The scam was so big it involved a fake gambling company that sponsored European football teams to show investors in Asia how legitimate it was.

The Australian accountant who drew up the legal structures for EuroFX was so confident that he sat down and gave the ABC an on-camera interview from his home on the Gold Coast. He'd done the consulting on setting up companies and left others to do what they wanted, he said, claiming innocence.

The schemes were based over different jurisdictions involving shell companies and multiple bank accounts. UK police ultimately handballed the investigation to Chinese authorities but it was a complex web for them and Australian police to unravel, particularly with the victims largely abroad.

The ABC had a team working on the story back in Sydney and even though it aired on the national program *7.30*, audiences were only interested up to a point. It was burned off in the early midsummer days of January when ratings are down and viewers are in holiday mode. The ABC devoted a day of coverage to the story but it didn't go any further and there was no follow-on from authorities to pursue the Australian involved. Despite all their desperate hope that the foreign media could help, the victims had overestimated the role we could play.

For months after the story, I checked in with the occasional WeChat message to Chao Ma. She continued to crisscross China rallying victims, her determination for justice undiminished.

―――

There were times, though, when the empathy from audiences surprised me and had a more immediate effect.

In 2018 a shy eleven-year-old boy unexpectedly stole the limelight in a documentary we made about China's recycling and rubbish industries. Mengnan had been dealt some shockingly bad cards in life. He was born in Henan, one of the poorest, most overpopulated provinces, and his father tried to sell him and his two brothers when medical costs for a terminal illness became too much. This wasn't a common story in today's China and I was shocked to hear the boy so nonchalantly explain it, unaware of how extraordinarily dreadful it sounded.

His uncle had intervened to save him but that didn't make life much easier. Mengnan was taken to Beijing to live with his uncle and aunt in a brick shack without running water or electricity, perched on the side of a makeshift rubbish dump. His uncle Wang Jindong collected rubbish to make a living, peddling a three-wheel cart around abandoned construction sites to gather whatever could be sold at scrap markets. Mengnan helped him sort it.

Stories like Mengnan's were a world away from the news agenda. For all of China's technological prowess and rapid development, there were still millions across the country who eked out a life in the gritty underbelly of the glistening new cities. They didn't fit the state narrative and weren't highlighted in government propaganda, but low-paid migrant workers were the glue that held China's cities together.

Mengnan's plight was particularly heartbreaking. We found him through a charity school set up for the children of migrant workers. It was on the south-eastern fringe of Beijing set among industrial blocks in a massive district called Daxing.

Mengnan's school was for the children of migrant workers who didn't have the Beijing 'hukou' residency permit. Under a longstanding system designed to manage the size of cities, you needed the permit to access local schools. With more than 20 million people, population management was a priority for

Beijing's government, but the hukou had created a caste-like system. With around 200 million workers leaving their home towns to keep the country's economy ticking, it was inevitable some brought children who needed schooling, creating a grey zone of schools that existed outside a city's official education program. Mengnan went to one such school.

All of the students were, relatively speaking, poor. But as the adopted son of a rubbish picker, Mengnan was at the bottom of the playground hierarchy.

'I don't get on with my classmates because they think I'm poor,' he told us, unaware how heartbreaking his words were.

We spent days following Mengnan and his uncle Wang Jindong, while filming the school, the rubbish dumps and the recycling depots where Mr Wang collected enough money each week to keep the family going.

My producer Charles Li and I made a donation to the school when we saw the great work it was doing. I didn't think much of the paper receipt that the principal wrote for me, but keeping it turned out to be a major stroke of luck.

Unbeknown to us, Mr Wang's brick shack was on land controlled by a local branch of China's military. The local commander was letting the Wang family squat against the wishes of district officials, who wanted to clear them out. One day while we were filming, the commander got out of his 4WD in plain clothes and demanded to know who we were and what we were doing. Once we explained, he admonished Mr Wang for going along with it. We thought our documentary would grind to an abrupt halt.

Thinking quickly, Charles Li told me to get out the donation receipt. Showing it to the commander, he explained that we were trying to help the family. When he saw our good faith, the commander relented.

Even though this was a minor victory, I assumed that the program couldn't really change anything and felt guilty for exploiting a family in dire circumstances to make a bit of 'poverty porn' for audiences abroad, especially when we returned for a final shoot to find the district government had built a brick wall to close off access to the shack in an effort to squeeze the family out.

But after we aired the program, something extraordinary happened. Emails flooded in from viewers asking how they could donate to help Mengnan.

Maybe while filming it and stressing over how to form a coherent narrative, I'd underestimated the emotional impact of what we were making. But when the editors sewed it together and added music, the piece brought tears to my eyes too.

The emails came thick and fast and we were genuinely stumped on how to deal with them. The migrant worker school wasn't officially registered and didn't have a bank account to donate to. Mr Wang didn't have electricity or a phone, let alone a bank account. And due to China's incredibly restrictive law for non-government organisations, there wasn't a suitable NGO to which we could entrust foreign donations.

And yet the emails and messages kept coming.

So we set up a GoFundMe page to collect the money while we worked out how best to distribute it. We tried to see if we could donate it to Mengnan's next school after he finished primary school, but no one was certain where he would go.

Even when he got a lucky break, it didn't come easy. At almost 20,000 dollars, with more coming in, unsure how we would transfer the money, we decided to close the page.

Eventually we had to settle for the most direct way. One morning in Beijing's early autumn we drove back out to the bricked-in shack. I poked my head above the wall to find Mr Wang inside, his rubbish cart bricked-in and unable to be used. He called for Mengnan, who as usual looked happy to see us.

I dropped the news on Mr Wang that we'd be taking him to the bank to set up an account. I told him the viewers of that show we'd made a few months earlier had donated close to 100,000 yuan—more than enough to pay for Mengnan's future school fees and rent a basic apartment with power and water.

Needless to say, Wang Jindong was thrilled.

My Chinese colleagues and I were a tad worried, however, that Mr Wang might not be the best custodian of the viewers' money, especially as his first response was to treat us to a lavish lunch at the nearest restaurant, insisting we drink Baijiu, the fiery Chinese rice liquor that wasn't well suited to eleven in the morning on a workday.

We declined, so he ordered us beers instead.

I couldn't begrudge a man for celebrating an unexpected windfall but Steve Wang and Charles Li kept reminding him that the money was for Mengnan, not him. As we left that day, our fear wasn't that Mr Wang would blow it, but that he would keep it in the bank for a rainy day, not seeing that Mengnan was in immediate need.

But there was only so much we could control, and the unexpected surge of generosity from viewers was a nice reminder that political differences don't always strip away compassion.

There were so many tough stories we covered in China, whether political or personal. It was nice for once to have a happy ending.

9

RULE OF LAW

It only took a few weeks of being posted in China before I found myself sitting in the back of a police car. And it was due to my own stupidity.

I was outside a prison. With a camera. Absolutely asking for trouble.

For weeks I'd been trying to find a way into a story that had unfolded before I'd arrived in China: the mass arrests of lawyers who worked on human rights cases. The raids on prominent law firms and lawyers across the country had been one of the defining moves of Xi Jinping's leadership, sending a clear message to those seeking to push the limits of China's claim of being a 'rule of law country'.

It was important for outsiders to understand what was happening, particularly as Australia's government was trying to complete an extradition treaty with China. Understandably, few involved in the field were willing to talk to the media, especially on camera. It was incredibly sensitive. Some of those detained were facing years in jail for state security crimes.

But one lawyer in Beijing wasn't scared. Instead, he seemed to relish speaking out. Yu Wensheng was a relatively recent convert to the human rights legal field but what he lacked in years of experience, he more than made up for with passion. He declared on the phone that he 'wasn't scared' and came to the ABC office to give a detailed account of his previous run-ins with authorities. Among other claims, the diminutive, greying lawyer said he had been made to keep his arms lifted up around the back of a large steel chair as a form of torture.

Interviewing him, I felt it could only be a matter of time before someone so outspoken fell foul of state security. The strength of his comments was so rare, a Chinese person directly criticising authority on camera, I feared for his welfare.

Yu Wensheng wasn't closely linked to the lawyers targeted for their human rights work, but he was outspoken in their support. He was short and balding, with fire in his eyes when he talked about the contradictions between China's stated legal principles and the reality.

He'd already had his licence to practise suspended, but he continued to crisscross the country seeking to represent people in need of help. One of them was a fellow lawyer, Wang Quanzhang, who was among the 300 or so lawyers detained during the raids. Unlike most, who were subsequently released, he disappeared.

From the photos I saw, Mr Wang didn't look like a rabble-rouser in his glasses, nondescript haircut and drab clothes. His wife, Li Wenzu, had endured years of her husband pursuing sensitive cases, representing victims of land seizures, followers of the banned spiritual movement Falun Gong and democracy activists. As a colleague of Mr Wang's told me, 'Those are the sort of cases you never win in China.'

But now with a three-year-old son, the stakes for Mr Wang were higher. His determination to persist in fighting for the underdog had led to many arguments, Ms Li told me, but she always supported him. The fire burned deep inside, she admitted, which was part of his appeal.

With all of Mr Wang's close colleagues caught up in the raids, Li Wenzu turned to Yu Wensheng to help. And with Mr Yu being such an outspoken type, this is how I ended up with him outside the prison where Wang Quanzhang was being held.

———

Yu Wensheng, probably against his better judgement, allowed me to tag along on his next visit to Mr Wang's place of detention in the city of Tianjin. Once a two-hour drive, Tianjin was now just a half-hour hop on one of China's shiny new bullet trains.

I asked Mr Yu if he was worried that having a foreign journalist in tow could cause him problems. I'm sure he knew it would, but he told me not to worry. I'd decided to film the trip myself instead of taking colleagues—less is more for sensitive shoots—but not being a cameraman, I had a pep talk first with the bureau's then-shooter Wayne McAllister, who told me that good stories live or die by the 'sequences' you film. He ran me through the need to get narrative shots from different angles that can be sewn together to tell the story.

'Focus on the small details,' he told me. 'Get the interviewee to walk past twice, direct them—you're making a feature story remember, not just covering the news,' Wayne lectured me.

It's the sort of stuff the journalist rarely thinks about.

I packed my Sony camera, a monopod and a small light and headed off early one autumn morning to meet Yu Wensheng at Beijing 'NanZhan', the mammoth single terminal station where trains heading south departed. Tens of thousands of people filed in and out, with trains arriving and departing every few minutes.

I only had a small camera but it wasn't long before security guards stopped me among the crowds of travellers in the waiting room, just moments after I'd started filming general vision of the ticket lines. They questioned me long enough that I missed the train, but my transgression was routine: not having permission to film in the station.

Eventually they put me on a later train in the front carriage where a guard could keep an eye on me.

After I met Mr Yu at the other end, we caught the subway from Tianjin station to the end of a line heading in the direction of the detention centre. During the journey, I interviewed Mr Yu, filming him as he described the purpose of his visit and what he knew about Mr Wang's case. Other commuters shifted away from us as he spoke, from an instinct that the foreigner with the camera talking to a bloke about a human rights issue could be trouble.

We emerged into the city's frontier: rural plots of land, low buildings and dozens of smoking men hustling their hire cars. Whether it was Beijing or elsewhere, you could judge when you'd crossed the city limits by whether the taxi drivers negotiated fares.

We settled on a heavy-set driver with a pet cricket in a tube chirping in his breast pocket. The cricket soothed him, he told me, as we drove towards the detention centre. The driver chatted away and agreed with Yu Wensheng's general complaints about authorities and little guys not getting a fair shake.

In general, Chinese cabbies could be relied upon to tell you that the common people, or *laobaixing*, were not being heard. My insistence on filming Mr Yu during the ride and his constant talk about national security cases didn't perturb the driver. He seemed not to care too much that he was driving a foreign journalist and a human rights activist lawyer towards a prison, as long as he got paid. And he understood why I had to crouch below the window as we arrived.

After seeing Mr Yu walk in to register at the front office of the prison, I realised how relaxed the scene was. Prisoners' family members were standing around in the carpark sharing cigarettes and chatting. Farmers from nearby fields walked past with goats. Courier delivery drivers came and went with packages. After several minutes crouching down trying to film secretly, I realised I had far more leeway than expected.

So a few minutes later when Yu Wensheng returned to the taxi having had his application to visit Wang Quanzhang rejected again, I hopped out and asked him if he could walk back to the prison gates so I could catch a clearer shot of him walking out.

Ever happy to oblige, Mr Yu agreed. I stood there with a handheld camera filming him stroll across the small carpark to the car.

'Stop, go back,' I said, getting into the swing of things.

I wasn't a cameraman, so I was relishing the rare opportunity to do a bit of directing.

'Okay, once again please.'

Yu Wensheng walked back and forth to the gates as I changed from a tight shot to a wide.

'Stop, okay, a close-up of your hand opening the door.'

I'd gone from hoping to get a few glimpses of a gutsy lawyer leaving a prison to filming a full-blown creative sequence. Angles, wide shots, close-ups. The cabbie seemed bemused by it all as he reclined in his chair, cricket chirping on his chest.

Unbeknown to me as I kept filming and directing Mr Yu, a crowd had gathered. I was so caught up looking through the lens that I'd failed to notice the uniformed prison guards and police forming a group behind me. And when I finally put down the camera and realised, it was too late.

Yu Wensheng had noticed the writing on the wall and hopped into the car. I jumped in with him and we directed the driver to take us back to the train station. But more police cars rolled around the corner and an older cop with a cigarette hanging out of his mouth jumped out and gestured to the cab driver to pull over. Busted.

For the next hour, a good cop/bad cop duo interviewed me in one of their cars while others interrogated Yu Wensheng. The driver was questioned separately.

Luckily, I'd swapped cards from the camera so they wouldn't delete my footage when they inevitably went through it. The police had an air of frustration about this bloody foreigner randomly rocking up to a prison and pulling them away from their lunch. They wanted to know how I knew Yu Wensheng and who'd introduced us. I told them I'd searched for him randomly online, and I was making a story about the average day in the life of a lawyer. Anything to not get him into deeper shit.

After an hour or so and several calls to their superiors, they told me I was free to leave, as was Mr Yu.

The cabbie's air of casual bemusement was long gone. He was fuming that we'd entangled him with the police and wasted his afternoon. Yu Wensheng wasn't deterred; he kept explaining how the authorities weren't legally entitled to reject his application, but the driver was having none of it. I paid him 300 yuan to make up for it and he drove us to the nearest train station, where he was glad to see the back of us.

I felt awful for having put Mr Yu in a police car for an hour. He said he wasn't in any immediate trouble but it's the sort of thing that would be recorded on a file somewhere.

It was a classic Journalism 101 of what a selfish foreign reporter shouldn't do—put their interviewee in danger just to get a better story.

And it was a good lesson: even when things look fine, you should use common sense. It's illegal to film outside prisons in China (as in many other countries) at any time, let alone when there's a political prisoner inside.

Yu Wensheng promised to keep me updated on the case. He walked into the station and caught a train south to tackle another case in a coastal city.

I returned to Beijing, cursing my stupidity but knowing I had the makings of a good story.

—

Wang Quanzhang's case was one of many, and we only stumbled upon it because he happened to be Mr Yu's unofficial client, but as the years went by, it became clear his case was the most serious of all.

His wife, Li Wenzu, was stoic and bold when we first met in her father-in-law's apartment in west Beijing in late 2015. About

30 years old with bright eyes and a short bob, she was friendly and welcoming to the strangers squeezing awkwardly into the apartment. Her three-year-old boy was playing on her lap as we sat on tiny children's chairs in his playroom, toys scattered around. She couldn't possibly explain to him where his dad was, so she'd said he'd gone away on a holiday.

She didn't seek the limelight, and when she opened up about the toll her husband's case was taking on her family, her sadness and anxiety came to the fore. But she held it together, tears at times rolling down her cheeks, although she never sobbed properly.

Unlike some other family members of detained lawyers, Li Wenzu thought staying silent wasn't going to help free her husband. She spoke of how determined he was, and she must have known he'd show a resilience in prison that others couldn't muster. Before coming to China, I wrongly assumed that the country's activists would walk on eggshells, constantly fearful of surveillance. But to my surprise many of them were the opposite—outspoken and boldly facing the prospect of harassment, prison and possibly torture.

It was almost as if some sought to be martyrs. Within the activist community there was a strong streak of Christianity. It wasn't uniform, but many of the boldest activists were driven by Christian ideals. This gave context to the Communist Party's suspicions about Christianity being politically subversive. A journalist friend of mine once said, 'They have a point.'

Other activists like Yu Wensheng seemed driven by a determination for justice, which helped him muster courage in the face of pressure. He had started a human rights group to link the legal community on Telegram, one of the encrypted apps, and he pressed on with efforts to legally be registered as Wang

Quanzhang's lawyer, making that train ride to Tianjin and submitting fresh applications at the front office of the detention centre gate each month, all of them rejected. Officially the reason was that state security agencies must give permission to allow lawyer visits in national security cases. But they rarely did.

As one year stretched into the next, others were sentenced or released from prison, but there was little movement and no contact in Mr Wang's case. He was being held in 'residential surveillance at a designated location', the euphemistic term for incommunicado extrajudicial prison. Li Wenzu told me, 'If he's being tortured, we don't have the faintest clue.'

The only word she received came six months after his disappearance when authorities said her husband was under investigation for state subversion. She believed that Mr Wang's refusal to crack and confess to anything was drawing out his case.

More than a year and a half after the meeting in her apartment, we met again with Li Wenzu, this time outside the gates of a prosecutor's office in central Beijing. I'd set up the meeting through a messaging app and brought along our newly arrived Australian cameraman, Brant Cumming, who'd come to Beijing from Adelaide via five years in the Middle East. He knew a sensitive situation when he saw one.

It was a strange scene. The prosecutor's office wasn't far from Tiananmen Square and the Chinese leadership compound Zhongnanhai, so the surveillance was intense. This was the most central part of Beijing, a mixture of traditional architecture and modern surveillance cameras on mostly quiet streets.

Li Wenzu and a friend were arguing at the gates with security guards and police who were not letting them in. Given the heavy police presence in the area, it didn't seem appropriate for two Westerners with a camera to join them, so we sat as inconspicuously as we could in a small park opposite, hoping the slight summer haze would help obscure us.

After a while Ms Li and her friend walked over. Ms Li wore a T-shirt with a sketch of Wang Quanzhang on the front. Despite the awful situation her family was in, she seemed to have blossomed from the anxious wife reluctantly thrust into the spotlight to a confident activist fuelled by a mission to free her husband.

We went back to our office compound, where she spoke not with tears but determination. 'On the news every day we hear China is a country with rule of law, but from my perspective, if you look at this case, there's no law at all,' she said. She and her son had been forced to leave her apartment. Paid goons followed her around filming on their phones to harass her. 'They told landlords not to rent houses to us. I spent ages trying to get my four-year-old son into a kindergarten, only for state security to pressure the school into not accepting him. He still hasn't attended school.'

Over a year and a half of this treatment, she'd gained the confidence to film them back, chiding and questioning her harassers. She showed me a video she'd filmed outside her front door of one of the paid goons, a young waif-like man, sitting curled up in a ball, head bowed in shame. He'd been paid to follow her around for days but she'd got into his head, questioning him about how embarrassed he felt to do that sort of work.

'You don't have to do this type of job, there are plenty of other jobs like in supermarkets, McDonald's or KFC,' she told him.

The man, who looked all of twenty in the video, kept his head buried in his knees, mumbling that he'd signed a document compelling him to do the work.

'If I quit, they'll send somebody else to replace me,' he muttered.

It was an extraordinary piece of footage, exposing the many complex layers of China's surveillance state. A young man employed to intimidate a mother was himself on camera trying to hide, mortified that his target had used logic and compassion to break him down. He was nothing but a low-paid migrant worker who felt he had little option but to do this dirty work. Now he was being forced to face the awful reality of what his job involved.

As Wang Quanzhang's case ground towards charges against him for subverting the Communist Party state, Li Wenzu tried creative ways to keep his case in the spotlight. She, along with the wives of several other lawyers caught up in the crackdown, shaved their heads bald. Then, at the 1000-day mark since his arrest, she set off on a twelve-day, 100-kilometre march from Beijing to Tianjin, where her husband was still being held.

By this stage she'd become a high-profile figure for the foreign media. Journalists and camera crews followed her as she began the walk, dressed in a bright red winter's coat, her son in a down jacket hoisted on her shoulder. With the exception of security goons, there weren't any Chinese cameras pointed at her. Like all prominent dissidents, Li Wenzu was now a star to the China-watching community abroad and the small community of dissidents in China, but completely unknown to the general public. To any Beijing driver rolling past the caravan of media on the footpath that morning, they wouldn't have had the faintest clue who the young woman in red was or why people were following her.

These parallel media worlds led to widespread perceptions that the Western media was mistreating China by focusing on obscure human rights cases. But the cases were obscure for a reason—China's Communist Party devoted huge resources to suppressing public information about them, ensuring the community of fellow activists received the deterrent message about arrests and punishments while keeping the broader public in the dark.

Li Wenzu didn't make it to the Tianjin detention centre. On the sixth day of her quest, she was stopped at a hotel lobby in an outer district of Tianjin and detained at a police station. According to her, she was questioned by a senior police officer from the city's state security bureau. After she was released later that evening, some friends picked her up and drove her back to Beijing.

———

As Li Wenzu's torturous personal saga was unfolding, Australia's Coalition government led by then-Prime Minister Malcolm Turnbull was trying to push an extradition treaty with China through the parliament in Canberra. The treaty wasn't new—it had originally been signed between Australia and China in the dying days of John Howard's government in 2007. That was during the peak of the mining boom, pre-Beijing Olympics, a time when relations were largely untroubled.

But even back during easier times, there was reluctance in the Australian parliament to ratify the treaty. Successive Labor governments didn't push it and nor did the Coalition when it regained power in 2013. The list of concerns was long. If a person was extradited from Australia to China, they would not be guaranteed a right to a fair trial or due process. The Chinese judiciary was not independent, recording a 99 per cent conviction rate in prosecutions. Plus, there was China's use of the death penalty.

In 2017, even as diplomatic tension was starting to simmer, the Turnbull-led government made the most concerted push to finally get the treaty into law. China's government had been supercharging efforts to repatriate corrupt fugitives, even sending undercover agents into Australia to pressure Chinese nationals to 'voluntarily' return home.

I had no trouble believing corrupt fugitives were a significant problem, as back in my Xinhua days a colleague had told me about a good friend who was now living in Melbourne because her dad, a mid-level official from central Shaanxi province, had absconded with government funds. She'd laughed about it as though it wasn't unusual.

Since Xi Jinping had come to power, he'd made a big display in state media of repatriating suspects from abroad, with a promise to swat both 'tigers and flies' as part of a massive anti-corruption drive called 'Operation Foxhunt'. The state news channel CCTV frequently went live to show commercial passenger planes landing from the United States or Europe before an unhappy-looking passenger in handcuffs was taken down the stairs by stern officers and paraded to the media.

There's little doubt that corruption had run rampant before Xi Jinping's rise, and foreign media investigations into the extraordinary accumulation of family wealth of some very senior leaders, including Xi himself, highlighted how deep the problem was.

But the ferocity and speed of his corruption purges, starting just after he took power in late 2012, were unprecedented. Initially it seemed newsworthy as provincial Party chiefs or city mayors were placed under investigation. A military chief and then a very powerful retired member of China's highest-level decision-making cabinet, the Politburo Standing Committee, were brought down.

But by 2015 and 2016, one of my colleagues compared it to 'a cricket score', so high were the weekly numbers of politicians and officials displaced and detained. Was it a genuine strike at deeply embedded corruption or a political campaign? Or both?

There was evidence that for all of its political elements, the anti-corruption drive worked wonders on the ground. When I was on a reporting trip to a factory in southern Guangdong, the Chinese-Australian owner bemoaned how he couldn't cut corners on safety requirements anymore because the local inspectors wouldn't dare take bribes.

With China's government so obsessed with results in its battle against corruption, this looked to be a rare area where Australia could garner some goodwill. 'We don't want to be a haven for fugitives,' the ambassador at the time told me. Australia already had a similar treaty with Communist Vietnam, she argued, saying safeguards on the Australian end should ease concerns about China's legal system.

As a journalist covering occasional legal cases, however, I was hard to convince. It wasn't just Wang Quanzhang's case that troubled me.

———

In the mid-2010s, a succession of Australian drug mules was arrested in southern China's Guangdong province, often at the airport with poorly concealed packages of methamphetamines. Around the same time, there was an upsurge in foreigners caught with commercial quantities of ice across the border in Hong Kong. While these suspects were all arrested in China in close proximity, the legal treatment they received differed enormously depending on which side of the China–Hong Kong border they were on.

In Hong Kong, which despite being a region of China had its own separate legal system, prosecutors ended up withdrawing charges against six Western suspects, including two Australians, judging they were the victims of a sophisticated West African crime syndicate that had duped them into becoming unwitting drug mules. Across the border in Guangzhou, where the circumstances appeared awfully similar, this line of defence didn't cut it in China's Communist Party-controlled courts. Among at least half a dozen Australians who were arrested, one had a learning disability and another had been involved in dubious get-rich-quick schemes.

Given China's well-known use of capital punishment for serious drug offences, it struck me as odd that people would walk through customs with poorly concealed packages of methamphetamine. Yet that's what happened, according to Chinese prosecutors, in multiple cases. Prosecutors pushed for the death penalty.

A father and former actor, Karm Gilespie was made to wait in a jail cell for more than five years between a two-day trial split between a hearing in late 2014 and a second one in early 2015, and the eventual verdict delivered in 2020. Prior to his ill-fated trip to China, he had left a string of videos and social-media posts about 'wealth creation' schemes. Years later, when his death-penalty judgment was announced, friends who thought he'd disappeared revealed he had originally been lured to Guangzhou in the hopes of signing some form of investment deal.

During those years he was interned we heard nothing about his case, from family, lawyers or diplomats. If his family thought that publicly staying silent would help, those hopes were cruelly dashed when the Guangzhou Intermediate Court announced their decision in the middle of a period of heightened diplomatic tension with Australia, describing it as an 'important case' (though not important enough to provide any details of the trial when I requested them). In June 2020, Gilespie was sentenced to death.

There was zero transparency, as we would understand it. In another case involving an Australian jockey from Adelaide named Anthony Bannister, who like Gilespie claimed to have been duped, the court refused to allow Australian reporters to witness his appeal against a suspended death sentence. There were others accused of similar offences who were made to wait more than six years in a Guangzhou jail cell just for their initial trial.

There's little public compassion for alleged drug smugglers, but the delay and secrecy around their cases would be scandalous in many other countries. Whether for sensitive human rights cases involving Chinese accused of trying to subvert the state or for more straightforward drug-smuggling cases involving foreigners, I saw little to assure me that any safeguard at the Australian end could ensure extradited suspects would face a fair trial.

Australian parliamentarians agreed, with a backbench revolt scuttling the government's efforts to pass the extradition treaty. I would be very surprised if any Australian government tries again to ratify it.

———

Wang Quanzhang had to wait three and a half years for his day in court.

When it finally came, the trial was announced on Christmas Eve 2018, when many foreign journalists were out of China. But I was staying in Beijing that Christmas, and I remember tucking into a 'Christmas orphans' feast with Stephen McDonnell, the two of us pledging not to drink too much ahead of the early trip to Tianjin the next morning.

I'd followed this random case in China's huge judicial system from an early point, astonished that it had become 'the' case of most significance. I needed to see it through.

The trial was taking place at a centrally located court complex but there was never any chance of us being allowed in. I took the train with cameraman Steve Wang and producer Cecily Huang, and we hired a car to take us to the court. We hopped out separately in a side street. I set off to walk to the front by myself, but a group of plain-clothes police stopped me to demand my press card.

'Where are you going?' they asked.

After showing them and explaining I was there to cover the trial, they asked if I had permission to attend, which no foreign media was able to obtain.

'The case has nothing to do with your country,' one officer told me, and advised me to leave, but they'd already anticipated a media presence. As I walked towards a position across the road from the front entrance, which had been sealed off, I was stopped two more times by police asking to check my press card. It seemed they wanted to record exactly who was there.

Steve and Cecily joined me and a small gaggle of reporters, undercover police, hangers-on and European diplomats, all standing around in the freezing cold. The diplomats had applied to observe the trial to show concern about human rights in China, but were also barred, so they stood shivering and talking among themselves to make a point. Occasionally a reporter would go to McDonald's and come back clasping a cup of hot coffee to bring feeling back to their fingers.

Missing from the gathering was Li Wenzu. She had hoped to see her husband for the first time in three and a half years, but twelve security guards turned up to her Beijing apartment to stop her travelling to Tianjin for the trial.

Three bogus TV news crews, operatives of the government, bearing a microphone flag that read 'Legal online', were also there, shoving their cameras in the face of Western journalists and sticking microphones in front of the diplomats to ask them why they were interfering in the case. It was pure performance art, with the crews deliberately walking into the backdrop when we filmed pieces to camera in an effort to ruin our shots. They were having a great time, laughing while harassing Westerners who dared to take an interest in the case.

When one of the bystanders started yelling in support of Wang Quanzhang, the police shoved him into a van. A media scrum formed to record it, and one of the fake cameramen tripped up a French photographer trying to get a shot. The Chinese cameraman claimed the photographer had assaulted him. Police quickly surrounded the Frenchman.

The fake TV reporters also called one of my Chinese colleagues a 'traitor'. It was an unedifying display that said a lot about how China's government viewed the law and the media.

We waited for hours across the road from the court. When I went to McDonald's for some respite from the cold, an undercover policeman also sheltering inside snapped into action and asked me for my press card, as though I needed it to buy coffee.

While this ridiculous theatre was unfolding outside, details of Wang Quanzhang's crimes were being revealed inside the courtroom. A lawyer posted pictures online of the indictment, revealing Wang was accused of subverting the Chinese state by conspiring with a foreign NGO to organise legal training for Chinese lawyers. He also was accused of subversion by representing practitioners of the banned spiritual practice Falun Gong. But whatever else was happening in the court, we clearly weren't going to find out, so by early afternoon we farewelled our media colleagues and our new acquaintances in China's security services and headed back to Beijing to file the story.

We later found out that Mr Wang had sacked his court-appointed lawyer within minutes of walking into the hearing, determined to make a point about the lack of independent representation. About a month later, Wang Quanzhang was found guilty and sentenced to four and a half years behind bars. If anything, this gave his family some relief, as his long time imprisoned before the trial counted towards the sentence. He was finally released in April 2020 and reunited with Li Wenzu and their young son. Their tearful embrace at home was captured by a friend and posted online.

———

While the release and reunion for Wang Quanzhang brought closure to a five-year saga for one family, the cycle was only just beginning for another. Yu Wensheng, the gutsy lawyer who had introduced me to Mr Wang's case, was now facing his own day of reckoning.

He'd been arrested by twelve police officers, including a SWAT team, in Beijing while walking his son to school. A government media outlet released a highly edited video of the arrest claiming Mr Yu had assaulted a police officer. It had happened just hours after he'd circulated an open letter advocating changes to China's constitution, including oversight of the Communist Party and democratic elections.

Our run-in with police at the gates of the Tianjin detention centre three years earlier was minor league compared to calling for multi-party elections! Clearly each setback spurred him towards a bolder form of activism.

Like Wang Quanzhang, Yu Wensheng was held incommunicado and eventually put on trial in a closed court. His wife made dozens of attempts to visit him and appealed to the international community to raise awareness of his case. Like Wang, he was convicted and sentenced to four years in jail for incitement of state subversion.

Another family disrupted, their lives altered.

But no matter how harsh the punishments, there were always those brave enough, or perhaps mad enough, to take a stand and face the consequences.

The fire burned deep within them.

10

TRADE WAR

'I don't blame China,' said Donald Trump, turning from the lectern to make eye contact with Xi Jinping.

The US president took in the round of applause that broke out among Chinese officials in the room as the translation reached their earpieces.

'After all, who can blame a country for being able to take advantage of another country for the benefit of its citizens?' he said, turning to Xi once more. 'I give China great credit.'

In the Great Hall of the People, in front of China's leader, Trump had, with a backhanded compliment, just delivered the clearest signal that he wasn't bluffing on his threat to launch a trade war.

That moment was the single most important comment to come out of Trump's visit to China in November 2017, to that point the most anticipated foreign-policy trip of his entire presidency (later eclipsed by his unexpected summit with the North Korean leader Kim Jong-un in Singapore).

The China trip, though, had a lot more at stake, coming after Trump fired up his base with scathing rhetoric about China during his campaign to become president. 'We can't continue to allow China to rape our country,' Trump had said on the stump to the wild applause of Midwest supporters. Talking tough on China was a classic campaign tactic for US politicians on both sides (Joe Biden once called Xi Jinping 'a thug'), but once in office they usually toned it down as the pressure of business lobbies and professional diplomats shaped their policies.

Donald Trump, though, kept going hard; his decision to take a congratulatory phone call from Taiwanese President Tsai Ing-wen after being elected caught Beijing off guard. Out of deference to China's sensitivity about Taiwan's sovereignty, no US leader or president-elect had spoken directly with a Taiwanese leader in 38 years, despite continuing to sell arms to the self-ruled island. Seemingly out of nowhere, Trump broke that convention, clearly rattling a Chinese leadership struggling to come to grips with the unconventional new president across the Pacific.

During his first year in office, Trump veered between praise and criticism for the Chinese leadership, backing down on a promise to designate China a currency manipulator but continuing to insist that the trading relationship between the world's two largest economies was heavily tilted in China's favour.

All the while, China's leadership put out soothing messages about 'cooperation' being beneficial to both sides.

Even after an early 'get to know you' visit by Xi Jinping to Florida, where the two men and their wives posed uncomfortably on a plush sofa in Trump's garish Mar-a-Lago resort, relations between the world's two strongest countries were defined by their uncertainty.

That made Trump's autumn trip to Beijing all the more tantalising.

Few of the foreign journalists could quite picture the bombastic US president in Beijing, let alone him sitting down to a two-man superpower summit with Xi in the Great Hall of the People. So on the morning when it happened, excitement was at fever pitch.

Trump had flown to Beijing via Japan and South Korea. I'd covered the reaction to his visit in Seoul and caught a glimpse of his motorcade passing by some of his more extreme South Korean supporters. They were mainly older, many were conservative Christians, and some had hung up posters calling on Trump to immediately bomb Kim Jong-un.

But Beijing was the main event. On the morning of his meeting with Xi, I decided to walk the four-kilometre stretch between the ABC office and the Great Hall. Trump and his entourage were staying at the St Regis Hotel just near the office, which was fenced off and surrounded by curious Beijing locals, all waiting to a get a selfie as the US leader rolled by. His two black presidential limousines were parked at the front entrance, so if I walked, I would catch the convoy as it rolled down an empty Chang'an Avenue.

Twenty minutes later, the two limos, flanked by twenty motorcycle police and another 40 vehicles, proceeded down the heavily guarded avenue before I'd even made it to Tiananmen Square, next to the Great Hall.

'Shit, I'm late,' I panicked, starting to bolt in my suit towards the Tiananmen gate, hosting Mao's portrait, past which stairs would lead down under Chang'an Avenue to the Great Hall.

As I neared Tiananmen, a policewoman rushed up to me.

'Hello, do you need some help?' she asked in a tone that made it clear helping me wasn't her priority.

Before I could answer, another two police in plain clothes, who had been lurking among the Chinese tourists taking pictures of Mao's portrait, had rushed up and surrounded me. Even on a day of extreme political sensitivity, the Forbidden City behind Tiananmen remained open to tourists, although I'd guess a decent chunk of them were undercover security agents.

'Where are you going?' the policewoman asked, her bodycam filming me.

This sort of security shakedown was so common for journalists in China, it felt really good to pull the media pass out of my pocket. 'I'm late and I'm scared I'm going to miss the meeting, how do I get across the road to the Great Hall?' I asked, genuine panic in my voice.

At the sight of my pass, her tone changed dramatically. She barked into her walkie-talkie to tell whoever was watching me on a surveillance camera that I was a *jizhe*, or journalist. She gestured for me to follow her to a crossing further up the road. She and the other police had an urgency that seemed to sympathise with how much trouble a journalist would be in for missing the leaders' meeting.

After multiple security checks, I met my cameraman Steve Wang inside and we made our way up to an elaborate conference room with crystal chandeliers and burgundy carpet.

Outside the front of the building, Xi and Trump were walking the red carpet and clapping along as Chinese and American children excitedly jumped up and down with flowers and mini flags, a cute North-Korean-esque touch that never fails to charm visiting leaders.

Inside the hall, there was row upon row of seating for officials in front of a long table reserved for dozens of business executives from both sides.

They were to take turns signing deals worth a total of 250 billion US dollars.

Two oversized 'leaders' chairs were at the end on a stage, reserved for the two most powerful men in the world. Many of the deals were just MOUs (memorandums of understanding) for projects that may or may not happen, but the headline figure was symbolic. Xi Jinping had ordered officials to frantically tally up as many dollars' worth of deals, either real or theoretical, as possible in order to dangle this extravagant carrot in front of the US leader. While it was normal for foreign leaders to ink lucrative agreements on trips to Beijing, 250 billion dollars was well out of the ordinary. It was a blatant attempt to get President Trump to back off on his threats of tariffs, and to keep the status quo going.

Quite clearly, it was a status quo that worked very well for China.

———

After waiting around at the back with the other media, Xi, Trump and dozens of CEOs walked in to music and applause. This was not supposed to be the main event of the day but rather a goodwill event prior to a joint statement to be read out in a different room in the Great Hall.

Up the back, a flustered US press official snapped at foreign journalists and Chinese officials, the stress of managing so many moving parts taking its toll.

'No,' she loudly said to one of the media crew members who was demanding more access to an event later that day. 'I told you only one pool photographer would be allowed!'

Seemingly not sure what to make of it, a Chinese official tapped her on the shoulder and offered her a seat.

Up the front of the hall, President Xi repeated the usual Chinese talking points: 'win–win cooperation', 'mutual respect' and so on. There were few surprises with Xi Jinping's speeches. Having tight control of an entire government and media apparatus meant anything he said had usually been foreshadowed by weeks or months of comments from officials and articles saying the same thing. He rarely said anything specific, and his speeches were designed to affirm him as the 'big picture' man setting the direction of a nation while those below him nutted out the details.

When he did spring a surprise, as with his 2019 decision to impose a national security law on Hong Kong, Xi never announced it himself. The official newsagency Xinhua would put out the statement, or officials at highly staged-managed press conferences made announcements on his behalf.

Xi never held press conferences where he could be questioned. If a policy was controversial or the subject of intense criticism abroad, like the mass internment of Uighurs in Xinjiang, his name would rarely be linked directly to government statements.

Seldom would his quotes be attached to any big new development. Only later on, when a policy program was established, would Xi usually make a speech or release quotes in the state media to put his signature on it. It was almost as though he would get the state media to test out an idea before taking the risk of being publicly associated with it.

For the looming trade battle with the United States, there was no new idea to test out. Xi was trying to stop Trump from instigating change, and although he didn't say it directly in his remarks, the 250 billion dollars' worth of deals sitting between the business executives said it more clearly than words. There were orders for 300 new Boeing jets, 50 new Bell helicopters, plans for huge Chinese investments in American shale gas and Alaskan LNG, letters of intent for huge soybean orders, promises of more American beef and pork for Chinese noodle soup bowls, vague plans for Dow Industrial to help a bike-sharing company in Shanghai design lighter-weight bicycles . . . It just went on and on.

From a distance, it looked like a treasure trove of riches. In detail, it looked like a lot of vague promises. But the message was clear.

The biggest question hanging over the hall was whether or not Trump would settle for these promises of riches and drop his threats of a trade war.

Even from the back, I was struck by how Trump looked exactly the same in person as he did on TV. So often people you regularly see on the screen appear taller or shorter or fatter or older in real life. Yet this man who was absolutely dominating the world's airwaves looked exactly like Donald Trump, golden hair glinting under the chandeliers.

And he sounded like Donald Trump too. 'Booootiful' deals, 'Wonderful people,' 'Amazing things happening' . . . It was classic Trump, and sounded very much like he'd take the bounty and keep his mouth shut about the trade imbalances and lack of reciprocity that plagued the economic relationship.

As he prattled on, I gestured to Steve to unplug his camera. The joint statement between the two leaders was happening straight after the business event in a room downstairs, and if we pulled out early, we might be able to get a prime position near the front. On the unlikely chance that these two 'strongman' leaders would take questions, I would be in with a chance.

As Steve began shutting down the camera, I pulled the cord from the audio splitter at the side.

And that's when Trump's tone changed.

The relationship is 'a very one-sided and unfair one', he said. He started talking about 'unfair trade practices', 'forced technology transfer' and 'the theft of intellectual property'.

'Turn it back on, turn it back on!' I hissed to Steve as I jabbed the audio cord back in a hole.

'But I don't blame China,' Trump went on, pausing with one hand theatrically raised in the air before delivering the backhanded compliment that some Chinese officials and business leaders awkwardly applauded.

All the while Xi sat there in an oversized leather chair, his poker face on as the translation came through his earpiece. It was, frankly, exhilarating to see a foreign leader be direct, critical and forthright in front of Xi Jinping on Chinese soil. For years I'd watched dignitaries roll into Beijing and play the diplomatic game on China's terms, as though they'd been overawed by the pomp and ceremony. I remembered Barack Obama's meek and evasive answer to a question about why the United States sells arms to Taiwan when he visited Shanghai in 2009. Even US presidents, leaders of the only country that China views with a degree of deference, shaped their language to fit Chinese diplomatic norms when visiting. Foreign leaders, even powerful ones, didn't publicly chide the Chinese in China. They were far more two-faced about it, criticising China's government abroad and then gutlessly staying mute in Beijing.

So to see a US leader throw the niceties out the window and accuse Xi's government of presiding over IP theft, unfair market-access policies and exploitative trade practices was simply remarkable. Trump's comments signalled a historic shift.

At the joint statement 'press conference' afterwards, the language was much more diplomatic. The two men, both deeply hostile to media that didn't praise them, didn't take any questions. As they wrapped up and walked out, the US press pack shouted questions across the room, momentarily stunning some of the Chinese state-media reporters unaccustomed to such forthrightness.

One question, yelled by a female American reporter, rose above the cacophony, quite likely reaching the ears of the two men leaving the stage.

'President Trump, do you still think China is raping our country?'

The US leader didn't turn around or acknowledge the question.

Four months later, he announced tariffs on Chinese exports.

China's economy ended three decades of socialist isolation with the Reform and Opening Up Policy in 1978, two years after the death of an ailing and wildly erratic Chairman Mao brought the disastrous Cultural Revolution to an end. Steady progress followed, but the economy really took off when the United

States and other member nations agreed to China's entry into the World Trade Organization in 2001.

When I was a child in the 1990s, I'd notice my toys, our kitchen appliances and pretty much everything plastic we had was 'Made in Taiwan'. As an adult, everything was 'Made in China'; the country went from a rising exporter to unquestionably the world's dominant manufacturing powerhouse.

While there had been a huge number of conditions placed on China's entry to the WTO, there was rising unease a decade and a half later about whether Beijing had lived up to its promises. Trump's rhetoric reflected a deep suspicion that the world's largest economy had let the wolf into the henhouse. After America lost an estimated 2 million manufacturing jobs in those years, Beijing was now coming for its high-tech economy.

The trade entanglements that the United States, Germany, Japan and other manufacturing nations had with China were unexpectedly fascinating to me. Australia's lack of sophistication in its economic offerings was apparent any time I tried to find Australian companies doing anything mildly creative in China. There was a start-up trying to market STEM education software and a few food 'incubator' entrepreneurs (in other words, they ran a restaurant), but Australians were few and far between in China's massive economy. And even when they attempted to sell the most uncreative product possible—meat pies—they still weren't any good at it.

I met three Australians separately trying to peddle pies to China's billion-plus mouths, and not one of them lasted more than a couple of years. Australians just weren't very good at tapping the Chinese market, except those back home who dug stuff up, grew stuff, milked cows or sold education and tourism services to Chinese visiting Australia. It was embarrassingly basic and a sign of Australia's dumb luck that even when China later started blocking various imports for political reasons, it couldn't stall the biggest one—iron ore—because Chinese steel mills needed it so badly.

This simplistic trade relationship explains why the Australian business lobby has been so consistently deferential to China, urging the pollies to say and do the right things so the Chinese keep on ordering more resources, wine and milk powder, and sending their kids to Australian unis.

But the Europeans, Japanese, Taiwanese and South Koreans were different. They made stuff, often high-tech stuff, that the Chinese wanted because they couldn't make it themselves and were rapidly trying to catch up. European aircraft, German cars and appliances, Taiwanese semiconductors that power smartphones, Japanese robots and South Korean OLED screens were just a sample.

As China emerged as a competitor for all of these exports, this remained the market they were all desperately trying to sell more to. It made for intriguing business stories about Chinese firms acquiring strategic German industrial robotics companies, taking large stakes in European car manufacturers and even a Swedish 5G equipment maker desperate to convince its government not to block a Chinese rival for fear it would be shut out of China in retaliation.

But it was the Americans who took the cake for the most interesting business entanglements with China. Under Donald Trump, issues that had simmered for years were finally out in the open. The blocking of major US tech companies, the stalling of American financial payment firms, the forced joint ventures for car companies seeking access to China's market, and demands to transfer valuable technology secrets in exchange for market access were among the many qualms US companies had about doing business in China.

Despite this friction, the Americans were selling more than ever to China. Sales of iPhones were surging, Boeing jets were clogging Chinese airspace, and American cars, most assembled in China, were charging down Chinese highways.

Chinese investment was flowing the other way too, with ridiculously cashed-up Chinese companies (with murky ownership) such as Hainan Airlines Group and Anbang Insurance Group buying everything from American hotel chains to Silicon Valley companies.

With so much Chinese cash flying around, there were plenty of reasons for the US government not to rock the boat. But by the time Donald Trump was in office, there was also a very clear pattern to what was happening. Since joining the WTO, China had effectively cherrypicked the markets it opened to foreign companies, allowing entry in sectors where it couldn't compete, such as aircraft manufacturing, and restricting or flat-out blocking competition in areas where it wanted homegrown companies to dominate.

The US payment giants Visa and Mastercard were often cited as prime examples. Despite a promise to open up its massive payments sector upon joining the WTO, China stalled. Even after the United States successfully challenged China in the WTO, Beijing delayed further, taking a tardy seven years from receiving Mastercard's application to offer local payment services before approving it. In the meantime, not only had China's UnionPay monopolised the market, but also a new group of digital payment providers were further eroding a market the American companies were still seeking to enter.

The pattern was repeated elsewhere, with American tech companies shut out supposedly for not bowing to censorship demands, allowing Chinese rivals to grow and flourish in a coddled market. It was quite clear that if China had a competitive advantage, for example, in low-cost manufacturing, it would enjoy open markets abroad to export those goods, creating factory jobs in places like Guangdong, while in areas where foreign companies had a competitive advantage, China thwarted them.

Sometimes these tactics were masked. McDonald's was everywhere in China, but its Chinese outlets were owned by an investment fund of the Chinese state. Buicks were common on the road, but a major Shanghai-based government-owned car company controlled half the business.

China was no longer the poor, backward country that needed special treatment. It had become a mercantilist rival to the United States while imposing higher tariffs on American goods than the United States was placing on Chinese exports. Wholly owned Chinese car companies such as Great Wall were exporting abroad, free from any requirements to enter joint ventures with local partners. The Chinese state was building a long-delayed rival to Boeing and Airbus (albeit with many US and European parts) and local smartphone makers such as Huawei, Oppo and Xiaomi were taking a bigger and bigger slice out of Apple's market. Yet China remained adamant that it must retain the designation 'developing country' at the WTO, a self-defined title that justified Beijing maintaining protectionist policies while continuing to expect 'developed' countries to remain open to its exports.

Beijing argued that because Chinese people on average were still considerably poorer than Americans, Europeans, Japanese and Australians, they deserved more favourable treatment to allow further economic development. With a GDP per capita one-sixth of the United States' and one-fifth of Australia's, China was becoming a middle-income country but still a long way behind Western nations.

That said, it had an advanced space program, the world's fastest supercomputer and some of the world's biggest tech companies, it was already the world's dominant manufacturer, and it had a 'Made in China 2025' plan to dominate emerging high-tech industries such as solar power and electric cars.

Put simply, for China with its 1.4 billion population to ever get anywhere near income parity with a country like the United States, it would have to absolutely dominate the world's industries and decimate the global market share of foreign competitors. Becoming the 'factory of the world' helped pull millions of Chinese out of poverty and made consumer goods cheap and accessible, but it did put many blue-collar workers in other countries out of work. And now with Chinese companies coming for higher-end sectors of the world economy too, it wasn't hard to see the pushback growing. Giving China trade concessions had helped to create competitors, backed by a government with a blueprint to dominate the industries of the future. Long term, it was helping Chinese companies compete against Western rivals on an uneven playing field.

The Trump administration decided to slow it down. If only it wasn't so clumsy about it.

As the trade war heated up, I felt happier than ever to be witnessing it from within China. Relations with Australia were becoming frostier, but I couldn't imagine at that point in 2018 that China's increasingly difficult relationship with Western countries would culminate in me having to leave. Back then the geopolitical tensions seemed less personal. The main game was clearly competition between the United States and China; Australia was just a bystander. There was intense interest from back home, a marked contrast to the early years of my posting when it was difficult to generate excitement for China stories.

When Donald Trump announced a 10 per cent tariff on about one-eighth of China's exports to the United States, it was an opening salvo rather than a full offensive. US trade officials had cherrypicked products for the tariffs that could avoid directly slugging American consumers with higher prices. Prices at Walmart would largely remain unchanged, but manufacturers using Chinese parts would notice the difference.

We headed to the technology markets of China's electronics manufacturing heartland in Shenzhen to gauge the reaction, but few seemed particularly worried.

'In the short term there will be an impact, but long term, it will make things harder for Americans than it will for us,' one electronics vendor at the massive Huaqiangbei market told me.

Huaqiangbei had to be seen to be believed: mall after mall, floor after floor of small vendors selling everything from semiconductors to switches to cords and tiny components. Young men, often shirtless and dripping in sweat, rolled boxes in and out of doorways on trolleys, orders coming and going. Completed consumer drones, Segway transporters and musical keyboards were for sale. Vendors specialising in one type of tiny component would man a stall next to a few hundred others selling the same thing. It was hard to imagine choosing who to do business with; they all represented factories in Guangdong province.

These were the people with the most to lose in a sustained trade war: small-time businesses and workers from small factories. Judging from the number of vendors, the domestic competition to become a supplier was already tough, and now they had to contend with a warning from the United States that the days of China being welcomed as the world's factory may be ending.

'Americans aren't happy when they see Chinese getting rich, are they? That's the truth!' a cigarette-smoking courier resting on his trolley told me.

'Beat the Americans to death!' yelled another man, obviously enjoying playing up for the camera.

Overall, the vendors in Shenzhen told me they were already doing it tough. The boom times were over, the economy was slowing and the pressure from the United States was another of many worries.

'This is something we can't control—it's an issue between countries—so we just follow the Communist Party on this,' one woman told us with a breezy air.

Whatever happened with the US tariffs, the vendors of Huaqiangbei looked like they would be sitting at their stalls, taking orders, for years to come.

———

Our trip to Shenzhen to cover the trade war had hit a speed bump. We wanted to film inside a factory but were having trouble negotiating access. The producer, my colleague Cecily

Huang, had pulled off a coup in getting us inside the headquarters of DJI, the Chinese drone maker that was rapidly chewing up competitors and making incredible consumer drones, but when we turned up, they let us nowhere near any production facility and gave us a white American spokesman to interview.

It didn't work visually to have this Yank speaking for a Chinese tech company about the US trade dispute. Frustrated by multiple knockbacks, Brant Cumming, Cecily and I ended the first day of the assignment at a swish German craft beer bar in Shenzhen's high-end CBD area.

Sitting next to our table were a rather stiff-looking German businessman and his Chinese business partner, a hard-drinking forty-something woman whose family owned a toy train factory. She told us she had a night off from her kids, so even though it was a business dinner, she was in a boisterous mood and double-parking her drinks. Her German counterpart, a toy train distributor, was jet-lagged and perhaps not as excited as she was to be in a fake German pub.

He bailed out, but she took a shine to us and said she wanted to introduce her friends at an Irish bar nearby. So we pressed on through the night-life of Shenzhen, walking past smoke-filled clubs filled with twenty-somethings looking at their phones and dance bars full of revellers. We finally made it to an Irish bar where Chinese, Africans and Westerners were downing booze with enthusiasm.

And that's where we met Ivy.

Ivy was a Hong Kong-based environmental activist originally from Shenzhen, married to a German banker who worked for HSBC. Warm and energetic, she pulsed with the enthusiasm you'd expect from someone who'd set up their own NGO. She bought us rounds of drinks and when we told her about our desire to film in a factory, she messaged a friend who ran a medium-sized solar panel production facility and told us she would help line it up.

It was rare for a night on the turps to be so productive. We parted ways with not only a ticket to a factory but also a pledge to meet again the following day to visit Shenzhen's highest building.

———

That next afternoon we ascended the 117 floors of the Ping An financial centre to film the sweeping views towards Hong Kong and the lush hills surrounding Shenzhen. I can't describe how thrilling it felt to be in southern China, far from the political conservatism and dusty, dry air of the north.

Shenzhen, a city of outsiders chasing opportunity, pulsed with a dreamer's energy. Nearly everyone was from somewhere else, including a Chinese Aussie we met who had abandoned a life in Sydney as a used-car salesman to sell computer components at the Huaqiangbei markets.

'It's tough to make it here, but if I stayed in Sydney, I'd still be kicking tyres on Parramatta Road,' he had told us, a takeaway flat white in one hand, a cigarette in the other.

Our new friend Ivy joined us at the observation deck on the 117th floor along with her German husband and a couple of his German friends. They were classic European business spivs in China, talking about opportunity and quizzing me on why Australia–China relations had begun to dive.

It was complicated, I explained. They didn't think concerns about foreign interference were worth risking a trading relationship for. But it was all very jovial and Ivy said she'd vouched for us to her friend, smoothing the way for filming at the solar panel factory the next day.

That night cameraman Brant Cumming and I decided to cross the border for dinner in Hong Kong, so we took the bus with Ivy and her husband. He revealed his political colours early when he asked me, 'Why is the Western media so negative towards China?'

I gave my honest opinions on reporting on China, dealing with the censorship, the constant obstruction, the 'us and them' nationalism and the increasingly dire stories we were hearing from far-western Xinjiang. It was the sort of honest conversation I could only have with a foreigner. Given that he was a German banker in Hong Kong, I assumed it was nothing he didn't regularly hear.

For his part, he questioned why the West was obsessed with democracy, saying that China was run like an efficient corporation: 'CEOs don't give employees a vote, so why should a government?'

The chat seemed pleasant enough and we bid them both farewell upon arriving on Hong Kong island. Brant and I had dinner and then a generous tally of drinks with Stephen McDonnell and a former ABC journalist, Sarah Clarke, culminating with us missing the last bus back to Shenzhen and crashing on the floor of her family apartment.

The next morning, with sore heads, Brant and I bussed back across the border, confident we'd get the time and address confirmed for the solar panel factory visit that morning. We packed the gear at the hotel, met Cecily (who, ridiculous as it sounds, wasn't allowed to nonchalantly cross the border like us because as a Chinese national she needed a pass card she hadn't brought) and waited for instructions.

And then the text message rolled in.

'Hi Bill, my friend cannot invite you and the ABC crew to the factory today because he is afraid you will twist the facts to do a story that is against China.'

I replied that we hear that a lot, but Ivy clearly agreed with her friend. 'Why does the Western media in China always focus on negative and harmful aspects? You need to focus on more positive things and work together for cooperation,' she texted.

'What the fuck?!'

This was an abrupt change of tone. Ivy had been nothing but friendly and helpful since we met her downing shots at an Irish bar 48 hours earlier. She'd made it out like getting into the factory would be a breeze. She lived in Hong Kong, ran an NGO and was married to a foreigner. I didn't take her for a raging nationalist reducing 'the foreign media' to clichés about 'positive' and 'negative' stories.

I suspected my lengthy chat with her German husband on the bus to Hong Kong must have been the turning point.

Turns out you have to be careful what you say to foreigners in China too.

———

Trump's trade battle rumbled on for the next two years with China countering each move, one heavyweight pursuing another, moving, feinting but landing few blows.

In the view of the United States, China had initiated a type of trade guerrilla warfare against America, poaching manufacturing jobs, forcing companies into joint ventures, demanding their technology secrets or outright blocking their entry into its massive market. There were persistent claims of hacking and intellectual property theft in the United States, in Europe and among private companies in Australia.

The IP theft aside, Americans still reaped massive benefits from the trade relationship. TVs and electronics were cheap, multinational companies that could access China, such as Apple, were tapping a massive market that didn't exist before, and China's purchase of US debt helped Americans to keep living well beyond their means.

The United States had opened its doors to exports because it hadn't seen Chinese companies as a threat to anything other than low-end manufacturing. Now that was changing, fast, and Washington was belatedly trying to catch up.

In China itself, among the fairly international circles that foreign journalists move in, there was a surprising amount of sympathy for what Trump was trying to do. Some of it was from Chinese liberals just glad to see a foreign leader finally stand up to the Communist Party. But others were pissed off with the higher import tariffs that China slapped on foreign goods and hoped the pressure might force the Communist Party to stop slugging Chinese consumers when they wanted to buy a fully foreign-built car.

Overall, the popular narrative was that the United States was unfairly targeting the country because it was insecure about China's rise. This only strengthened domestic support for the government standing firm.

The American tariffs aimed to get the Chinese to the bargaining table to make some concessions, and China said it was more than happy to talk, an acknowledgement that some of the American grievances had merit.

When Trump came to power, China had a fast-growing annual trade surplus of around 350 billion US dollars. Trump wanted to shrink that by getting China to purchase more American goods. But the deeper problems were around access for foreign companies to China's vast market. Trump wanted undertakings that China would allow US companies to fairly compete, would stop requiring them to give up their Research and Development (R&D) to Chinese partners, and would stop stealing US intellectual property. Other Western countries wanted the same, but were too cautious to say it aloud.

But as the tariff campaign rolled on, the flaws in Trump's strategy and execution became clear. His trade team in Washington must have overestimated how much leverage America still had. While the United States remained China's biggest export market, it purchased less than one-fifth of all Chinese exports.

Although it remained the world's factory, China's economy was increasingly shaking off exports as its main driver of GDP growth. Placing a modest 10 per cent tariff on just a portion of those exports to the United States wasn't much of a blow to China, which was nonetheless worried about it, judging by the intense focus on the issue in state media.

Over time, Trump would up the ante, announcing tariffs on further exports and threatening to raise the percentage to 25 per cent. He would announce it on Twitter and get the US Trade Representative office to prepare lists of products to target and then just as quickly backflip at the slightest sign of a Chinese compromise.

As the tit for tat continued, China did make some concessions, reducing import duties on foreign-made cars, ending a local partner joint-venture requirement for auto makers, allowing a bit more access for foreign financial firms, and banning the export of fentanyl, a hospital-grade anaesthetic that was quietly wreaking havoc in communities gripped by the US opioid crisis.

At times, Trump moved the other way, abruptly cancelling trade talks and pushing ahead with higher tariffs. But as 2018 moved into 2019, it became pretty clear that he wasn't willing to launch a proper offensive. With China retaliating against the more limited range of American products arriving in Chinese ports, Trump was cautious not to trigger an electoral backlash from pissed-off soybean farmers in the Midwest or lobster fishermen in coastal towns.

With no ballot box to worry about, Xi Jinping could handle whatever discontent was brewing, and reports of elite-level dismay at his unwillingness to make reasonable concessions never eventuated into anything more concrete.

The United States was trying to inflict pain on its rival without the stomach to cop many blows itself. And the Chinese leadership knew it.

With an American election looming in 2020, China's leaders waited Trump out, assuming he would cave as the urgency to win votes became paramount. Frustrated by the lack of progress, Trump finally pulled the trigger in late 2019, labelling China a currency manipulator and then extending tariffs to cover all Chinese exports to the United States, some at a crippling 25 per cent, others at 10 per cent.

But it was all a bit late. China had played him for time, and Trump quickly backslid, agreeing to a 'Phase One' trade deal that committed the Chinese to buying more American agricultural products that they wanted anyway in exchange for the Americans dropping some tariffs and reducing others. The core problems of market access for American companies were left for a 'Phase Two' deal that Trump never got to negotiate.

China had stared the United States down.

The Americans failed to fix the fundamental problems in the relationship and, even though some Chinese exports still had tariffs on them, Beijing realised its economic ascendency was unimpeded.

———

I was left with no doubt that Trump's early moves to impose tariffs genuinely rattled the Chinese leadership. Speaking to US business leaders in China, it was also clear that Beijing had lost the support of corporate America.

Faced with a confrontational, unpredictable US president and a frustrated American business community no longer willing to take Beijing's side, China's government looked flat-footed. The repetitive commentaries in state media and statement after statement from officials spoke of an anxiety rarely seen in Chinese diplomacy. If the Americans followed through, maybe the Germans, the other Europeans and the Japanese would too?

China's debt-fuelled growth model was running out of puff. Exporting higher technology goods and services was the next frontier if China was to keep growing and avoid the infamous 'middle-income trap'. A coalition of trade partners putting up barriers to protect their own workers would, on the other hand, throw it all into turmoil.

But the Trump administration never sought to build an effective international coalition. Instead of trying to rally the EU and Japan, Trump separately embroiled them in tariff disputes, managing to piss off the economic allies he needed to confront China.

His incremental tactic of applying small tariffs and expecting China to come to the table offering compromises also showed an appallingly bad read of how much the balance of power had shifted. Had he gone in hard at the outset with high tariffs and been willing to risk a bit of political pain back home, he wouldn't have given the Chinese the impression he was bluffing. Instead, he reaffirmed Chinese perceptions of how vulnerable democratically elected leaders are to domestic interest groups.

There was one area where the Trump administration was successful, though: curtailing the rise of China's tech giants.

Hailing from Australia, I was familiar with Huawei, the Chinese tech giant from Shenzhen that was banned from building Australia's National Broadband Network in 2012. A Labor government decided it was too much of a security risk and a Liberal government reaffirmed that assessment the following year. But elsewhere, Huawei wasn't as contentious and it was rapidly building fifth-generation mobile network equipment throughout the world.

Who controls Huawei? In the company's telling, it's a private enterprise owned by its employees through a shareholding system and doesn't answer to the Chinese state. But as its annual reports make clear, it has received at least a billion dollars' worth of Chinese government funding through various subsidy schemes and fits the mould of a 'national champion', a company given favourable treatment to innovate and compete on the world stage.

I visited Huawei's campus-style headquarters in Shenzhen twice, where American, Canadian and Australian PR employees would manage our visits, shuttling us around in air-conditioned buses. Inside the slick showroom, American telco engineers who once worked for giant US corporations would soothingly take us through Huawei's technology. Delegations from Africa and the Middle East were being toured through the high-tech display too, and it was a superb sales job that left you in no doubt Huawei's technology was the best and the cheapest. The PR reps told you about the huge number of PhD graduates working in R&D and the impressive sales figures of the company's ventures into smartphones, laptops and operating software.

On our second trip, we were given a sit-down interview with the head of Huawei's Global Cyber Security and Privacy office, an Englishman named John Suffolk. He had the title of senior vice-president, but my instinct whenever a giant Chinese company puts up a foreigner to interview is that they can't be anywhere near a decision-making level of real substance.

Suffolk repeated the same lines: the company had a great track record on security, it was the most scrutinised equipment provider and it would be delighted to build a 'cyber security excellence' centre in Australia if that's what it took to convince the politicians to allow Huawei in.

Australia wasn't exactly the biggest market around, but Huawei threw a sizeable chunk of resources at trying to win over the policymakers. It sponsored the Canberra Raiders, the capital's rugby league team. It hired Australia's longest-serving former Foreign Minister, Alexander Downer, to sit on its Australian board and say soothing things about the company in the media (can you ever imagine a former Chinese Foreign Minister joining the board of a Western tech company?!).

It also hired a well-regarded former Victorian premier, John Brumby. The company even approached a retired navy admiral, John Lord, to be the public face of the company in Australia.

At an end-of-lunar-year banquet and talent show for staff at the Xinhua News Agency, Beijing, January 2011, with colleagues dressed as paramilitary police for a performance. Xinhua was a good insight into how a state media newsroom worked and a great introduction to China during a less difficult time in Beijing's relations with the West.

Paramilitary police stand guard outside a football match at Beijing's Workers Stadium, August 2016—there were also nets around the pitch to stop fans hurling bottles at the players. The matches were a rare chance for Beijingers to gather in large numbers and let off some steam. I was a regular, and lived in an apartment overlooking the stadium.

Foreigners were few and far between for school students in Shaanxi province, October 2016. This was one of my first assignments to a rural area and the reaction to a foreign news crew was a world away from attitudes in Beijing.

A man at a rural wet market in Zhidan, Shaanxi province, November 2016. Outdoor meat markets were a fairly normal feature of rural areas until an early cluster of coronavirus cases linked to a Wuhan wet market in late 2019 prompted the government to clean them up.

The Communist Party General Secretary, Xi Jinping, addresses the 19th Communist Party Congress in Beijing, October 2017. It was best remembered for him enshrining 'Xi Jinping Thought' into the Party's constitution. He was yet to face the challenges of Hong Kong's uprising, a trade war with the United States and the global pandemic, all of which strengthened his personal power.

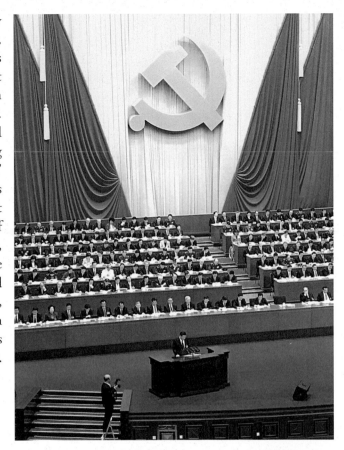

Li Wenzu outside a prosecutor's office, campaigning for the release of her lawyer husband, Wang Quanzhang, November 2017. Wang ended up being the most prominent lawyer jailed in a targeted crackdown on legal activists, spending four and a half years behind bars before being reunited with Li in mid-2020.

With my partner, Yinan Cai, a journalist for the German media who I met over a craft beer in Beijing. Partly due to the increasingly bleak situation for Chinese staff of foreign media, she later quit to set up a theatre company with friends.

With ABC Beijing colleagues Charles Li, Cecily Huang and Steve Wang at the Great Hall of the People, March 2018. It was as close as we were allowed to get each year to China's decision-makers.

Mengnan, the eleven-year-old adopted son of a rubbish picker, a migrant worker, walks across a brick wall that local authorities built to hem in the family shack and force them out, Beijing, June 2018. His plight struck a chord with viewers, many of whom donated money to help his family find a better place to live.

Young women in Miao traditional dress at a festival near Guiyang, Guizhou province, October 2018. While ethnic minority groups are officially celebrated to showcase diversity, the Chinese government's treatment of some other ethnic minority groups, in particular the Uighurs of Xinjiang, became one of the defining stories of the Xi era.

A boy with his grandfather at a poverty alleviation event, Danzhai, Guizhou province, October 2018. Poverty alleviation is one of the signature achievements of the Communist Party and, while milked for domestic propaganda purposes, the improvements on the ground are noticeable.

New office towers rising in Guomao, in Beijing's east, November 2018. By this time, the building frenzy of the early 2000s had slowed in major cities, but still continued in smaller cities and remained a key way for local governments to stimulate economic growth.

On a beach in southern Taiwan for military drills with General Chen Zhongji, Kenting, Taiwan, May 2019. Taiwan's military is being increasingly outgunned by China's, and Xi Jinping has declared democratic Taiwan must be under Communist Party control by 2049 or even earlier, ensuring it will become a more important flashpoint as each year ticks by.

With cameraman Brant Cumming and producers Mark Corcoran and Cecily Huang on the Kinmen islands—controlled by Taiwan's government, but just off the coast of China—in June 2019. As we wrapped up this shoot, a much more urgent crisis was brewing in Hong Kong.

The view down Hennessy Road, Hong Kong island, 16 June 2019. The protestors opposed closer legal ties with mainland China and called for more oversight of police. Estimated attendance ranged from hundreds of thousands to 2 million. It was a stunning display of people, but not people power, as their demands ultimately weren't met.

At ground level during the biggest street march of the Hong Kong protests, 16 June 2019. Despite an intense focus by China's government on violent elements, the vast majority of protestors were peaceful.

Clearly the fortunes of Huawei in Australia meant a lot to the former PLA engineer who founded and still presided over the tech giant, Ren Zhengfei.

When all that lobbying came to naught with a 2018 decision by the Turnbull government to again block Huawei from building Australia's 5G network, you could see it wasn't just the private Shenzhen company that was upset. Within a day, China's Cyberspace administration had blocked the ABC's website. The ABC's Beijing bureau chief, Matt Carney, was subjected to multiple hostile grillings by Ministry of Foreign Affairs officials when trying to renew his visa.

China's government sure took a deep interest in the fortunes of this private company.

———

I felt a bit sorry for Huawei. No matter how much the central and Guangdong governments pumped it up with subsidies, cheap land and whatever else, its global ambitions were also being unintentionally thwarted by Beijing. China's government published a new security law in 2017 that stated in black in white that 'any organization or citizen shall support, assist and cooperate with the state intelligence work in accordance with the law'. When this was put to them, Huawei's various spokespeople came up with a counter line: Huawei always follows the laws of the country where it's operating. Given general suspicions in the West about espionage and the Chinese state being behind cyber attacks, it required a giant leap of faith.

China's broader anger about Australia blocking Huawei was more likely about a potential domino effect. Australia's moves would be closely watched in Washington, the United Kingdom and other European countries. And it was the Americans during Donald Trump's presidency who most enthusiastically led the charge against Huawei and a fellow Chinese equipment maker, ZTE.

Under Trump, the United States didn't just block Huawei, but also pressured other Western allies to do likewise. While the Europeans were reluctant to succumb to a widely disliked US administration and ditch a cheap and advanced supplier, the Americans put them in a tight spot.

Countries such as the United Kingdom, France and Germany thought they could mitigate the risk of Huawei's potential spying by only installing the Chinese equipment in non-core sections of their networks. That didn't satisfy the United States, which was concerned that its alliances with countries such as the United Kingdom would be undermined if sensitive communication over British 5G networks was prone to interception.

So Trump's team increased the pressure. The United States started restricting the sale to Huawei of semiconductors, the advanced microchips that power electronic devices and network equipment. Google's Android disappeared from Huawei smartphone operating systems.

But many of the American-designed chips Huawei used were made in Taiwan, so the White House upped the ante by placing a trade ban on companies abroad that used licensed American technology to manufacture chips.

It was an effective strike, cutting off Huawei from a reliable supply of top-notch chips and exposing how reliant China's tech champion still was on advanced American technology.

It also threw Britain's plan to include Huawei in its 5G rollout into turmoil. Without the American-designed chips powering

Huawei's equipment, the British got spooked and announced a seven-year plan, later fast-tracked, to phase existing Huawei kit out of the network. France followed suit, and Sweden banned Huawei from its 5G network, although the Germans, who had hitched their economic fortunes to a Chinese future, pushed ahead with a plan to include Huawei's gear despite serious doubts.

It wasn't just Western countries shunning Huawei. Japan, Taiwan and Vietnam, countries with a far better understanding of China, used various means to exclude Huawei from their networks. Governments in those countries didn't make a lot of noise about it, but they too were drawing lines in the sand about how to engage with China. Doing business was one thing, but having China's government-supported companies supplying your most sensitive critical communications networks was another.

Huawei has continued to prosper, with China's government responding to the US chip bans by pouring huge resources into developing China's own technology in an accelerated bid for self-reliance. The company also locked in contracts to build 5G across Africa, the Middle East, Russia, Pakistan and South East Asia.

The world became increasingly split along technology lines.

———

There was one other major division brewing, which will only intensify in the years to come. Living in China, you're aware of how American technology companies control your daily digital lives.

That's because, with a few exceptions, they are absent from the Chinese internet.

My colleagues back home never seemed to quite comprehend how effectively China's Communist Party had thwarted the world wide web. They'd send WhatsApp messages and wonder why I didn't receive them. They'd email on Gmail expecting quick replies. Friends would use Facebook's Messenger to chat, unaware of how difficult it was to get a VPN to connect so that I could use it.

Even sites that weren't blocked didn't work properly. They were slow and pages lagged. Services such as iTunes or Apple News were blocked, meaning devices couldn't be used to their full potential. Multiple news sites, not just the ABC, had also been banned, while China's own social-media sites started implementing regulations against foreigners who live streamed, sometimes blocking feeds if a foreign face appeared.

The government obsession with controlling what people do on the internet was utterly pervasive and extraordinary. China had well and truly decoupled the internet; it will go down in history as one of the most far-sighted economic and strategic moves any country has ever made.

As the rest of the world, including Europe, allowed the American tech giants to monopolise their markets, China put up a great firewall early and created a protected space for its own burgeoning tech companies to thrive in. In 2010 at Xinhua, colleagues were already trying to sign me up to a flurry of social-media sites that would go on to fill the void. When I came back to Beijing in 2013, WeChat had emerged and was cannibalising rivals, becoming the indispensable platform for daily life in China.

The official line from defenders of China's oppressive internet censorship policies is that American companies refuse to modify their products and implement mass censorship on their platforms in China. Hence they aren't banned; rather they choose not to comply with China's laws.

In reality, Google did create a censored version of its search engine and originally gained entry into China's market but withdrew because of what it said were major hacking attacks on the Gmail accounts of Chinese political activists. While nationalists framed Google's departure as a 'retreat' from China because it was losing the market share battle to local rival Baidu, it seems doubtful any multinational would forgo a business because it was 'only' capturing 29 per cent of the world's largest and fastest-growing internet market.

Funnily enough, Google's claim to a principled stand didn't stop the company trying to get back in. In 2017 I spent several days in an ancient canal town that had been rebuilt as a tourist attraction, centred around a convention building that hosted an annual 'World Internet Conference'. Google representatives faithfully turned up to the annual get-together, which promoted 'Internet Sovereignty', China's vision of a world wide web not only decoupled but divvied up into national borders through censorship.

I wasn't in the town of Wuzhen for the conference, but rather for an ancient Chinese boardgame. In an attempt to emulate the battles between chess champion Gary Kasparov and IBM's Deep Blue in the 1990s, Google had acquired a British artificial intelligence company that had applied its algorithms to a chequers-like game of strategy called Weiqi. In English, it is called 'Go'.

The AI software, called AlphaGo, used machine learning and something its engineers called 'neural networks' to decide which move to play out of roughly 30 million possibilities. In a major publicity push, Google organised a three-game series against the world's top-ranked player, a young Chinese genius named Ke Jie.

Weiqi is a bit like chess in that it is slow, complicated and makes for terrible television. With intense excitement about the match in China, we went down to Wuzhen only to realise we wouldn't be able to interview Ke Jie or film anything remotely interesting. But I'll always remember Google's Executive Chairman, Eric Schmidt, using the tournament to ingratiate Google with the Chinese public. He sat down for a 'fireside' chat with a Chinese host who was clearly being paid not to ask anything sensitive, and spruiked Google's products.

As expected, the AI defeated the frustrated Chinese champion, who memorably chided a local journalist for daring to ask him a question in English.

'You are Chinese, why are you speaking English!?' he said to loud applause from the live audience, tapping into the classic stereotype of China's 'angry youth'.

Google should have been angry too. Just minutes before the first match, with online interest peaking, China's government ordered internet services and broadcasters not to stream the games live. It was a little reminder from the Communist leaders in Beijing that Google was still unwelcome.

———

At least Google was creative in its efforts to get back in. Facebook's Mark Zuckerberg simply tried blatant ingratiation. In the years after Facebook was blocked, Zuckerberg learnt Chinese and showed off a basic command of it during a talk to university students in Beijing. He jogged around Tiananmen Square on a smoggy day, ensuring his PR team publicised a photo of him as he passed the famous gate with Chairman Mao's portrait. He chummed up to China's chief internet censor, Lu Wei, to no avail. (Lu was later was purged for corruption.) He reportedly even asked Xi Jinping to give an honorary name to his unborn daughter during a dinner at the White House, which Zuckerberg's PR team later refuted.

Either way, it was clear 2.7 billion worldwide users weren't enough. Reports filtered out of Silicon Valley about Facebook looking at ways it could offer its services to Chinese users that complied with the strict censorship laws. Simply building a censored version closed off from the rest of Facebook defeated the purpose. So it was never quite clear what an acceptable version of the world's biggest social-media platform would look like. In the end, a bit like Rupert Murdoch many years before, Zuckerberg gave up, realising that authoritarian Communist leaders have no incentive to allow foreign internet platforms in.

And even if they did, it was all too late.

China's protectionism worked a treat. Not only had it stopped information it couldn't control reaching most of the population, it had also fostered some of the world's biggest and most creative technology companies. Tencent's WeChat (known as Weixin in China), Sina's Weibo, Alibaba's Taobao and Ant Financial's Alipay plus search giant Baidu were the leaders, but there were many more. Even online services that weren't sheltered from competition such as ride-hailing service DiDi Chuxing still vanquished their overseas rivals, tapping into an environment that heavily favoured the domestic companies. Uber lost its war with DiDi and was swallowed up in a 'merger' that forced the American company out with just a minor equity stake.

For China's billion-plus online community, Chinese services were convenient, entertaining and left no desire for any of the international services. Mobile payment technology raced ahead of what was happening abroad. Cash became redundant, and QR codes were king. Only the small minority with personal or work connections abroad, an overseas education or an elite job needed to use VPNs to get around the controls.

While many people bemoaned the censorship, it remained an inconvenience rather than a focus of anger for most. China's internet companies were thriving in their massive fishbowl. American companies, unable to jump in, were dominant outside. But then one Chinese internet service jumped out of the bowl.

———

I first heard of TikTok when I met a friend of a friend at a function who had come back from India, where she was helping to build 'market share' for the company. The short video looping app was taking off in the world's other billion-plus population giant, and it was quite common to come across young hard-working Chinese tech and marketing types who were crisscrossing between the two countries.

The Chinese companies were targeting India because it resembled the China of ten years earlier, with a rapidly growing online population and a domestic industry in its infancy. The Western tech rivals were there but hadn't had a smooth run, particularly Zuckerberg, who fell foul of Indian popular opinion with his 'Free Basics' program. His offer would have connected hundreds of millions of poorer people to the internet, but it limited them to a pre-set list of websites including, of course, Facebook. Regulators grounded the idea.

The country's massive population and fast economic growth still left plenty of opportunity for Chinese rivals to gain a foothold. As TikTok signed up millions of users in India, it was also making significant gains in the United States and the rest of the West. The app exploded in America, where its parent company, Bytedance, claimed more than 100 million active monthly users by 2020. That number might have been a stretch, but the quirky videos filled an entertainment void that Zuckerberg and other US tech titans had somehow missed.

While TikTok styled itself as an entertainment app, it had its share of political content, and activists claimed the app censored content critical of the Chinese government's treatment of Uighurs and its political crackdown in Hong Kong. Internal content moderation documents reported by *The Guardian* explicitly outlined censorship guidelines that included purging content on Falun Gong, framing it within a broader ban on groups that 'promote suicide'.

Content about national leaders was also to be censored, but Bytedance later said the instructions were old, and it had updated content moderation guidelines to better reflect local markets. Either way, any Beijing-owned company would be under tremendous political pressure not to host content critical of Xi Jinping or the Chinese Communist Party, even if it's in foreign languages on a site banned in China (TikTok is blocked on the mainland, where its heavily censored Chinese version Douyin is one of the dominant streaming platforms).

The Trump administration was well aware of these concerns but decided that the most potent threat was Chinese companies collecting the data of US citizens. This wasn't any different from the vast amounts of data that Facebook, Twitter and others vacuumed up about their users, but under Trump it became grounds to ban TikTok and WeChat in the US market.

Sitting in Beijing, where for years I had to pay for multiple VPNs and wait while they connected before loading Google, Twitter, YouTube, WhatsApp, Instagram or even the site of my employer, the ABC, I was sympathetic to the American attempt to square the ledger. Why should Chinese services in the United States have free market access when American sites are largely blocked in China?

But the personal data of users seemed to be a less important issue. China had blocked all of these American sites from its market, claiming they needed to fundamentally change their services (censor them) to gain entry. Even when they did, in the case of Google, they faced hacking attacks. From a trade protectionism standpoint, the Americans had a very strong case to treat the Chinese tech companies in a reciprocal way.

But long term, there's another issue. TikTok and particularly WeChat were doing to American users the inverse of what China feared about US tech: applying the Chinese Communist Party's censorship beyond China's borders, imposing it on US citizens in America. It was the same for users in Australia or anywhere else.

On TikTok, the content moderation was hard to detect. Was it censorship? Or was it just the algorithm curtailing the viral spread of content critical of China's government? At least journalists were writing about it, even if the young user base couldn't care less.

On WeChat, it's a lot more blatant. The public accounts that distribute news in Chinese rigidly adhere to Beijing's ever-tightening lists of what can and can't be said. Even the accounts registered overseas have to comply with the speech restraints of the platform. And those overseas registered public accounts aren't even visible to users with a mainland account.

But that doesn't mean they're brimming with 'dangerous' content.

Whether it's popular outlet *College Daily* in the United States, or *Today Sydney* and *Today Melbourne* in Australia, the WeChat news accounts catering for Chinese communities in the West never cross censorship lines laid out for them by an authoritarian government in Beijing. At times they're scathing about the politicians in the countries where they are based, but not when talking about Chinese leaders.

In Australia, much of the content of these proliferating WeChat public news accounts is trashy and apolitical. Often they copy stories from the *Daily Mail* or *The Sydney Morning Herald* and translate them into Chinese. But there is also a large focus on discrimination against Chinese. 'Shocking!' the headlines read. 'Two Chinese murdered in point blank shooting', the top story on the daily update for *Today Sydney* once said. I clicked on it to find that the murders happened in Cambodia.

'Shocking! A Chinese female student insulted and humiliated on campus', another headline stated, only for me to click and realise it occurred in the United States.

There were real cases of racism in Australia against Chinese and other Asian people, particularly in the aftermath of the coronavirus outbreak in Wuhan. The mainstream media in Australia covered these but not their full extent. In some cases, WeChat platforms helped push these issues out into the open. But the constant focus on discrimination, whether or not it happened in Australia, helped fuel the Communist Party's 'century of humiliation' nationalism that some young university students increasingly displayed on campus.

Of the cases that made it to the media, students at Australian universities would increasingly demand lecturers or tutors remove content they deemed critical of China. One University of Sydney tutor had to apologise after displaying a map in class that didn't adhere to China's version of territorial reality. He pushed back when nationalistic students challenged him (they leapt on his Indian heritage to claim he deliberately chose a map that favoured India's border claims) and covertly recorded the conversation, giving it to the sympathetic *Today Sydney*. The university, hooked on fees from Chinese students, made the tutor apologise.

In another case, a Monash University student studying a course called 'Data in Society' complained to *Today Melbourne* about a teacher assigning two articles from the journal *Nature* as required reading. They detailed the Chinese government's use of electronic data in Xinjiang, surely the most appropriate study of pervasive digital surveillance of a society anywhere on earth.

'The articles spread rumours about China's government, are suspected of disseminating misinformation, stir up racial issues and have a strong anti-China tendency,' the student told the media outlet. The teacher told the students they could choose two alternative articles to analyse, but the aggrieved student was unhappy that the original readings remained in the course.

Many WeChat accounts appeal to Chinese students abroad, so the Chinese information bubble is quite understandable. But WeChat is also the predominant app among first-generation Chinese migrants to Australia, the United States and other countries. That's understandable if Chinese is your first language, and it's natural to seek out news sources in Chinese about the country you've migrated to. With family members and friends back home banned from using any of the social-media sites that are popular abroad, WeChat is indispensable for staying in touch. But with Beijing's censorship guidelines making it impossible for the ABC, SBS or other foreign media to create real Chinese-language news services on WeChat, it leaves only those patriotic, censored sites to fill the void. At election time, particularly in electorates with large Chinese-speaking populations, WeChat becomes a big problem.

Long term, permitting WeChat to embed the Communist Party's censorship in the news environment of Australian citizens is creating a major opportunity for foreign interference. It's the same anywhere, but particularly in countries with a large Chinese diaspora such as Australia, New Zealand and Canada, where the platform is a major campaign tool in certain seats.

The madness of WeChat's use in liberal democracies was perhaps best exposed during a rift between Australia and China over a tweet in late 2020. China's chief provocateur at the Foreign Ministry, Zhao Lijian, tweeted a digital artwork of an Australian soldier holding a knife to the throat of an Afghan child, in reference to the Australian government's investigation of war crimes committed years earlier by SAS soldiers.

Zhao posted it on Twitter, enjoying the Chinese government's freedom to get its messages out to overseas audiences while so rigidly restricting voices abroad from reaching people in China.

In response, Prime Minister Scott Morrison posted a message in Chinese on his 'official' WeChat account (which like all accounts, has to be registered to a random Chinese national back on the mainland). Morrison's post wasn't particularly provocative but attempted to get his message directly to members of the Chinese community without the heavy distortion of China's government media.

Within hours, WeChat deleted his message. In its place, a notice went up advising that the prime minister had violated the rules of the platform.

———

The Trump administration's attempts to ban new downloads of updates of TikTok and WeChat followed the failures of his trade measures. He muddied the waters by demanding Beijing-based parent company Bytedance sell TikTok's American operations to a US company or face a ban, and then, when China's government moved to block a sale, Trump's team used a national security rationale to force the major app stores to block new downloads of the two services.

A US court struck it down, with a group of California plaintiffs arguing that blocking WeChat would cut them off from relatives in China and violate free speech. Given that text messaging, email and the good old fashioned phone call still existed, it seemed like a dubious argument, particularly as the reason the relatives abroad were supposedly cut off was because of another country's repressive policies. But the judge sided with the plaintiffs, slapping down the ban and deciding that the Trump administration had provided insufficient proof that the sites provided a national security threat. Once again, Trump's moves to even things up with China failed, this time due to the checks and balances of the US system.

China's tech giants, protected at home from US competition, would continue to thrive another day with unfettered open-market access to America. But in India, the advance of Chinese tech had come to an abrupt halt.

———

In the middle of the 2020 summer, China and India's long-standing border dispute took its bloodiest turn in four decades. In the darkness, high on a ridge in the remote Ladakh region in disputed Kashmir, a group of unarmed Indian and Chinese soldiers came face to face in a skirmish that ended with soldiers being stoned, clubbed and thrown off the side of a ridge. In the freezing high altitude, twenty Indian soldiers were killed. China refused to confirm how many of its troops perished.

In India, anger was boiling. Chinese troops had stepped up their border efforts in recent years and, the way the Indians saw it, were encroaching on India's territory. Now Indian soldiers had died horrific deaths, prompting the country's highly nationalistic media to commence an intense focus on China.

Within days, India's regulators announced the country would ban dozens of Chinese apps, including TikTok and WeChat, citing them as a threat to the 'sovereignty and integrity of India'. Delhi ignored outrage from Beijing, doubling down with further app bans in the months that followed. By the end of 2020, it had prohibited more than a hundred.

As with Huawei's ambitions and the national security law, Chinese tech dreams of embedding themselves in India's market had fallen apart due to the actions of China's government, this time its military. India had learnt the lessons taught by China a decade earlier: to block technology from a country seen as a threat and develop your own. Chinese tech companies, which had grown so creative and powerful in the fishbowl of China's protectionism, were getting a taste of their own medicine.

11

HONG KONG

The biggest stories are the ones you don't see coming. Hong Kong's uprising, by far the biggest story of my time in China, was so unexpected that only a few months earlier I decided to make a documentary about Taiwan instead.

'It's all gone a bit quiet in Hong Kong,' I remember telling Matthew Carney, the executive producer of the *Foreign Correspondent* program, who agreed.

But it wasn't unexpected for the Hong Kongers, whose protests had been building for years as China's government chipped away at the autonomy the former British colony had been promised. When the breaking point came, its ferocity would change forever the wider world's understanding of China.

———

My earliest impressions of Hong Kong were formed during a stopover en route to a backpacking trip to Europe, and it's fair to say I got a very limited picture.

I was eighteen, travelling with two schoolmates. One, Charlie Noble, had an uncle who worked as a surgeon at a hospital on the Peak, overlooking the dizzying towers and bright lights. He drove a Ferrari and took us three starry-eyed boys to bustling dim sum restaurants and on ferry tours of Victoria Harbour. He organised for us to stay in unused staff dorms on the Peak itself. We only stayed a couple of nights and went on to spend weeks in Europe, but that short stay in Hong Kong was my highlight of the entire trip.

It was pretty typical of the Hong Kong many Western visitors saw: yum cha, hiking, cocktails and shopping on Hong Kong island itself or Tsim Sha Tsui just across the harbour. 'Honkers' was staggering under its colonial hangover. Many Westerners experienced the Rugby sevens, the sleaze of Wanchai and the boozy nights at Happy Valley racecourse. The bright lights, crowded streets, markets and rooftop pools made it easy to overlook the cramped, overpriced apartments or the elderly garbage collectors pulling trolleys of recyclable cardboard to survive. It was truly a city of haves and have-nots.

Many years after that backpacking trip, I went to Hong Kong on visa runs from China in my mid-twenties, staying in tiny hotel rooms and devouring steaming bowls of salty egg noodles and barbecue duck at hole-in-the-wall restaurants. They were cheap and cheerful visits that only deepened my love for the city. Later when I was working for the ABC in Beijing, Hong Kong never failed to dazzle. It was a refuge of mountains, water and multiculturalism, geographically close but culturally distant, a truly international, liberal outpost. It was under the Communist Party's control, but gossipy books on Chinese leaders were sold on the streets and people spoke freely. Fears that the Communists would crush the city's autonomy after the 1997 handover from Britain seemed overblown.

There were plenty of warning signs, though, none bigger than the 2014 'Umbrella' protests that saw students and activists block major roads for the best part of three months, a seemingly drastic action to pressure China's government to give them genuine democracy, the ability to freely nominate and vote for the city's chief executive.

China's government, still keen to project an image of commitment to the 'One Country, Two Systems' promise of elections and consultations, had countered with an alternative offer: you can all vote as long as we choose the small handful of candidates you're allowed to vote for.

When I arrived back in China in 2015, the Occupy protests seemed like a last hurrah. The protestors had blinked and been cleared from the streets, sometimes by police, sometimes by organised men who appeared to be triad members. There was a sense of futility about the movement's failure to achieve its goals. Beijing, clearly, was not for turning. And yet it still felt like the day of reckoning—when the liberal, open city had to integrate with the authoritarian, censored mainland—was still far off in the distance. I never could have guessed it would be just over the horizon.

So Hong Kong was a low priority for me, but on the occasional trips I did make there, the threads of deeply embedded resentment were slowly coming together.

———

The fate of the three men I interviewed on my first assignment to Hong Kong for the ABC says a lot about the direction the city has taken. One is now in jail, one fled to Taiwan, and the other has been feted in Beijing.

It was mid-2016 and the news agenda in China was still ticking along fairly slowly, especially as Beijing had settled in for a long summer lull. I was bored and one of two correspondents in the bureau, along with Matthew Carney, sharing the scraps of news about China that editors wanted amid the US campaign between Donald Trump and Hillary Clinton. I'd been looking for a reason to get out of the capital and do an assignment in Hong Kong but there was rarely a big-enough trigger. But a feature about all of the small ways that the city was changing fit the bill, and so I'd made the three-and-a-half-hour flight to Hong Kong with veteran ABC cameraman Wayne McAllister. From Beijing it was a solid day's travel when you factored in the time to get all the camera gear through customs.

Wayne is the sort of bloke you want in a crisis—well over six-foot tall, with a big build and a big beard; you could mistake him for a bouncer if he wasn't so friendly. I felt guilty for having shacked us up in one of the smallest matchbox hotels on Hong Kong island, a Catholic-mission-run establishment high on the hills and far from the action. Most of the large cases of equipment were stacked in Wayne's tiny room, and I doubt the bed was long enough for him, or the shower high enough. We were on assignment for the *7.30* program and while the editors were keen for a story about Hong Kong's political precariousness, they had a tight budget.

We stuffed all the camera gear into the boots of Hong Kong's notoriously outdated red taxis and shuttled from interview to interview. The first of the unlikely trio we met was Edward Leung, whom we had agreed to catch up with at one of the city's concrete soccer grounds where his friends had gathered for a weekend game. Edward was running late, making me sweat in the tropical heat. The arrangements had been difficult. As a leader of an emerging student-led 'localist' group that campaigned against mainland Chinese influence, he kept his communications guarded. I'd had to contact him through elusive intermediaries, and as I sweated under the mid-August sun watching local soccer teams play on the baking concrete, none of them knew where he was.

Eventually Edward did turn up, but he was in no hurry to sit down and do an interview. Skinny, with round thin-rimmed glasses and a sharp undercut, he appeared both intellectual and kind of hip. He watched a game, chatted with friends and took the occasional selfie with strangers who approached him to express their support. He was the rising young star of Hong Kong's political movement and definitely the edgiest.

Edward Leung's political party didn't just call for Hong Kong independence, but also ran campaigns against mainland Chinese traders who bought up items such as milk powder in Hong Kong and took them across the border to sell at a profit. His platform was seen as discriminatory by some and radical by many. Fewer than one in five Hong Kong respondents in surveys supported trying to break away from China's control. More autonomy seemed to be the pragmatic compromise most Hong Kongers were comfortable with.

But Edward Leung's passion struck a chord and his slow, calm, determined way of talking when he finally did sit down for an interview underlined his appeal.

'People have hatred against each other,' he told me, describing the deep divisions within the city. 'Some people started to submit. Some people started to leave Hong Kong permanently. Some people already gave up.'

Leung was a contradiction. Born on the mainland, he came to Hong Kong as a child but called his movement 'Hong Kong Indigenous'. It was this backstory that nationalistic critics in mainland China couldn't get past—that one's political identity doesn't have to be rigidly tied to their ethnicity and heritage.

'Freedom, I think, is the most essential value of Hong Kong because our descendants came to Hong Kong seeking freedom and liberty,' he said. He denied accusations of discrimination against mainlanders, saying his group only targeted the behaviour and actions of some mainland Chinese in Hong Kong.

In an early sign of the vast political restrictions to come, Edward Leung was banned from running in local elections due to his platform. He promoted other candidates but, at the ballot box, his party remained on the fringe.

On the streets, meanwhile, it was front and centre of Hong Kong's political conflicts. As Leung chatted to me that day, he was awaiting trial on charges of rioting after a violent clash with police that erupted one night at a local street market. Police had turned up to issue fines to unlicensed street vendors in the working-class suburb of Mong Kok, and Leung's group rallied a couple of hundred protestors to try to protect the hawkers. All-night clashes erupted with protestors smashing up a taxi, pelting police with bricks and burning bins. Riot officers used pepper spray and fired warning shots as things got out of hand. Vision of an officer being knocked unconscious as protestors advanced hurling sticks and bins was an ominous warning of the ferocity that would erupt a few years later.

Edward Leung was among the dozens arrested in the aftermath and, while it didn't dent his popularity, it would severely disrupt and upend a young life with so much potential. His case took another two years to work its way through the courts from when I met him, and in 2018 the then 27-year-old was convicted of assaulting a police officer and given a six-year jail sentence.

Little could he have known that just two years after he entered prison a protest movement far bigger and with far more ferocity than that night at Mong Kok would ignite.

Edward Leung wasn't at the 2019 Hong Kong protests, but many viewed the jailed political figure as the spiritual leader of the movement. 'Liberate Hong Kong, revolution of our times', the slogan adopted and chanted everywhere by the protestors, was his slogan. It was spray-painted on walls and echoed off buildings as protestors marched, chanting it from street to street.

It had the power to unite, to symbolise struggle. Too much power for Beijing. In 2021, under a new national security law, China's government outlawed it, declaring the slogan contained 'separatist connotations' and could be interpreted as grounds for a state subversion charge.

———

From the heat of the streets to air-conditioned offices, Wayne and I lugged our gear around Hong Kong. Our next interview was inside the offices of one of Hong Kong's pro-democracy parties. There's nothing like the blast of overzealous air conditioning chilling the sweat down your back as you cross from the humidity of the streets into Hong Kong's icy offices and shopping malls.

As with Edward Leung, there were intermediaries involved. Lam Wing-kee wasn't half as exciting, but he had a more interesting story to tell.

Pushing 60, with a grey mop, a skinny frame and a sling bag, Mr Lam looked like a man who would run a quirky bookshop. He didn't speak English or sufficient Mandarin, so I had to bring in a Cantonese translator.

He spoke of his curious ordeal with the air of a man not particularly fond of recounting it, but it was an extraordinary story.

Just weeks earlier, Lam Wing-kee had been released from eight months of detention in mainland China. He had been detained while crossing the border from Hong Kong into Shenzhen, whisked away, blindfolded and placed on a train for ten hours. He wasn't sure where he ended up, but it turned out to be a detention centre in the city of Ningbo. He spent the next eight months imprisoned there, facing daily interrogations culminating in a confession that was broadcast on China's state TV.

'Everything was a forced act with scripts and lines to remember,' he told me.

The reason for Mr Lam's ordeal was that he sold political books, some about Chinese leaders, that would never be allowed across the border. But he wasn't just selling them in Hong Kong. Lam Wing-kee was also mailing books to customers on the mainland. Given how sensitive it was, I did wonder why he would make regular trips to Shenzhen. It sounded utterly crazy when you're in that line of work.

He had a girlfriend there, he said, and while he wouldn't be the first man to take unwise risks for a woman, he also probably didn't suspect his situation would get so serious. As was often the way for politically active types in China, everything seemed normal until suddenly it wasn't.

By crossing the border, Lam Wing-kee made things easier for the agents who targeted him. He had colleagues and associates who were also swept up in the operation. One was last seen on Hong Kong island delivering books, and another disappeared while on holiday in Thailand. They all subsequently emerged in mainland China detention centres, sparking fears that Chinese government agents were kidnapping politically sensitive types from the streets of Hong Kong and even abroad.

Lam Wing-kee was one of the luckier ones. Not long after he emerged on state television confessing his guilt, he was back in Hong Kong. His handlers on the mainland, he said, had ordered him to return to the city and gather the records of customers, then bring them back across the border.

Instead, Lam Wing-kee called a press conference. In front of dozens of journalists and cameras, he described what had happened: a tale of secret agents, interrogations, padded cells and false confessions.

For one of his associates, the saga ended differently. A prolific author of political gossip books, Gui Minhai was apparently abducted from his holiday unit in Thailand and taken to mainland China, where he too emerged in Ningbo to confess to a hit-and-run accident years earlier that killed a woman. Even when his sentence for that crime was up, he still wasn't free, with agents detaining him for 'illegal business operations'.

He also popped up in state-media 'interviews' claiming he went to mainland China of his own free will, and refusing help from Sweden, where he held nationality. He later claimed, according to Chinese authorities, that he wanted to renounce his Swedish citizenship and restore his Chinese nationality. As his case dragged on year after year, it claimed the job of a Swedish ambassador, who tried to rope in Gui's Swedish-based daughter to broker a deal with shady middlemen. They had suggested to the ambassador that they could help in securing Gui's release, and in apparent desperation, the diplomat set up a meeting with Gui's daughter without approval from Sweden's Foreign Ministry. The story plunged Sino-Swedish relations to new lows.

Four and a half years after he vanished, just as the global coronavirus was spreading from China to the world, Gui Minhai was sentenced in a closed court to ten years in jail for 'illegally providing intelligence overseas'.

Back in Hong Kong, Lam Wing-kee had seen enough. He packed up his life and left the city that was no longer safe enough for his bookshop. He moved to Taiwan, the last refuge of free speech in the Chinese-speaking world, and reopened the shop.

The third person we interviewed saw things from a different angle. He was the counterbalance to the activist and the book-seller, a former broadcaster named Robert Chow who had set up a social-media group called 'Silent Majority for Hong Kong'. It was far from certain that people who shared his pro-Beijing, anti-protestor views were the actual majority, but he blamed the disquiet on Hong Kong's declining prosperity, the frustration that mainland cities were rapidly advancing while Hong Kong had seemingly stalled. He predicted that a pro-independence movement would boil over into violence, foreseeing the petrol bombs and Molotov cocktails that would become common among more radical protestors three years later.

'Do we want Hong Kong to become another Syria?' he asked me as we sat in his small office.

It sounded a bit dramatic, but Robert Chow firmly believed that China should be allowed to bring prosperity and stability to Hong Kong. Like many firm supporters of Beijing's rule, he took a fairly generous view of the level of freedoms on the mainland.

'I think China is already moving up to its own kind of democracy, they have a lot of freedom in China,' he told me. 'It used to be that you can't move from city to city. Now you can do that quite easily, now you can change jobs whenever you like. In the '60s and '70s you were given a job and you couldn't change or move.'

Pro-government figures would often use the low bar of China's Mao-era policies to point out that China was a lot more open than before, and even though it was not as open as Hong Kong, it was striking a good enough balance.

'Go down to a bar or wherever in Beijing and talk to the Chinese people. Since when are they worried about talking about the government?' he said. 'It's not Iran or Iraq, right?'

As the protests later showed, the silent majority of Hong Kongers weren't of this view, but it wouldn't matter. Those who went all-in on embracing the Communist Party's stewardship of Hong Kong had time on their side. About a year after our meeting, Mr Chow travelled to Beijing, where his group met top government officials in an event celebrated on state television. It was a high-level blessing for the political work Chow and and his allies were doing in Hong Kong. They were choosing the winning team and knew whatever Hong

Kongers themselves thought, the Communist Party on the mainland had the power.

With the story in the bag, Wayne and I packed up the camera gear and, after three days of shooting between stifling heat and freezing air conditioning, we flew back to Beijing.

There was a simmering discontent in Hong Kong in 2016, but it seemed increasingly marginalised. I couldn't imagine how dramatically things would change.

12

TINDERBOX

When Hong Kong's protests broke out three years after that initial assignment, I was on the wrong disputed island.

As word of a 'massive' demonstration planned over an anti-extradition bill reached me, I was 500 kilometres to the north-east on islands that were supposedly Asia's next flashpoint but felt like a place time forgot. Kinmen is a story every journalist covering Taiwan will at some point do: a pair of islands so close to China you could almost wave to people on the other side. And yet they're controlled by the government in Taiwan, more than 300 kilometres away across the Taiwan Strait. Look at it on a map and it's comical, but the islands are a significant chess piece in past and future conflicts.

It made for a good curiosity item in a *Foreign Correspondent* program we were doing on Taiwan, but clearly the urgent story was brewing in Hong Kong, where hundreds of thousands, possibly up to a million, people were taking to the streets.

As I wrapped up filming for the documentary, Beijing cameraman Steve Wang and the ABC's then-South East Asia correspondent, Kathryn Diss, flew in to cover the march. Both were convinced something had changed. Within a day of getting back to Beijing, cameraman Brant Cumming and I were on a plane again, flying down to Hong Kong.

It was impossible to tell at the time how pivotal the next few months would be in Hong Kong's broader history. They would change the city forever, setting the scene for a political crackdown that would help shift perceptions of China's government in Australia and further abroad.

When we arrived, the protestors were plotting to rally midweek. All signs indicated it would be big. Asia's greatest hub and most international city was heading towards a prolonged standoff with China's government, but like so many big stories in the history books, it wasn't immediately obvious how significant it would turn out to be.

Brant and I arrived in a city on edge with an unexpectedly Christian twist. Hundreds of young protestors had gathered around the Legislative Council building repeatedly singing a 1970s American Easter hymn. In the warmth of a midsummer night, they sang 'Sing Hallelujah to the Lord' again and again and again. It was monotonous and droning and really quite annoying, but in the initial weeks the Christians seemed to play an outsized role in the movement. Aside from their ability to mobilise through Church groups, the Christians also tried to play a protection role, seeking to utilise a law that prevented police shutting down religious gatherings for 'illegal assembly'.

That night Brant and I filmed and interviewed young protestors under a perfectly clear Hong Kong sky. Many pledged to stay out all night ahead of a mass demonstration the following day, when Hong Kong's Legislative Council was scheduled to debate the bill that historically will be seen as the straw that broke the camel's back.

The government of Carrie Lam—indirectly installed by Beijing via a 'democratic' ballot of just 1200 voters representing special interest groups—was seeking to pass changes that would allow suspects for certain types of crimes to be extradited to jurisdictions with which Hong Kong had no extradition treaty. The catalyst, according to Lam, was a murder case involving a Hong Konger who killed his girlfriend while in Taiwan, but the one jurisdiction everyone cared about was mainland China.

Lam offered safeguards: political offences would not be grounds for extradition and the law was a pragmatic change reflecting Hong Kong's gradual legal harmonisation with the mainland. The change 'strengthened' the promise of One Country, Two Systems, she said.

To most Hong Kongers, though, it would be the first proper crack in the wall that separated the Communist-controlled legal system from Hong Kong's British-style common law courts. While the structure of the Legislative Council had always been rigged to ensure a pro-Beijing majority would vote for Lam's proposals, large-scale mass opposition had scuttled previous attempts to push through unpopular bills. The Christians praying and singing were pinning their hopes on that happening again.

Brant and I did interviews for a few hours, bought a 'silver bullet'—a chilled can of Asahi sold at the many 7-Elevens around town—and returned to our run-down hotel near the government buildings in Admiralty to write and edit stories for the morning.

As on my previous trip with Wayne McAllister, the ABC budget didn't stretch beyond the bare essentials. Brant and I squeezed camera boxes into a tiny elevator at our hotel. The overpowering stench of antiseptic cleaner in the rooms with the mix of bright white lino floors and stained lime-green curtains made it look like the hotel equivalent of an old iPod.

'Looks like the sort of place where clients bring prostitutes and drug dealers get murdered,' I quipped to Brant.

We resolved if the story dragged on, we'd change hotels.

———

The next morning we made a late start, expecting a long day and night ahead. I had that 'fear of missing out' journalists get when I read on Twitter that early-morning clashes between protestors and police had already taken place near the Legislative Council building.

It was shaping up to be stunning day—sunny with occasional bursts of pelting rain that made the towers on Hong Kong island glimmer. At street level, everyone was wearing yellow plastic construction helmets and black shirts. Cling wrap covered their skin in anticipation of tear gas. The Christians were still singing, but they were vastly outnumbered by a seemingly endless mass of young people handing out supplies and passing on information from further up the road.

The mood was slightly festive but tense. These weren't young people indulging in the novelty of protest, but a generation hardened by the failure of mass demonstrations just five years earlier. They'd either taken part or watched the students occupy the streets and walk away after almost three months with nothing tangible to show from it. They were unified in seeking to make it a leaderless movement so no one would be especially targeted.

Brant and I strolled into the protest zone poorly prepared. We'd hastily organised a local fixer who would translate Cantonese and knew the lie of the land. We'd also tasked her with picking up some basic protest safety gear, and when we found her among the tens of thousands she was brandishing construction helmets and extremely flimsy high-visibility vests that looked like they'd come apart when the heat was on. I looked comical in the over-sized bright yellow helmet, like a boy reporter masquerading as a conflict journalist. But it's all we had.

At least our fixer's commitment to the cause was obvious. She was a Cathay Pacific flight attendant who regularly flew routes into mainland China. She'd called in sick that day, as had thousands of colleagues, to attend the protest. Cathay Pacific would later be named and shamed by China's government for not targeting staff supportive of the protests. Eventually top heads rolled and the airline was coaxed into taking such a firm stance that both Hong Kongers and mainland nationalists boycotted it, each for supporting the other side.

By mid-afternoon, the tension around the Legislative Council had risen. Police who had earlier kept formations around adjacent roads withdrew, and by now fifty to a hundred thousand protestors were blocking some of the biggest thoroughfares on Hong Kong island. The protestors already had one victory, managing to block legislators from entering the Council and voting on the extradition bill. News of this spread and only encouraged more people to come out onto the streets.

Brant and I went back to our budget hotel a few blocks away to file stories and eat, but when we returned the mood had soured. A veteran of five years in the Middle East, Brant could smell the pepper spray on the wind. We affixed our goggles—the sort students would wear in a science lab—and headed back into the thick of it.

As rumours and panic spread among the protestors, the lack of police on nearby streets was disconcerting. They surely weren't going to allow another Occupy movement to ferment? Knowing that Hong Kong government officials and the police leaders were inside adjacent buildings, plotting what to do, built the suspense further.

The protestors didn't seem to have a coherent plan. Debates about what to do were raging on their medium of choice, the encrypted app Telegram. People we spoke to on the ground said they were waiting on a consensus to emerge, but they stressed that the movement was leaderless. While avoiding the mistakes of the Occupy movement, this strategy was leaving them without clear direction.

As the afternoon humidity intensified and the protestor numbers swelled, everyone expected police would move in after nightfall. Teenagers and those barely old enough to call themselves adults were frantically handing out goggles, anti-irritation solution and helmets, counting down the hours to sunset and an inevitable clash. Some sat in circular groups, conserving energy for a long night ahead.

And then, suddenly, it erupted.

Hundreds of police with batons, shields and tear gas came running from the major roads surrounding the protest area. Tear gas filled the air as police moved in, swinging batons and firing rubber bullets, while protestors dispersed like a large school of fish. As long as you weren't at the front line, you could avoid being beaten, but still plenty of hardcore demonstrators manned the barricades, raised umbrellas and dug in.

I'd never covered civil unrest. It rarely happened in Australia, and on the Chinese mainland protests were stopped so effectively that by the time you heard about them, they were already being snuffed out.

So the sting of pepper spray on my arms was a novelty. It lingered on the skin with an irritating burning feeling. The taste of tear gas made your heart rate rise. If you smelled a little, you knew a lot was probably coming your way. And as you coughed and spluttered, an instinct kicked in to move away.

Brant, eyes red and nose running, was shooting near but not directly at the front of clashes. He refused my offer of a flimsy eye mask and seemed to have a higher tolerance than most.

Just when the effects of the tear gas subsided and things became calm, another cloud of it wafted over from elsewhere, as police cleared protestors from adjacent streets. The skirmishes raged on the overpasses too, like a game of cat and mouse.

Live pictures were now being beamed out around the world of Hong Kong's glistening financial towers emerging through thick clouds of tear gas, the streets below an urban battle scene. A presenter from ABC Newsradio, oblivious to my coughing, rang for a live cross to get me to describe what I was seeing.

Soon the police had effectively cleared the area around the Legislative Council. Riot squads now occupied the streets, and debris and discarded masks were all that was left. The protestors had dispersed up Hennessy Road, the main thoroughfare of Hong Kong island.

Brant and I madly filed, trying to get enough signal to push out the pictures by deadline. The afternoon assault by police took us by surprise. They'd clearly been ordered not to wait until the evening and to end the protest swiftly. I described it in an article as a 'swift and forceful crackdown', a marked contrast to the slow and tolerant approach police had taken five years earlier.

The young protestors gathered on Hennessy Road were devastated. A young woman in tears told me she was 'heartbroken' by what the police did. A young man barely past adolescence, with the curious chosen name of 'Hale', pledged to return to the streets within a few days. They got the confrontation they sought yet seemed surprised police weren't nicer about it.

This became a theme over the following months as many protestors took a hysterical view of police, accusing them of heavy-handedness and sexual assault, drumming up conspiracy theories about murders and assigning them an almost mythical level of cruelty. It turned into a self-fulfilling prophecy, as exaggerated fears of police impunity and authoritarianism at the outset of the protests became real when Beijing increasingly empowered the Hong Kong Police Force to implement control. At the beginning, police issued permits for peaceful demonstrations and responded when a predictable core of radical protestors turned violent. It frankly was surprising how long the police kept issuing permits, given the predictability of the violence, but the vast majority of protestors were peaceful, and the authoritarian state just above the border may have created an extra layer of vigilance in Hong Kong society about police misusing their powers.

But within months, they'd stopped issuing permits, owing, they said, to the inevitable violence committed by the black-clad frontline demonstrators.

By the following year, police were swarming the streets on key dates, stopping and searching young people and carrying out mass arrests before any protests could even begin.

———

As the day stretched into night on Hennessey Road, the last protestors were making a stand. Brant and I were drenched in sweat and tear gas residue but with so many platforms to file for, we remained out on the streets.

Things had become eerily calm. Further down the road a stand-off was still ongoing but we were lingering at the back interviewing weary protestors out of harm's way, or so we thought.

And then suddenly, panic. Hundreds of young Hong Kongers started running towards us. Someone yelled that police had raised the warning flag.

'Thwack, thwack'—two distant shots came from the barrel of a tear gas gun—and then, just like a cricket ball, a cannister bounced once in front of me and hit me square in my leg before ricocheting onto the ground a metre away and releasing its white cloud.

Caught off guard, Brant and I weren't wearing our flimsy masks, and as we began to bolt, a young woman in the crowd accidentally tripped Brant, who fell face first onto the cannister as it spewed out the gas. He and the heavy broadcast camera around his shoulder hit the deck. I had the tripod in one hand and helped pull him up with the other before we set off again.

Brant's tolerance for tear gas was high but he was now running blind, a big camera weighing him down, a bleeding gash on one arm from his fall, and his eyes and nose running like open taps. We were coughing and spluttering and running and sweating and we must have covered a couple of hundred metres to get clear of the scene.

Hunched over and recovering on a quiet road, I spotted a 7-Eleven and went to get some water for Brant, who took it gladly but needed a more soothing tonic.

So I returned with a couple of silver bullets, straight out of the fridge. Covered in blood, sweat and tears, Brant cracked his open and enjoyed one of the most well-earned beers of his life.

That was day one.

13

DEADLOCK

Within days of the Legislative Council protest came a rare backdown. Carrie Lam announced she would shelve the contentious extradition bill, apparently in an effort to offset another planned protest.

But it was too late. Deep distrust had set in and Hong Kong's pro-democrats focused on her refusal to formally withdraw the bill from the Legislative Council's schedule. They suspected her of a tactical backdown; they wanted the proposal shelved for good.

Deepening the crisis was a new set of demands that rapidly became the mantra for the entire movement. 'Five demands, not one less' started circulating in the days after the Legislative Council protest. Activists were furious about how the police had moved in with force, and even more upset that Lam blamed the protestors, describing some of them as 'rioters'. The slogan flew around the messaging apps first. Within days the 'five demands' were scrawled on a makeshift banner hung over the scaffolding of a shopping mall under renovation. A 35-year-old lone demonstrator in a yellow raincoat put it there.

As with the overall movement, I underestimated the seriousness of his protest. It was the first Saturday since the midweek demonstration that ended in tear gas and I walked from our new, slightly better hotel just down Hennessy Road to Pacific Plaza, where word of the lone protest had spread.

Fire crews were on the street below inflating a large yellow landing cushion, while friends of the man, only named later in the media as 'Leung', yelled at him to come down. He remained standing, his back turned to them and the street, his head covered by the yellow hood. Whatever they were yelling in Cantonese, it didn't appear to move him.

I remained on the street for ten minutes or so but figured he would give himself up to the emergency crews. As passionate as the protestors were, I couldn't imagine anyone giving their life for the cause. So I went back to the hotel.

That Saturday evening I was having dinner with the freshly arrived reinforcement Nick Dole, whom the ABC had dispatched from Australia. I had more or less forgotten about the lone protestor; we were preoccupied with expectations of a huge turnout for another rally planned for the Sunday.

It was only when I got back to the hotel that I saw the news. The man had fallen while trying to get away from rescue workers. They had advanced towards him on the scaffolding to try to secure him, but Mr Leung had tried to climb away. He lost his balance and plunged not into the inflated cushion, but onto the footpath below.

He had died for the cause, all to draw attention to those five demands written on his banner:

'No extradition to China.'

'Total withdrawal of the extradition bill.'

'We are not rioters.'

'Release the students and injured.'

'Carrie Lam step down.'

Suddenly the city's rising anger was no longer about the extradition bill. It was about everything that had come before it. Many Hong Kongers had decided this was the do-or-die moment in their city's history.

———

The day after Mr Leung died, the biggest collection of Hong Kongers in history hit the streets. It was absolutely extraordinary to witness and, coming from a country that's fairly apathetic to large-scale protest, somewhat hard to take in.

Nick Dole and a veteran cameraman flown in from Brisbane, Craig Berkman, were with me. We'd initially suspected the ABC of overegging the coverage by sending Nick and Craig in. I assumed Carrie Lam's move to withdraw the bill from imminent debate in the parliament would quell the numbers, but once again I underestimated Hong Kongers.

The morning was quiet, the city seemingly normal, but by lunchtime small groups dressed in black started making their way towards Victoria Park, to the east of Hong Kong's CBD. By early afternoon, the crowd had grown and solidified, like football fans heading to a vast stadium. Some were on foot, while many were below the ground on Hong Kong's MTR.

By mid-afternoon we were in the thick of it, interviewing protestors and filming from overpasses around Wanchai Station. It was a big crowd, no doubt about it, but the scale was hard to grasp from one section alone. Young and old, some with families, all were heeding the organisers' advice to wear black, symbolising the darkness of what they feared the future would bring for their city. As the crowds spilled over from Hennessy Road to parallel streets and police gave up trying to contain them to the original route, it was becoming clear that the numbers far exceeded expectations.

Like a sea of humanity, on they marched, hour after hour. We filmed among them and tried to beam out pictures live, at times failing to get reception and needing to bolt several blocks away until we found a signal. We hunched over our Live U transmission kits in alleyways and tried to convince security guards to let us into the lobbies of quiet office buildings to record our voice reports. With the size and enthusiasm of the protest, it was hard not to get caught up in the atmosphere, but we had recurring deadlines to meet and were barely managing to meet them. The protest we were supposed to report on was engulfing our ability to communicate it.

Having given up trying to get to the end point near the Legislative Council building, we instead stayed in place near the Ozo Hotel, our slightly better digs that would become a de facto ABC bureau over the following months. It was basic but clean and pleasant and perfectly located. I had a corner room with a view of the masses streaming past below. From the twelfth-floor window, I took a photo that showed just how dense the crowd was.

And they kept coming. Hour after hour, the sea of humanity didn't stop.

It was an extraordinary display of people, but not necessarily 'people power'. There was pessimism among those we spoke to that suggested the protest wasn't a means to an end, but the end in itself. There was little hope that such an enormous outpouring of opposition would force the people in power to change their positions.

Nick Dole and I felt we were pushing shit uphill with our vox pops. Usually protests are the easiest places to get random people to talk, but nearly every protestor would tell us that 'We are Hong Kong people', have a long chat about why they were protesting, make a passionate argument about the demands they wanted, and then, when we asked if we could quote them, declared: 'No, you cannot interview or quote me! But please tell the world our message to stand with Hong Kong!'

Frustrating as it was, it reflected just how cautious many ordinary Hong Kongers had become. Fear was already a tangible commodity in this supposedly free city, and would only increase in value as Beijing tightened its grip.

———

Hong Kong is notorious for its tiny living spaces but there were some people with space to spare, none more so than Jimmy Lai, one of Hong Kong's richest men and Beijing's most wanted political target.

A child of Guangdong province just across the border, Jimmy Lai was born less than a year before the Communists seized power. He had escaped on a boat to British Hong Kong as a child, tasted chocolate for the first time and by his own telling, was hooked on everything Hong Kong had to offer.

He built a fortune selling clothes and then turned to media, publishing *Apple Daily*, a boisterous, trashy tabloid that developed into the most fervently anti-Beijing newspaper in the city.

There was plenty more to the back story of Jimmy Lai, including a vicious feud with newspaper rivals, but it was his activism and position as the city's most prominent media tycoon that made him integral to the Hong Kong uprising story.

Getting to Jimmy Lai wasn't too hard; he often took a prominent role in street protests and spoke to the media regularly. But to get to his mansion one morning in the middle of Hong Kong's protest movement, we had to go through an American middleman. Mark Simon, a tall, large, confident American with thick dark hair, dressed rather formally for a Sunday morning in a suit, was not who I was expecting to meet when I walked up millionaire's row on Kadoorie Avenue, an enclave of beautiful houses not far from the hustle and bustle of shopping district Mong Kok. But Simon, who for years had been an executive at Jimmy Lai's company Next Media and who had fended off accusations by pro-Beijing types of being a CIA operative, was clearly pulling the strings.

I could see why Jimmy Lai's critics were suspicious—smooth-talking Americans weren't commonly part of Hong Kong's political fabric. But I was also surprised by the presence of a young cameraman waiting across the road from the house.

'Oh don't worry about him, he's always there,' Simon said.

It turned out the photographer was one of the many that Jimmy Lai's main rival newspaper, the *Oriental Daily News*, employed to tail him and write negative stories. One of the reporters once sued Lai for using intimidating language, a charge that was dismissed in court.

Lai was clearly no ordinary figure.

He was nowhere to be seen when we turned up, so we were left to marvel at the luxurious colonial-era house while a domestic helper cooked up a decadent-looking breakfast. She laid it out: bacon and egg omelettes, sausages, bread and French press coffee, all served on a round dining table in a sunroom overlooking an expansive, leafy garden.

By coincidence, we had two nights earlier filmed inside one of the city's infamous 'cage houses', where landlords divided apartments into dozens of bunk-style spaces and rented them to people down on their luck. They were overcrowded, hazardous and seen as a symptom of Hong Kong's outrageously expensive and crowded property market.

It was a tale of two cities.

Finally Jimmy Lai turned up in a buttoned-up shirt and sandals, semi-formal for a Sunday morning. He insisted we eat breakfast together before he dived straight into politics over the dining table, talking about why he didn't fear speaking to the media.

'The world has to understand what's going on,' he told me in a matter-of-fact way.

There was something of a street quality to Jimmy Lai, despite his billions of dollars and his slightly British Hong Kong accent. At times he talked with a mouth full of food, too urgent and determined to swallow his rolled omelette. His closely shaved head of grey hair made him look like a mob boss who'd left the mean streets behind, but no mob boss would pick a fight with the Communist Party of China. It would be bad for business, and the advertising revenue for *Apple Daily* had been squeezed after pro-Beijing interests launched a boycott campaign. Despite its general popularity, the paper was on the financial ropes.

After polishing off breakfast, we moved to the living room to set up the interview, and Lai delivered the sort of comments that

TV journalists live for. Clear, strong and sharp, the 70-year-old told me, 'We cannot stop, we are bound by duty.' The protest movement must keep going. He warned that if Xi Jinping sent in troops to quell the unrest, he would have to 'face the world's sanction'. He rejected claims that he worked with the CIA and spoke of his newspaper being the voice of the people.

It was stirring stuff, and a far cry from many of the protestors I'd met on the streets who were too fearful to be quoted.

Jimmy Lai was already high on Beijing's radar but he was happy to make himself as clear a target as possible. During the protests, he travelled to the United States to meet with Vice-President Mike Pence and regularly called for US support at a time when thousands of protestors brandishing American flags were calling for the United States to scrap special trade privileges with Hong Kong and continue a separate economic relationship with Hong Kong, conditional on the state of human rights in the city.

Some protestors had started to regularly bring American flags to demonstrations, and on one afternoon there were thousands of US flags flying through the centre of Hong Kong island as protestors marched to the US consulate—a sight that would be regarded as unbelievably treacherous and offensive on the mainland. Against this backdrop, Jimmy Lai met a US vice-president and the Secretary of State in Washington. It was amazingly brazen.

We packed up the camera gear and left the leafy surrounds of Kadoorie Avenue before venturing back to the vertical districts of Hong Kong island. I wouldn't cross paths with Jimmy Lai again but would report on him from afar as the protests continued and Beijing responded.

About twelve months after our meeting, Jimmy Lai hit the international headlines again for different reasons. Two hundred police raided his newspaper offices and arrested him under the sweeping national security law that Beijing imposed on the city in response to the protests.

The reason for his arrest? Collusion with foreign forces. The maximum penalty? Life in jail.

Led away from his office in cuffs, Jimmy Lai looked like a man who'd been expecting such a day for a long time. Ever defiant, he was released on bail and returned to a hero's welcome from his staff. He told them his arrest would just be the beginning.

He was right.

Within months, he wasn't just back behind bars, he was being publicly paraded in shackles.

14

BLACKOUT

If my time in Chinese and foreign media has taught me anything, it's that censorship works. But it has its limits and that's where propaganda comes in. It too works—if anything, more effectively.

The initial weeks of Hong Kong's protest movement in 2019 were completely blacked out in mainland China, despite the images being beamed around the world. The march with upwards of a million people on 9 June to oppose the extradition amendment bill? No reporting. The surrounding of the Legislative Council that ended dramatically with tear gas and rubber bullets? Nothing. The extraordinary sight of possibly 2 million protestors filling Hong Kong's streets on 16 June? No coverage either.

The occasional story about small pro-government rallies or Foreign Ministry condemnation of 'foreign interference', on the other hand, were sprinkled through China's internet but not in a way that could even begin to inform people. And it continued this way, even as the protests began to take a violent turn.

By week three the ABC had sent me back to Beijing, assuming the story had hit a stalemate. Covering Hong Kong was costly; you'd work through the weekends when the protests happened but then the city would switch back to normal on Monday morning, leaving you with little to do. It was the most comfortable civil unrest imaginable. The shops and restaurants were all open, the hotel was fine, there was even downtime to catch up with mates or hike the many scenic trails around the island.

We spent the weekdays arranging interviews, filming feature stories and writing, but the cyclic nature of the protests made deployment decisions difficult. Should we stay or go? If we finish filing on Monday and fly back to Beijing on Tuesday, will we need to return on Friday? Maybe we should just stay put.

These sorts of discussions bounced back and forth between Hong Kong and Sydney, with each decision a gamble. Extending or renewing assignments cost money, so the story had better be worth it. After three weeks, was the audience still interested? Six weeks? Twelve?

I was happy to remain in Hong Kong, as the story was generating far more interest than most of the topics I filed on from Beijing. Australian audiences could relate far more to Hong Kong than to the mainland. But after two straight weekends of coverage, we packed up and gave it a rest. The protestors were vowing to reconvene for an annual march on 1 July, the anniversary of Britain's 1997 handover of Hong Kong back to China.

When I returned to Beijing, the media blackout was extraordinary. In a world of digital interconnectedness, China's Communist Party leaders had managed to cut off the vast majority of the population from knowing what was going on in their own country. Domestic social-media sites were scrubbed of posts, videos flying around in groups on WeChat deleted one by one. As always with China's censorship, it wasn't about blocking 100 per cent of the population from knowing, but rather a critical mass. The system wasn't airtight, as information leaked, and it had to flow freely and in great detail to those in leadership positions and relevant government departments. Those who travelled between Hong Kong and the mainland were also aware of what was happening, as were the elite section of the population that used VPN software to circumvent the censorship and read international news.

But they were a minority, probably well under 10 per cent of China's total population, and many were middle-class beneficiaries of the broader system.

The automated keyword and content blocking, along with armies of human censors employed by both government and private media companies, are very effective but there is usually a time lag between content appearing and the system detecting it. The speed of the censorship depended on priorities. A local protest in a rural province could evade censorship initially as higher-level officials in China's Cyber Space administration only belatedly took note of it. Local officials fearful of bad news spreading upwards would shut down information first, but they only controlled their patch.

On the other hand, if politically damaging news was spreading about senior leadership—for example the Bloomberg and *New York Times* investigations in the early 2010s of family wealth belonging to former Premier Wen Jiabao and Xi Jinping—then firm instructions forbade any mention.

Hong Kong's protests were placed into that latter category.

Given the amount of information online, it would have taken an extraordinary level of organisation to scrub China's domestic internet of news. And yet they did, for as long as they could.

———

Within a month, the censors had reached the limits of blocking information and were moving to shape it instead.

I was back in Hong Kong with yet another cameraman, our other ABC bureau shooter Steve Wang, a tall, bespectacled Beijing native who spoke with the capital's guttural accent. Steve and I are the same age and forged a tight bond through those long nights dodging tear gas and getting the right shots followed by hours of editing and writing at the hotel, only to get back up at the crack of dawn to beam in live to morning news bulletins in Australia.

It was exhilarating and exhausting and all the trickier for Steve, who as a mainland Chinese national could only spend a maximum of fourteen days in Hong Kong on any one visit. There are so many injustices to irritate mainlanders about Hong Kong, but needing permission from the Exit/Entry administration each time and being denied the luxury afforded to foreigners for long stays in the city rank highly among them. For Steve, it meant shuttling between Hong Kong and Beijing to help accommodate a growing roster of Australian correspondents being rotated through.

The step-up in coverage had a lot to do with the events of 1 July 2019. It was the first major protest since the epic '2 million march' in June. (Organisers claimed almost one-third of Hong Kongers took part, surely an exaggeration, but a lot closer than the police guess of 338,000.)

Those numbers couldn't be maintained, but the 1 July turnout was still large. As before, it culminated with protestors surrounding the Legislative Council building, next door to the People's Liberation Army garrison, a tall, inverted pencil-shaped tower inherited from the British colonial days.

I couldn't quite imagine what those PLA soldiers posted to Hong Kong must have been thinking, looking down from their air-conditioned barracks at the huge crowds. It would be bad enough at the best of times looking out from a prime harbourfront position and not being able to take proper part in that glistening city. But now they could clearly see how different the city was from the image portrayed through state media.

Already speculation was swirling that the Chinese leadership might resort to using military or paramilitary force to end the political unrest, a move viewed as a 'nuclear option' that would solve one 'problem' yet create many new ones.

The night of 1 July drove that speculation to fever pitch. Outside the Legislative Council, the police had withdrawn. The streets, the nearby park and the overpasses belonged to the protestors, young, wearing black shirts and yellow or white helmets. They cut down the Chinese national flag outside the Legislative Council and replaced it with their own design, a black version of Hong Kong's flag, the orchid in the middle symbolically wilted. It fluttered in the midsummer evening darkness like a pirate flag on the bow of a ship. A successful mutiny, destination unknown.

For hours the protestors milled around, debate raging both in person and on their digital devices. Should they storm the Legislative Council? Or is that exactly what the police were encouraging them to do by withdrawing? Was it a trap? Or was escalation necessary?

In the late afternoon, some hardcore protestors had tried to smash through the glass doors of the building, ramming a rubbish cart into it and taking to the glass with metal poles. But going 'all in' and ransacking the chamber was a step-up many seemed hesitant to take.

I got talking to a skinny young protestor just below the flagpole. Like most, he would only give a first name: 'Andrew'. He didn't seem too sure that busting into the city's parliament building was a sound idea, but, in his words, 'What other choices do we have? Some people might be turned off and they might turn against us but I don't see any better choices at the moment.'

The mood that night was a far cry from the 'Hallelujah' singing of the initial weeks. The Christians were still there but were isolated voices among a much more radical crowd.

Steve Wang and I knew it wasn't a matter of if but when. We were taking a rest a few blocks away when word spread that the protestors had smashed their way in. We ran over and witnessed the most provocative display towards China's government since the 1989 Tiananmen Square uprising. Thousands of Hong Kong students were spray-painting walls, smashing their way into offices, logging onto office computers, destroying symbols of the government and ripping down portraits of past leaders from the walls. The fire alarms were ringing, protestors were blowing whistles and the corridors of power were a cacophony of yelling in Cantonese. On one wall, someone spray-painted 'Xi Jinping is a pig'. Elsewhere protestors were trampling on a picture of him.

Maybe the years of living and working inside the political straitjacket had sharpened my awareness of the danger around open criticism. To witness thousands of people throwing caution to the wind was shocking to me, but probably less so to Hong Kongers. The distance makes a big difference.

The protestors roamed around for a couple of hours, looking for light switches, open doors and symbols to deface. It took them a while but they found their way onto the main stage: the Legislative Chamber, the building that was supposed to represent the voice of Hong Kongers but had so clearly failed.

It wasn't clear who the leaders were that night in the chamber; the protestors seemed to work it out as they went along. Some hoisted a black sign decrying government descriptions of them as 'rioters'. Others arranged a line of pictures depicting the politicians they deemed responsible for the extradition bill that triggered the uprising. Perhaps most provocatively, one protestor hung the old British colonial flag over the dais, a message to Beijing that the Western imperialism against which the Communists fought so hard was preferable to being ruled by mainlanders.

It was an unprecedented display of rebellion, one that I thought might tip public opinion in Hong Kong against the protestors, but as I found out in subsequent days, many older people who didn't approve of their actions still focused their anger on the police and government. The bitterness towards Carrie Lam, the Hong Kong Police Force and ultimately Beijing was deep enough to tolerate extreme actions.

The next day China's government would continue to tightly censor reports of what had happened that night, but there were too many cracks in the information wall. Within days, China's government decided to flip the script and make Hong Kong front-page news, with headlines decrying 'violent criminals', 'thugs' and 'terrorists' destroying Hong Kong's stability at the urging of 'hostile foreign forces'. Pro-government rallies on a scale not even a quarter of the size of the protests were splashed over mainland media.

Pictures of the 2 million-strong marches in June were absent, as were pictures of the greatest affronts—the graffiti insulting Xi Jinping and the draping of the colonial flag. But there were images aplenty of 'rioters' smashing, looting, vandalising and causing havoc in a city that, in the eyes of mainlanders, already received favourable treatment. For many Chinese people reading the coverage for the first time through official state media, it was shocking and surprising that people seeking 'democracy' would behave this way.

Pro-Beijing spokespeople from the establishment political parties in Hong Kong were the only voices heard in state media. Whether the coverage was online or on CCTV, the mainland viewer was left with the impression that the protests were violent, that the majority of Hong Kongers abhorred the demonstrators and that the original grievance was just an 'excuse' for violence. Add to that a nationalistic campaign focused on 'standing with Hong Kong police' as they battled rioters for national honour, and it was a radically different narrative being presented.

China's domestic propaganda, although increasingly sophisticated, was still a blunt instrument. Many were happy to believe it, taking comfort in a type of nationalistic tribalism not dissimilar to what you might have seen at a Donald Trump rally.

But not everyone bought into the narrative. When I returned to Beijing, many ordinary people asked me what the 'true' situation in Hong Kong was like.

I felt lucky to have a foot in both worlds, able to tease out how people on both sides of the border viewed it.

I couldn't imagine that, just over a year later, police in Beijing would be asking me who I spoke to in Hong Kong as part of an interrogation that led to my departure. That the Australian government would be issuing safety warnings for travelling in Hong Kong. That the events unfolding before my eyes would sweep me up in their broader fallout.

———

Back in Hong Kong, the freewheeling local media was in overdrive and live streaming was the medium that shaped coverage the most. Young journalists, sometimes with a separate cameraman filming on a phone, would roam the streets chasing the action from site to site, calmly commentating on events.

People across Hong Kong would tune in, including Uber drivers and cabbies with upwards of six smartphones rigged to their dashboard. Many viewers relied on sites that combined split screens of up to eight simultaneous live streams. It became invaluable to us on nights when there was action in multiple districts and we had to decide where to go.

Out in the city, people would hunch over their phones at diners watching the split screens late into the evening, while restaurants nearly all had a TV tuned to the public broadcaster TVB, which had its own crews out on the streets.

'The revolution will be live streamed' could have been the slogan.

Steve Wang and I left the smashed-up Legislative Council building on that fateful night of 1 July with the demonstrators inside still in full flight. We had waited a long time for the police to surround and advance on the protestors inside the building, but our deadline got the better of us. On our way back to the Ozo Hotel, we passed by the expat bars of Wanchai. It was the early hours of the morning and we were lugging our equipment.

Outside one of the open bars, a group of overweight, cherry-faced white men were nursing beers, watching football, oblivious to the chaos unfolding just two blocks away.

Hong Kong's protests were like that—always one block away from normality.

I suggested to Steve that we dump our gear on the ground and write the story over a cold beer. It had been a long, intense day. We found a table and ordered two Heinekens. Steve connected the camera to the Live U, never straying from the job at hand. I started tapping away on my phone, trying to reduce the historic scenes to two 30-second radio voice reports.

Just as the beers arrived, one of the tubby British expats watching the screens said, 'They're going in.'

I looked up. They'd ditched the football and were glued to a live stream of the Legislative Council. The police were moving on the protesters. On multiple TVs from different angles were scenes of tear gas and havoc.

The barflies were just as hooked as everyone else.

I looked at Steve and he didn't have to say anything. We picked up the gear, affixed our gas masks and bolted towards the Legislative Council, the tear gas already wafting our way.

Our beers remained on the table.

15

PATRIOTISM

As Hong Kong burned in late 2019, Beijing was readying tanks to roll past Tiananmen Square. Missiles too.

Week in, week out, the protestors in Hong Kong had elevated their efforts, from occupying the international airport and stopping all flights to creating a popular alternative anthem played by an orchestra in full protest gear. 'Glory to Hong Kong' could be heard at every protest, a stirring musical rallying cry.

All the while the protests continued with weekly running battles across multiple districts that ended in tear gas, arrests and, increasingly, mob clashes between civilians of different political stripes. The mobilisation of Chinese paramilitary troops in a sports stadium just across the border in Shenzhen further fuelled speculation that China's government was contemplating a crackdown.

When news broke of the troop build-up, I crossed from Hong Kong to Shenzhen to cover it but spent two hours detained at the border, where public security officers questioned me and asked to see stories I'd written about Hong Kong on my laptop.

'What do you think of the protests?' they asked me.

'I think they've kept me busy,' I told them.

As the protests continued, we had already started to face delays and questioning at Beijing airport when flying to Hong Kong, but the border crossing at Shenzhen was different. They put me in a waiting room with one guard and his body cam watching me. I wasn't allowed to touch my phone and tell my cameraman outside what was happening.

I wasn't alone, though. A disgruntled older man had been stopped at the border for unclear reasons. He was swearing at the guards and trying to make small talk with me, incurring the wrath of the increasingly annoyed guard.

All I could do was wait, well aware that questioning, temporary detention and delays were part of the fun of reporting in China. From the government's point of view, Western reporters were not to be trusted. It must be frustrating to have to let these pesky foreign journalists run around and besmirch China's image.

After multiple calls to superiors and many photos of my passport and journalist card, the border officers got the all-clear to let me through. Legally, I had a visa and a press card, so stopping journalists from entering mainland China as the world focused on Hong Kong would be a big move that I would, of course, report.

As the paramilitary force, the People's Armed Police, performed drills in the stadium under security that was deliberately loose enough to allow media to capture a few distant images, demonstrators across the border in Hong Kong continued to rage. They seemed surprisingly blasé about the prospects of troops on the streets, most believing it wouldn't happen, while some hardcore protestors almost welcomed it.

'It will show the world the true face of China,' a young woman told me one night at a protest outside a university.

Back in Sydney, my bosses were increasingly concerned that I might get trapped in Hong Kong if they shut the border, leaving the ABC without a reporter in mainland China. So I continually shuttled back and forth, making a point of flying Cathay Pacific in quiet support of the fixer who took a day off to help us report the first day of the protests. Her airline was the subject of relentless pressure from China's government to change management and rein in staff who voiced support for the protestors. A mainland boycott meant the cabins were almost empty.

Police officers waited at the airbridge in Beijing each time a Cathay flight arrived. They always boarded the plane after the last passenger had walked out, when the crew were still onboard. I was never sure if they were searching for banned materials or interviewing the staff. China's Civil Aviation regulator had started demanding lists of staff from the airline working on mainland routes and declared those involved in the protest to be a 'safety threat'. One pilot who used the PA to urge passengers on a Hong Kong in-bound flight to 'add oil'—meaning 'Go' or 'Fire up'—was later ousted by the airline.

It was clear Cathay was being targeted. When I took the government-owned Air China back to Beijing, the police weren't waiting.

———

Usually returning to the capital felt like I was leaving the only big story audiences cared about that year. But as October neared, Beijing became front and centre again.

The Communist Party was preparing to celebrate 70 years since it 'liberated' China and instituted the longest continuous one party-state in history. According to tradition, ten-year anniversaries meant a huge military parade featuring tanks, missiles and marching troops down Chang'an Avenue past the 'Heavenly Gate', Tiananmen, for the paramount leader to inspect.

On the bucket list of spectacles, a Chinese parade would have to be near the top. The North Korean equivalent in Pyongyang is often cited as the pinnacle of Communist pageantry, but the Chinese are better resourced and do it on a much bigger scale. Although Xi Jinping in 2015 managed to sneak an extra parade in to mark the 70th anniversary of the victory over Japan in the Second World War, such spectacles usually happen once per decade, far less frequently than in North Korea.

For more than a year, the Beijing bureau had been talking about the parade. Everyone was looking forward to it, knowing that each spectacle had to outdo the previous ones. I was especially excited, having been left in the fog at a different extravaganza earlier that year, the biggest naval fleet review in China's history at the port city of Qingdao. It was supposed to be the largest show of muscle the Chinese Navy had ever assembled on the water, and Steve Wang and I were going to be on a Chinese warship to witness it, an amazing gig to get. Unlike some previous epic flotillas China's PLA Navy had organised, this one would be bolstered by seventeen ships and craft from other countries, including one frigate from Australia. Even as late as 2019, Australia was still on good enough terms for some military cooperation with the Chinese Navy. We were rarely allowed to attend anything related to the PLA, but an Australian ship for an exercise that showcased 'international cooperation' allowed us to get the royal treatment.

The PLA Navy had organised for the media to stay in the five-star Shangri-La Hotel in Qingdao's glossy CBD. We were invited to a reception where we made small talk and posed for smiley photos with the Chinese military spokesman, Colonel Wu Qian. We were bussed to a waterfront park to witness the 'battle of the Navy bands', which, sadly, Australia didn't participate in. It seemed a lost opportunity to forge a bit of goodwill, but I noticed only a few foreign navies willing to bring bands.

While the Chinese, Bangladesh and Myanmar bands took things quite seriously, playing stodgy military standards or versions of popular Chinese songs, it was the Indian sailors who brought down the house with Michael Jackson covers. Their irreverence was charming, and although most of the audience were Chinese sailors drilled to remain in their chairs and wave plastic clappers, the foreign journalists at the back were dancing.

All of these festivities were fine, but the PLA's insistence that we attend the elaborate four-day program of activities was a bit excessive. We were only there for the naval parade, and the Shangri-La was becoming a bit of a gilded cage. In typical Chinese-government style, the security around the hotel was intense. The waterfront of Qingdao harbour had been blocked off and our minders were so nervous about losing track of us that they falsely told me Qingdao's famous maritime museum was shut.

With a couple of Russian media colleagues, we took a taxi anyway, and sure enough found it open and bustling with domestic tourists scampering over the old warships and admiring fighter planes of a bygone era. I interviewed some of the tourists about the massive naval display and caught the sort of exchange that summed up so many things about modern China.

A retired Chinese man with neat grey hair, a khaki fishing jacket and an expensive camera dangling from his neck was happy to talk to me. He looked like the classic intrepid grey-nomad traveller and he had timed his visit to Qingdao with the naval fleet review.

But he had a bone to pick.

He was excited and patriotic about this display of Chinese naval might and happy to see the warships of other nations. But authorities had blocked off all vantage points around Qingdao's impressive harbour, which he believed was excessive caution.

'The people should be able to watch it,' he exclaimed, as a small crowd gathered to listen. He was especially frustrated with a suggestion from a Qingdao local official to just watch it on TV.

As he spoke to me, another older couple interrupted, shooshing him and telling him not to complain.

'*Mei guanxi*,' the husband and wife said over him, meaning 'no problem'. 'We're happy to watch it on TV, don't listen to him,' they told me, before drowning him out and correcting his gripes about the excessive security.

'It's for safety,' the husband yelled.

'Yes, safety, other countries are the same,' his wife chimed in, showing disapproval that this man was airing China's dirty laundry to a foreigner. No matter how legitimate his gripes, displaying national unity was all-important.

It was typical of what I encountered over those five years in China. No doubt it predated my time and will continue for years to come.

I didn't have the heart to tell the old fellow that I would be on a PLA warship watching the ships and submarines pass by at close range. That would be rubbing salt into his wounds.

———

The morning of the naval fleet review involved hours of security checks. Xi Jinping was going to be onboard another warship to inspect the fleet, so nothing was left to chance. Every piece of equipment we intended to take on board was rigorously inspected and approved. We were lined up into little groups and bussed from security check to security check.

After getting through the final check in a special locked-down zone of Qingdao port, we were finally taken to a wharf and walked towards a PLA training ship called the *Qi Jiguang*, named after a heroic Ming dynasty general known for fighting off Japanese pirates.

The weather wasn't looking good: grey, drizzling, plenty of coastal fog. Steve and I were nonetheless extremely excited to get on board. Along with the other media and the military attachés, we were ushered to a mess room where sailors in crisp white uniforms provided snacks, fruit, tea and coffee. A boxed lunch set not dissimilar to what you'd get on a budget airline was provided, branded with the PLA's logo celebrating 70 years of its naval arm, a rare souvenir. On the walls were pictures of famous scientists from China and abroad. The theme of this training ship, we were told, was science and knowledge.

Before long we were chugging out of port and through the heads, but because the mess room had small windows, it was hard to get a grasp of what was outside. After an hour or two when we finally were free to race to the observation deck, we realised the answer—not much.

To our great disappointment the clouds seemed to hang lower off the coast, and thick grey fog obscured everything but the water closest to us. As military band music started to crackle from speakers and commentators announced that Chinese submarines were passing, we jostled for position but struggled to see much. Red flags flapping in the rain were the only colour on top of dark grey submarine hulls that were silently gliding by, mainly submerged under the freezing grey water.

I'd banked on seeing a spectacular display but was left with every shade of grey imaginable. Chinese warships started to pass at a distance of about 100 metres, the crisp white uniforms of sailors on deck the only way to make out the shape of the hull. Before long we were told the star of the review was coming—the 304-metre-long aircraft carrier *Liaoning*, once a Soviet-era hand-me-down, refitted to be the first of many Chinese carriers projecting power far from the motherland's coastline.

But the rain was only getting heavier and all I could see was the dark shadow of a behemoth. A photo taken on my iPhone failed to catch it, and Steve Wang's professional zoom lens only fared marginally better.

I couldn't help but laugh—this was Xi Jinping's effort to project enduring images showcasing the growing might of China's naval fleet for both a domestic and global audience, he was just one ship away from us, inspecting each passing vessel in what was meant to be a display to inspire awe and fear, and the worst weather imaginable had literally rained on his parade.

When more than 30 Chinese ships had passed, we were treated to the deafening roar of flyovers. The fighter jets were low and close; you could hear them, but not see them in the dense clouds above. And then, as the visiting ships began their procession, along with the military representatives we rushed to the other side of the deck. The showers intensified.

After a few warships from Russia, Vietnam and India, the moment arrived that justified our attendance.

'From Australia, guided-missile frigate HMAS *Melbourne*,' crackled the voice on the speaker.

'You ready, Steve?'

'I can't see it,' he said.

'Nor can I.'

The Australian warship passed as the appalling weather reached its nadir.

Steve's lenses didn't catch it, let alone my smartphone.

More disappointed was the Australian Defence Attaché, Paul Deighton, squinting into his Konica camera. He'd played a key role in organising the Australian ship's visit and had been counting down the hours until the sailors from home emerged, standing proudly on deck.

But with that moment passed (we assumed), I turned to him as he scrolled back through the series of images he'd snapped.

'Could you see it?' I asked.

'Not really.'

Lost in the fog, but at least not the fog of war.

———

After the disappointment of Qingdao, I was all the more excited for the 70th anniversary military parade in Beijing.

The ABC's bureau in a tall old building on the street that turns into Chang'an Avenue would have been perfect to watch the late-night rehearsals. Its ageing balcony has a multimillion-dollar view of China's most important street and looks east towards the gleaming new towers of Guomao. The crops on farm fields three decades ago are gone, replaced by glass towers that grow towards the sky like wheat. When the setting sun hits them on clear days, they shine with the promise of prosperity and power, and still they grew, new buildings rising higher every time I gazed out. It was in the shadow of these modern towers that the tanks would line up before rumbling down the avenue, leading a charge towards the west.

Given our vantage point, we thought about setting up a camera to catch vision of troops and tanks practising for the parade. It would have formed one heck of a contrast to the scenes of rebellion down in Hong Kong. But Brant Cumming's efforts to set up a small camera were thwarted by security guards.

Like all tenants in the Diplomatic Residency Compound, we'd been given orders to vacate our office for the days leading up to the parade. Even the manholes were inspected and sealed with tape to ensure nobody could sneak into the sewers. There were no ifs or buts: windows in apartments were to be shut, curtains closed and office staff made to work from home.

But big colourful floats are rather hard to hide, so even though the missiles were kept under wraps, many of the civilian floats were parked at the Workers' Stadium, just across from my apartment.

I lived on the 25th floor of my fairly modern building, called HuaYuanZhiXing, translating as 'Star of China' but not really.

The name sounded good; the meaning was less important. It was the only tall modern building in an old residential community that was otherwise made up of two dozen red-brick walk-up buildings. There were small vegetable shops, a butcher and an older woman who cut hair on the street for 20 yuan, although I always gave her 30, still an embarrassingly low amount compared to what hairdressers charged in a salon.

But HuaYuanZhiXing was perfectly located next to the Workers' Stadium, one of the 'Ten Great Buildings' constructed in 1959 to celebrate a decade of Communist rule. It was a wonderfully outdated relic in a fast-changing city, and I'd spent many a night watching the local football club Beijing Guoan play, tens of thousands of foul-mouthed fans chanting 'stupid cunt' at the referee, the opponents and the visiting fans. You couldn't buy food or beer inside, so market stalls clogged the footpaths on game days selling fried quail eggs, oily pancakes and warm beer, which the vendors poured into giant plastic cups.

A night at the football on a balmy summer evening was Beijing at its best, and even though bulldozers were hastily tearing down the stadium in the days before I had to leave, they were plotting to rebuild a modern version in line with the original design.

But during that late summer of 2019, all football was played elsewhere as the floats depicting giant Communist flags, rockets, copies of China's constitution and rainbows were practising laps of the stadium behind newly erected temporary walls. Soldiers guarded the site but people in adjacent buildings could get a sneak peek.

With the parade on 1 October rapidly approaching, I was becoming increasingly anxious about whether I could attend it.

Relations with Australia were severely strained and despite submitting applications, none of the other Australian media correspondents could get a pass. We were all furiously checking with colleagues from other countries and as the days ticked down, the Australians appeared to have been singled out for a snub.

With more mass protests planned in Hong Kong for 1 October, I had to make a call on whether to stay or go. Having covered so many protests already, I was far more determined to stay in Beijing. But there wasn't much point reporting on a spectacle you have to watch on TV.

Two days before the parade, the Foreign Ministry was holding a welcome reception for media at a government press centre in Beijing's west. My college, the veteran ABC producer Charles Li, had been working the phones with our minder at the Ministry, Mr Ouyang, who was giving little away about the chances of a last-minute pass. Charles thought it necessary we attend the reception, even though another correspondent had been told no Australians would be invited.

The whole thing had left me pretty bitter. Relations between Australia and China had been unravelling for a while, but blocking us from witnessing a mass display designed to generate as much media attention as possible was a blow.

Charles' advice to me was to say some niceties to Mr Ouyang at the reception just in case he could come up with a last-minute pass. Mr Ouyang was a middle-aged veteran of the Foreign Ministry who appeared to have little interest in what we reported or even keeping tabs on us. Due to his relatively rare two-syllable surname, I could never remember his full name. He was always just 'Ouyang'.

I would have preferred to have more regular contact with my minder, but like many of the officials at the MFA, he was much more comfortable speaking to me through my Chinese staff. Only once did I have a proper chat with him during a visa renewal, but it left me underwhelmed. He said my reporting on Hong Kong was very biased but didn't bother to find an example when I asked for one. Nor did he mention an interview I'd broadcast a couple of months earlier with Taiwan's Foreign Minister, which really should have warranted a rebuke from a Beijing official. It appeared he wasn't even aware of it.

Like many officials, he'd been ordered to get across certain talking points (at that time, Hong Kong was the primary one), and anything outside of that remit was unnecessary. It meant that our small talk was a bit forced and transactional. I left the reception thinking I'd been conned into turning up and giving face to the Ministry while they snubbed the ABC.

It seemed a classic power play, getting us to turn up to ask for something, and then not giving it to us. But I was wrong.

The day before the parade, Mr Ouyang called Charles and told him he'd managed to secure one pass for me, which he portrayed as a great favour. Unlike, say the American CNN crew, which had a large space in the media section in prime position, Australia's entire media contingent received one pass about 30 rows back.

But at least I was in. With no cameraman or space to shoot anything, all I needed was a suit and a selfie stick.

———

The morning of the parade started in the late summer darkness of 2 am. Bleary-eyed journalists gathered for rigorous security checks at a media centre well away from the middle of Beijing, and then were put on buses for more security checks closer to Tiananmen Square.

It felt like the whole city had been counting down to this day and as I strolled past Chairman Mao's mausoleum onto the vast expanse of concrete at about five in the morning, volunteers slept in their portable camping chairs, having no doubt put in some long days and nights, maybe arranging the tens of thousands of seats facing Chang'an Avenue and Chairman Mao's portrait on the Heavenly Gate.

My section near the middle was an enclave of foreigners among thousands of locals who likely snagged their tickets through positions at state-owned enterprises or Communist Party membership. Of the 80,000 in attendance, everyone felt lucky to be there.

Most of the people around me were delegates on a 'Belt and Road' media tour, primarily from African and Middle Eastern countries but some from southern Europe too. By pure chance a visiting reporter from the *New Yorker* magazine, Evan Osnos, was seated next to me. He'd been in Beijing during the years when I first took an obsessive interest in China, and his book *Age of Ambition* beautifully captured the first decade of the century when the sky seemed the limit. He was back to write a feature about the trade war and growing US–China rivalry. The age of ambition had given way to an age of tension and suspicion. Parading missiles down the street only added to it.

Many hours passed. The square was blanketed in brilliant sunshine and sweltering heat. Spectators fanned themselves and watched the pale foreign journalist lather himself in sunscreen.

By late morning, the moment had arrived. Brass band ceremonial music heralded the arrival of Xi Jinping on the Tiananmen rostrum in a traditional black tunic suit. He and a few dozen of China's top leaders past and present fanned out into position, not a single woman among them. They were just tiny specks from where I was sitting, but the spectators around me enthusiastically cheered. This was a gathering of the loyalest of the loyal; a hushed reverence consumed the square as hundreds of meticulously drilled soldiers began a slow ceremonial march to raise the national flag. More than 50 cannon fired round after round from the back of the square as the soldiers set a slow, rhythmic drumbeat with their boots.

With the flag raised and the national anthem sung, you could almost hear a pin drop as the huge crowd awaited Chairman Xi's speech to open the parade.

And right as he stepped up to the microphone, my phone rang.

The lunchtime radio program was calling me for a pre-arranged live cross, a scene setter to describe what I could see. 'Well, there are only two people talking in all of Tiananmen Square right now—me and Xi Jinping,' I told the presenter.

It was mortifying. Everyone in my section looked at this disrespectful foreigner chatting away on the phone during the Chairman's speech.

I tried to hide under my suit jacket and crouch behind the seat in front, whispering through the phone and hoping the presenter would wrap up the cross. But, of course, she didn't. She had a direct line to Tiananmen Square where extraordinary scenes were unfolding and wasn't going to keep it tight. It was only a few minutes but felt like an eternity.

I slid sheepishly back upright, careful not to make eye contact with the many people staring at me.

Thankfully, they soon had more interesting things to stare at. First came the troops, column after column, rifles at the ready, each step precision-drilled. Army, Navy, Air Force, they marched with an intensity designed to inspire faith in China's unofficial religion—patriotism—and inspire fear beyond China's borders.

The military had matched the soldiers for height and with China's lack of widespread ethnic diversity, the effect from afar looked like an endless army of clones. The faces, their character, their individual stories were all dissolved by the whole. This show was about the power of the state.

Chairman Xi inspected the troops, greeting each battalion with 'Hello Comrades, you're working hard', before hundreds of tanks rumbled past Tiananmen Square. In a country where the events of June 1989 are still determinedly censored, it's extraordinary to see a large number of tanks on the very place where they once fired at protestors. With speculation swirling in Hong Kong about a Tiananmen Square-style crackdown, it was surreal. All news of the Hong Kong protests had again been censored, leaving no risk that those opposing the motherland's nationalistic embrace could rain on the parade.

I doubted that many people in today's China would have made the connection. The narratives within and outside the country were parallel universes. Generations of Chinese have watched tanks roll past Tiananmen once every decade. The vision of the tanks being put to their violent use to clear out protestors had been ruthlessly suppressed. Those holding on to memories of 1989 were a speck of China's population.

After the tanks, we watched hundreds of massive inter-continental ballistic missiles, anti-ship missiles, anti-aircraft missiles and short-range missiles on the back of trucks. Columns of mobile communication vehicles, stealth drones and even a mini-submarine rolled past, while fighter jets and bombers roared overhead. Helicopters flew over with three flags, re-inforcing China's singularity. The flag of a political party—the Communists—always precedes the national flag. The military, which remains the army of the Communist Party, not the nation, flies third.

For hours it went on as spectators strained their necks to see the hardware and used whatever they could to fend off the sweltering sun.

The last military truck didn't signal the end, just the beginning of the civilian parade, a much more interesting display showcasing China's achievements. Like everything that day, the scale was hard to comprehend. Tens of thousands of dancers accompanied individual floats. There were suit-and-tie lawyers waving copies of China's constitution, Winter Olympics athletes rollerblading around a giant slalom, high-school students waving sunflowers dancing around a float showcasing China's renew-able energy, astronauts, doctors, bicycle riders, robots, labourers, people dressed as birds and dolphins.

There were tributes to economic projects, to China's domes-tically made passenger jet and floats showcasing the highlights of each province, from satellite manufacturing to agricultural production. Tibetans danced in front of a mini-scale replica of Lhasa's Potala Palace and Mount Everest. Kitesurfers in boardshorts shared the Hainan province float with a rocket representing the island's Wenchang space launch centre. Giant doves were affixed to many of the floats. Portraits of Communist Party paramount leaders including Xi Jinping elicited huge roars from the crowd.

It got to a point where I wanted to go home. Like a huge banquet where the dishes just keep coming, it was an assault on the senses, leaving me and others exhausted.

Two and a half hours after it all began with soldiers hoisting the flag, came the final act.

By now there were hundreds of thousands of people in the square and on the twelve-lane expanse of Chang'an Avenue. Spectators and participants had been whipped into a frenzy of singing, flag waving and patriotic joviality. The conductor of the military band, after more than two hours of gyrating his hands and holding the soundtrack of the show together, seized a quiet moment to snap a selfie in front of Mao's portrait. A rare slip of discipline, but who could blame him?

As the spectators and performers started singing the classic Red song 'Me and My Motherland', tens of thousands of doves that must have been gasping in cages at the back of the square were released. In a mesmerising pattern they darted and turned direction, weaving in and out of flocks as the human masses cheered. A symbol of peace to end a display of sabre rattling. A message to a billion people watching at home that China's Communist Party will keep the peace by being strong. A message to those abroad that the region can maintain the peace, as long as it's on China's terms.

———

As I found my way out of Tiananmen Square that day and hugged the route of the parade walking east along Chang'an

211

Avenue, the spent civilian floats rolled past me. They were now devoid of music and empty of people, destined for another decade of hibernation before being refitted and rolled back out for the 80th anniversary. These colourful, oddly shaped floats cut an unforgettable image as they passed on an empty highway under the giant concrete rainbow that marks the point before Chang'an Avenue crosses a giant ring road bridge at Jianguomen.

After the rigidly perfect display we'd just witnessed, it was hard to believe anything going on that day in Hong Kong could top it. I'd heard the protests were in full flight, but few up north in the capital were paying attention.

With thousands of people making their way out of Tiananmen Square, I was just looking for a path out of the security cordon to walk home, but I caught a moment that stuck with me.

A group of five security guards who had been employed to stand there all day finally had a moment to relax. They had abandoned the rigid shoulders-back pose and were snapping selfies as the floats rolled by, a memory to send home to Mum and Dad or their girlfriends and wives, a souvenir of the day they guarded China's parade.

Seeing me walk by, the young men seemed to hesitate. They flashed a look at each other, as though wondering if they should stand guard again and not let their hair down in front of this foreign visitor.

Instead, they just smiled. I smiled back. We had all witnessed something truly extraordinary.

16

THE SIEGE OF POLY U

Late in November 2019, Hong Kong's anger reached its peak in a frenzy of Molotov cocktails, tear gas and rubber bullets. At the moment the police launched an assault on protestors at a major university to bring the six-month battle to its finale, I was stuck in a toilet block missing the moment.

The siege of Polytechnic University, or Poly U, was the most emotionally draining act of the 2019 rebellion, and it left me deeply sad and pessimistic about Hong Kong's future. It was the explosive result of six months of unanswered anger. An unelected government had given barely any concessions, and a sizeable group of protestors decided insurgency was their only remaining option. The violence in the city had escalated into horrific street beatings—one protestor belted a man in the head from behind with a manhole cover, in an attack that could have easily been fatal.

An information war had erupted online with out-of-context short videos flying around cyberspace showing either

213

heavy-handed police brutality or gang beatings by protestors. The city had turned upon itself—neighbour against neighbour, students against teachers and, in some cases, parents against their own children.

At its heart was an enormous power imbalance. I had no doubt that the majority of Hong Kongers either supported or were sympathetic towards the protest movement. Local district council elections confirmed this, with a huge turnout and a devastating swing against pro-Beijing parties. Pro-democracy candidates rode a wave of popular anger to make huge gains, and the biggest pro-Beijing party, the DAB, received little sign of a quiet wave of resentment against the chaos of the protests. The majority were really, really angry at China's government, its proxies running Hong Kong and the city's police force.

But China's government still controlled the city's fate. The people could march in their millions, shut down the airport, burn the city down with Molotov cocktails and capture international support, yet they were powerless to change their future. The Communist Party was not for turning.

As the weeks of protests in June and July turned into months, I had to find increasingly creative ways to justify the expense of assignments in Hong Kong. It wasn't just me. A rolling circus of ABC journalists and cameramen swung through the city during that summer as concern mounted about a possible military crackdown and, even worse, not having journalists there to cover it.

So our weekends were consumed by chasing the protestors and police around the city, the weekdays by trying to carve out curiosity features about the bigger picture. We looked into whether the city's housing shortage and stagnant economy was really fuelling the anger, as Chinese government media claimed (the answer was not really). We looked at whether a school course called 'Liberal Studies' that taught critical thinking played a role in pushing students towards the protest movement, as pro-government critics claimed (probably). Other journalists looked at the impact on Hong Kong's economy, and during an especially quiet week, ABC veteran Greg Jennett even toyed with a story on the downturn for Hong Kong's love hotels (the idea didn't get past the editors).

I hung out with a group of pro-Beijing retired men whom I met at a rally to support the police. They bemoaned that the young'uns didn't remember the 'bamboo ceiling' that the British imposed in the colonial days, and they called the protestors 'cockroaches'.

One of them, a jovial and very fit retiree in his sixties named William Cheung, expressed his horror at the vandalism the 'rioters' had unleashed, smashing up traffic lights and shopfronts, and breaking ticket machines on the MTR. One of his friends had had a very bitter falling out with his adult son over politics. This friend told me he was ashamed his son was taking part in the hardcore frontline protests; too ashamed to speak to me on the record.

I understood where they were coming from. They were retired cops and businessmen who didn't remember colonial rule quite as fondly as the teenagers and twenty-somethings who now waved Union Jack flags on the streets. They were patriotic Chinese and relished being part of a powerful nation, even though it meant making some reality adjustments about the nature of Communist Party rule. Pro-Beijingers in Hong Kong rarely identified as socialists or embraced the authoritarian aspects of the Chinese state, but they were proud of 'One Country, Two Systems' as a creative and benevolent compromise the Party made when it could have done away with the legacies of Britain's rule.

They chose a very sympathetic understanding of the more authoritarian aspects of Beijing's governance. William Cheung asked me what I personally thought of the extradition plan that triggered the six months of upheaval. He supported it strongly. I pointed out that an Australian citizen with a curious past named Yang Hengjun was languishing in a Beijing jail cell on unspecified national security charges, without access to lawyers for nineteen months, which struck me as a pretty good reason for Australians not to ratify an extradition agreement. William told me that it was no different from the Americans locking up prisoners at Guantanamo Bay, as though that excused the excesses of the Chinese state.

Others I came across at pro-government rallies, primarily older men, took a generous view of mainland China's internet censorship policies, telling me it didn't matter because 'everyone has VPNs' (they really didn't).

There also seemed to be quite a few older Western men, usually British, who were some of the most enthusiastic supporters of Beijing. One, a suited banker caught up in a demonstration while on his lunchbreak, told me the 'kids' protesting had no idea what they were doing.

'They're on the doorstep of the biggest economic opportunity in the world and they want to destroy it,' he told me during a protest at Causeway Bay on Hong Kong island.

Another older Brit named Peter Bentley became such a regular contrarian that Chinese state media turned him into a minor star. He'd lived in Hong Kong for decades and I first spotted him at a small weekday protest near the Legislative Council, angrily lecturing the young Hong Kongers, telling them they would take the city's democratic development back by 30 years.

He cut a lone figure during a much larger demonstration months later, standing in the middle of Hennessey Road, soaked in the rain, holding a 'Reject violence, protect stability' sign, an official government slogan heavily pushed by state media, as thousands walked around him to protest police brutality.

I had to give it to him: it took no small degree of dedication to be the lone counter-protestor.

I stopped to speak to Mr Bentley during the rally as the rain poured down.

'Have you even been to mainland China?' he asked, telling me the protestors hadn't actually been there to understand it themselves. 'They still think it's like in Chairman Mao's time.'

After I told him I lived in Beijing, he was surprised that I didn't agree that everyone in China had unfettered internet access through VPNs.

An Australian man became a star of China's nationalistic state media when he lambasted protestors after they caused flight delays at Hong Kong airport.

'The sooner Hong Kong actually becomes a part of mainland China, the better it's going to be,' he told a group during a heated exchange on a viral video.

It was by no means universal, but the older Western man opposed to the young protestors was a theme I repeatedly came across.

———

By November, things were getting out of control. Emboldened young protestors surrounded a policeman who opened fire and shot one of them. It was all caught on live stream. The young man survived but the incident supercharged the anger in the city.

Foreign journalists had generally marvelled at the police's restraint. We often spoke about how if groups of people ran around Sydney or London hurling petrol bombs and smashing up infrastructure, the police would have used their weapons months earlier.

There were horrors on the other side too. The omnipresent live streamers caught black-clad protestors dousing an older man they were arguing with in petrol and casually setting him ablaze. The Chinese staff in our office gathered around my phone to watch it in a state of shock.

When spliced up into clips showcasing the worst excesses of both police and protestors, the city appeared to be on the brink of collapse.

When Steve Wang and I flew back in November, the mood was post-apocalyptic. Young protestors controlled the streets at night, faces obscured in black masks and goggles, some smashing traffic lights, others digging up footpath bricks to scatter over the roads. We watched and tried to film as a protestor sought to light a street electricity box on fire.

The days of interviewing protestors on the streets were long gone. Just pulling out the camera could trigger an angry reaction. At best, the protestors would open umbrellas to block filming of their vandalism. At worst, they would surround you and question who you were working for.

I wasn't too worried for myself, but as a mainlander Steve was on edge and I didn't want to risk an angry mob turning on him. If anyone asked, he said he was Korean.

The bitterness in the city was also fuelled by changing police tactics. On the mainland, many people couldn't understand why the Hong Kong Police Force was so 'soft' on the 'rioters', 'mobs' and 'terrorists' roaming the streets. Such antics wouldn't be tolerated on the mainland, further fuelling resentment towards the entitled Hong Kongers.

Police were now using other methods, dressing as black-clad protestors and infiltrating the protests only to turn on their 'mates' and slam them to the ground before putting them in cuffs. Cameras captured images of older police officers in their thirties in balaclavas and black protest gear, flinging skinny teenage protestors to the ground, knees on their backs. Thousands were arrested, although, much to the chagrin of China's government and its supporters, most were released on bail only to return to the streets.

The police's changing tactics ignited paranoia within the protest movement and turned people further against each other. Ordinary bystanders who expressed a contrary view were accused of being informants.

Brutal brawls made weekend live streams addictive, with public broadcaster TVB cutting up a highlights reel each night of the most vivid action. Pro-government supporters were urged by China's government to rat on colleagues or employees who attended protests. Suspicion rippled through Cathay Pacific as the company, under pressure from Beijing, started picking off staff who expressed support for the movement on social media. Public servants and teachers too were in the firing line.

No one could see an end in sight.

China's government didn't deploy the military, which would have scared off the city's international financiers, who still played a vital role in outward-bound Chinese investment. For all of the talk of Shanghai replacing Hong Kong, the common law courts really did make Hong Kong irreplaceable. Global companies needed a jurisdiction where they could be assured of a fair day in court. Close to two-thirds of Chinese outbound investment was funnelled through Hong Kong, making the city an indispensable gateway. Putting the military on the streets, imposing curfews and emergency laws, would not only shatter confidence in One Country, Two Systems, but also make it hard to unwind. I was left with the impression that China's government genuinely wanted to keep Hong Kong going as a distinctive legal jurisdiction and financial system, as long as it could clamp down on its politics.

With no military intervention in sight, and with Beijing-backed leader Carrie Lam instructed by her bosses in Beijing not to give any further concessions, there was no way out.

It was demoralising for the people on all sides. Police were overworked, overstretched and increasingly angry at young protestors calling them murderers and rapists. The protestors certainly tended to interpret everything police did in the worst possible light. They set up a continuous vigil at Prince Edward MTR station in Kowloon, where police had chased protestors one night and blocked the journalists from following them down to the platform. Somehow rumours spread that the officers had murdered protestors without any cameras around and dumped their bodies in vats of acid to leave no trace. No family members had come forward to claim missing loved ones, but that didn't deter dozens of protestors from laying flowers, lighting candles and telling anyone who asked that MTR's refusal to release surveillance camera footage of that night proved the cover-up.

I felt sorry for the police, but sorrier for the protestors. At the root of the problem was a minority—unelected Beijing-backed politicians—ruling over a majority and defying demands that would be reasonable elsewhere: for example, democratic elections and an inquiry into police behaviour. A Marxist–Leninist nationalist political party, determined to rectify the historic shame of losing territory to British imperialists, was hell-bent on controlling a liberal, multicultural, international-minded city that thrived on open borders and freedom of speech.

There was no possibility of a win–win resolution.

———

The week before the siege of Polytechnic University, a similar confrontation took place at a different campus, the Chinese University of Hong Kong, north of the city.

Protestors had abandoned claims that violent elements were seeking to frame them by hurling petrol bombs at the police during clashes. The young demonstrators, many just out of their teenage years, were openly brandishing Molotov cocktails, saying they needed them for protection against the police. It sounds wild in hindsight that thousands of young people running around Hong Kong with petrol bombs had become normal.

Some weekends, masked protestors in black turned up to restaurants owned by pro-Beijing sympathisers and completely trashed them as shocked diners ran for cover. As the end of the year neared, a group ran riot through a shopping mall, setting alight a massive Christmas tree as a middle-aged security guard working the night shift looked on, helpless.

I'm sure many Hong Kongers were horrified by this violence, yet there was such popular sympathy for the movement, and such antagonism towards the police force, seen to be acting with impunity, that the criticism was always muted.

By the time the protestors turned their attention to Poly U, it felt like something had to give.

Polytechnic University is a large brick campus on the Kowloon side of the harbour. While it has a decent reputation, it doesn't have the academic prestige of other universities in Hong Kong. But its position near a major cross-harbour tunnel made it strategically important. Protestors gathering there could block the tunnel and maximise the havoc. Over several days in November that's exactly what they did.

Reports had seeped out that the students were accumulating huge numbers of petrol bombs and storing them on campus. On the streets around the university, protestors had scattered bricks and large nails, set up roadblocks, taken apart fences and smashed the traffic lights. At first, the vandalism seemed senseless. The subway operator MTR had given in to Beijing's pressure to stop services at stations near where protests were planned, so smashing up the MTR stations had some justification. The traffic lights on the other hand . . . I was never quite clear on why they were targeted, unless it was for general disruption.

Inside the Polytechnic campus, we passed a haphazard security checkpoint set up by the protestors. Nineteen-year-olds scrutinised our press cards. Fortunately they didn't ask Steve where he was from. These were depicted as menacing 'mobs' and 'rioters' by state media and certainly, if you were in their firing line, it was a fair description. But I was always struck by how softly spoken and polite many of the protestors were. They were still so young.

One evening months earlier, I tried to talk to a group of hardcore frontliners near the Legco building. Their English skills weren't great, so I tentatively asked if we could speak Mandarin—a language many protestors strongly associated with the mainland's encroachment upon Hong Kong's Cantonese culture. I braced for a negative reaction but the young protestors laughed through their masks and goggles and were happy to chat, excited a foreign journalist was asking for their opinions.

Their anger against Beijing didn't extend to its language, although I also spoke to mainland Chinese students in Hong Kong who weren't given such a friendly reception. As always, the Western experience of the city was a world away from what mainland Chinese saw there.

———

The scenes of destruction outside Poly U contrasted with the camaraderie within. Thousands upon thousands of students ran around stockpiling blankets, food, umbrellas and protest supplies. Demonstrators in masks had taken over the canteen and were serving meals. Groups of construction students were building brick walls to block the entrance routes, trowels in their hands mixing mortar. Others were wheeling around trolleys of

Molotov cocktails and setting in place butane canister bombs, taping six cans together with disconcerting determination.

The scene inside the campus was absolutely fucking wild.

On the upper terraces of the main building, some students with IT skills had created a split screen of twelve live-stream feeds showing where the police were gathering outside. Others were making a giant slingshot to propel rocks at police a couple of hundred metres away. A big enough engineering mechanism was lacking, so protestors were using their bodies as the anchor for the slingshot. We stood on a middle terrace watching them try to sling the rocks further, but they always came up just short, crashing into the no-man's-land separating the police line from the students.

Throughout the afternoon, police tried to recapture roads around the campus using a large water-cannon truck that sprayed a peppery-flavoured blue liquid that stung the eyes and skin. Protestors from the archery club countered with bows and arrows, hitting an officer in the leg.

The police kept firing tear gas, and a canister landed through a window, clearing out a floor of the faculty building. Its taste lingered in the air for hours, adding to the chaos inside. Water was leaking through a roof. Fire alarms were ringing. The carpet was a mess. It was like a college frat party, but the only booze was ethanol in the Molotovs.

Above us, police helicopters hovered, while just across from the university, People's Liberation Army soldiers watched from a suburban barracks, a soldier in green fatigues with binoculars retreating once we pointed our camera his way.

As this all unfolded, the afternoon sun started to set, leaving everyone guessing what would unfold after darkness. The students, hopeful of laying siege to the university, were bunkering down for a long stay. There was a convention in Hong Kong that police wouldn't enter a campus unless invited by the university, so the protestors figured they had a right to defend it with force if need be. But they were pushing that argument by occupying public roads outside the campus.

In the uneasy darkness of early evening, we left the campus to take up a vantage point in a building across the road. But we had a problem with our fixer.

Our normal go-to fixer in Hong Kong was an absolute gun. Kelly, a final-year university student with perfect American English, had the cynicism and humour needed to deal with civil unrest. She judged the more extreme protestors to be the 'weird kids' who didn't fit in at school, and scoffed at demonstrators' exaggerated claims about police. But she could still use her networks to snag us interviews with high-profile key figures in the movement such as Jimmy Lai or Nathan Law. Kelly said her Chinese medicine doctor, whom she saw once a week, didn't approve of her going out to work among the protests, saying all the running around was bad for her health, but she'd come anyway, cracking jokes and pointing out the best dim sum restaurants along the protest routes. She was a young, bright Hong Konger a step removed from the fervour: exactly what you needed in a journalist.

She really stood out. Throughout our time in Hong Kong, we'd hired local fixers and translators, but there was a high turnover and huge demand from other TV crews. Some fixers were protestors in disguise and seemed to be far too obsessed with local minutiae about police, which was of limited interest to our audience abroad. Others were happy to organise interviews over WhatsApp but reluctant to come out in the field.

Then there were those who had never worked with the media before and weren't sure what we actually needed them for.

But during the week of the siege at Poly U, Kelly was taking a break from running around her home city chasing protestors and cops for the foreign media. She'd recommended a friend of a friend, a student named Vanessa who, unlike Kelly, was very green and very caught up in the fervour. She'd watched for months as friends volunteered to be researchers and translators for the foreign media, all in the name of publicising the cause, and then joined the fray herself just when the stakes were getting too high.

As darkness surrounded Polytechnic University, police announced over a loudspeaker that they'd sealed off access to the campus. And for the first time during the protest movement, they dramatically upped the ante.

'Anyone who doesn't have a press card or a paramedics ID will be arrested and charged with rioting,' a commander announced over a loudspeaker.

A look of absolute fear came over Vanessa's face. She didn't have a press card; she was just a student helping out for a day. An uneasy feeling knotted in my stomach too. What had I got her into? We couldn't take the risk of leaving and having our twenty-year-old casual employee arrested and charged with a criminal offence. So we stayed put and bunkered down for a long night, waiting for the inevitable police assault.

As the hours passed, the protesting students continued their on-again, off-again battles with police. An armoured police vehicle attempted to drive through barriers the protestors had erected on a bridge and was pelted with so many petrol bombs that it retreated in flames.

Steve and I went out to film near the front line, but it was bloody dangerous. A rock hurtled past our heads, and people around us were hit by police pepper balls. The further we pushed towards the bridge, the harder it was to work out what was going on. The flames glowed, the smoke billowed and the lines of helmeted, masked protestors thickened, their umbrellas a flimsy shield that obscured our view. If police on the other side were about to charge, we'd have no warning. It was chaos and confusion.

We retreated back to our vantage point near the entrance of the university to watch protestors clash with police from another side of the campus, the piercing siren of the water cannon echoing off adjacent buildings. Protestors, glued to their phones in between throwing bricks at police, told us a police spokesman had warned that officers may need to fire live rounds to quell the unrest. Elsewhere, protestors had mobbed an ambulance and attacked an injured policeman who was being treated inside.

That night at Poly U felt far more serious than previous protests. An anxious-looking Vanessa became resigned to our strategy of staying until daybreak, probably regretting getting involved with foreign media. But this stand-off wasn't going to end well and we needed to be there to see it.

The protestors on the street continued their occasional charges at the police lines but, as the night wore on, the routine of skirmishes fell into a lull. They'd been at it for days.

Our position was pretty good: a protected vantage point, with a public toilet block in the carpark basement. We talked about our strategy if, as the police threatened, Vanessa would be arrested when we tried to leave. I promised her we would spend the next day doing what we could to bail her out and find a lawyer, although we didn't have much time to get embroiled in a legal tangle. We just hoped daybreak would bring some sort of change.

At about 5 am, as things seemed relatively quiet, Vanessa told me she wanted to go to the toilet in the carpark. Because of the threat of arrest and a general rule we had about not separating, I accompanied her and waited outside. We took our gas masks and helmets, just in case.

I waited at the door, mindful that police were likely gathering nearby.

And that's when all hell broke loose: a cacophony of fire as police moved in on the campus from all sides, the stealthy black-clad members of the unit known as the Raptors darting past me, blue lights around their necks identifying them in the darkness. Hundreds of riot police in green converged, firing round after round of tear gas. There were explosions as protestors, suddenly awakened, hurled whatever they had at the charging police— petrol bombs, butane bombs, rocks, bricks and glass bottles.

Fire and fury echoed off the buildings as thousands of students guarding the university desperately bolted for the main entrance. A bottleneck formed as students on a terrace above frantically hurled bottle after bottle of flaming kerosene.

I could hear all this but what little I could see of it had quickly become lost in the fog of tear gas. To make matters worse, my phone rang—it was the ABC's Hamish McDonald calling for a breakfast radio cross we'd pre-arranged the night before.

Through a gas mask and with the sounds of pops and explosions, I explained what I could see, or at least I tried. Hearing the chaos, Hamish asked me repeatedly if I was safe.

I felt a tugging on my arm and it was Vanessa, a look of

pure panic on her face. She'd emerged from the toilet as the onslaught began. She was terrified that one of these stealthy Raptor police would pin her to a wall and make good on that promise to arrest everyone without credentials for rioting, and she was looking to me for protection.

I ended the cross, and we made a run for it, hugging a wall and back up to the terrace. As we raced up the stairs past other media crews, we found Steve Wang, eye glued to the viewfinder, in the perfect position to witness what was unfolding.

He turned around, a sly smile on his face.

'You missed it,' he said.

As the sun emerged, the campus was on fire, small explosions erupting every few minutes. Hundreds of students were inside, while police cleared up the streets around the campus, biding their time.

We were frisked and searched by riot police as we left the university, but our daybreak strategy worked. They seemed to care less about their promise to arrest people like Vanessa and to be more interested in checking my credentials. Having a press card issued by China's Foreign Ministry always helped.

Just outside the cordon in the streets around the university, hundreds of young people in normal clothes waited in silence as we emerged. They were just standing there, some looking at their phones, desperate for news about their friends inside. All of them looked so young.

Maybe it was the lack of sleep, but emotionally it hit me. Their determination to support their friends against all odds was a stoic display of unity and fortitude.

Over the next 48 hours that unity developed into something quite extraordinary, the likes of which Hong Kong will probably never see again. Thousands of young people heeded a call to gather in the streets around the campus to surround and distract the police. They dug up bricks to block roads, formed human chains to pass supplies, and gathered then dispersed at speed in the streets around the university to confuse the police.

There were still elements of a nasty underbelly. A man suspected of harbouring pro-government views was beaten by a mob in front of me just as I was about to go live on air. But generally Hong Kong's young generation was working together, tireless in supporting each other and united in trying to free their comrades inside.

Some people organised scooters to whisk away protestors who abseiled down ropes from an overpass in an extraordinarily daring escape. Others helped their friends inside evade the police by escaping through the sewers. By the evening, much of Kowloon was brought to a standstill by the army of young protestors occupying the streets.

The ABC's Tokyo correspondent, Jake Sturmer, flew in to relieve me and hit the ground running like an excited Jack Russell, madly snapping away at scenes I'd become accustomed to. Japan clearly didn't offer up anything as vivid.

The Poly U stand-off continued into a second night. When we returned to the campus the following day, we saw colleagues from other news agencies doing a staff changeover. The police would allow one in to replace one coming out of the campus under siege. This freedom of movement for the media was one of the great contradictions of the Hong Kong protests: for all of the hysteria about authoritarianism, the police were far more open and accessible than we would deal with back home. I couldn't imagine Australian police being so accommodating if a major siege happened in Sydney.

Later that night, as we waited at a checkpoint we chatted away with a young officer who said he'd never pulled so much overtime in his life. 'The protestors are crazy, you never know what's next,' he told me casually.

But sympathy was a volatile currency and there were always officers who managed to ruin it. That night a group of twelve students made a run for it right in front of our eyes, bolting down a road from the campus straight towards where we and about fifteen police were waiting. The heavily armed police crash-tackled them to the ground before cuffing them, interrogating them and leading them towards buses to be taken to the lockup.

A group of older people waited near us, including a mainland man who had spent the protests opening a succession of WeChat accounts trying to beat the censors and tell people in mainland China what was truly going on. He and the others were there for solidarity and protection.

'We yell to them to ask their names and phone numbers,' said a middle-aged woman who would only tell me her first name, 'Iris'. 'We try to organise lawyers for them, because they're trying to protect our city.'

The movement was intergenerational. Hong Kong's youth might be leading it, but they had a supportive community behind them.

Before long, riot police were confronting the supporters, pushing the small group back and holding bottles of pepper spray to their faces, fingers on the trigger. The police were notorious for liberally shooting capsicum spray in people's eyes point-blank. A young aggressive officer was yelling at the mainland WeChat man and threatening to spray the burning liquid in his eyes. The man calmly held his ground before retreating a few steps, even though the group was already well away from the road.

For all of the violence generated by protestors, it was difficult to feel sorry for the police. They ultimately had the power. And within a year, they would run the streets with impunity, backed by Beijing and a new set of laws that made the protestors' once-exaggerated claims of a police state a reality.

In 2019, Hong Kongers stood up to Beijing in the biggest rebellion the city had ever seen. In 2020, Beijing got its revenge, jailing key figures, forcing others into exile and supercharging plans to curtail free speech, destroy the independence of the judiciary and end the legal separation of Hong Kong's courts from the Communist Party's control.

In one extraordinary year, China's government confirmed the worst fears that much of the world has about it—that it's driven by a ruthless desire to control others and a determined hostility to the values that Hong Kong and much of the Western world share: free speech, independent courts and a pluralism of views.

With the siege of Polytechnic University signalling the last hurrah of mass protests for 2019, the new year was always going to be a test of will and patience. As the coronavirus rapidly spread out of Wuhan in January, Hong Kong's government found a legitimate way to suppress attempts to reignite the protests. Social-distancing limits on outdoor gatherings gave police new powers to stop, arrest and detain people trying to gather for demonstrations.

Xi Jinping had already chosen a de facto new leader to spearhead Beijing's counter-offensive. A Beijing loyalist, Chris Tang, was appointed the city's new Commissioner of Police at the end of 2019. In a major signal of what was to come, he changed the force's longstanding slogan, 'We serve with pride and care', to 'Serving Hong Kong with honour, duty and loyalty'. There didn't need to be an explanation of who the force was loyal to.

Within days of his appointment, Chris Tang was in Beijing promising top Communist officials to use 'hard' measures to target violent protestors while being more 'humane' for lesser offences. He led a recruitment drive and began to flood the streets with police on the mornings of planned protests. Young people were stopped, searched and interrogated. 'Illegal assembly'—protesting without police approval—became the main legal offence, and the coronavirus restrictions added to the law enforcement arsenal.

It became clear as the months rolled on that the 'humane' measures weren't designed to tolerate protests in this supposedly free city, but to nip them in the bud. At times it was ludicrous. A lone teenage protestor was surrounded by nine police officers at a metro station for reading the *Apple Daily*, Hong Kong's popular tabloid that firmly backed the protest movement.

That was only the beginning of it. At 11 pm on 30 June 2020, China's government formalised its response to Hong Kong's year of tumult. It went further than many expected. Thirty years on from Tiananmen Square, China's government had learnt lessons and adapted. Those who feared that troops would be deployed on the streets had it all wrong. Xi Jinping had a far more effective tool at his disposal.

The first the public heard of it was in May 2020, when thousands of delegates in masks gathered for the annual political congress in Beijing, which had been delayed due to the pandemic. China's rubber stamp parliament announced it would 'debate' a new national security law for Hong Kong. The Communist Party had long tried to extend the mainland's national security rules to the former British colony, but mass protests in 2003 spooked local pro-Beijing politicians from pushing it.

Now Beijing was ready.

The standard way of changing laws involved the city's Legislative Council approving them. But the violence of the uprising gave Xi Jinping the perfect excuse to impose national security laws on the city by decree—a nuclear legal option that was always available to China's government but previously seen as too explosive to use.

In the weeks that followed the congress, China's government didn't let Hong Kong's officials read the draft law, let alone the public. Just one Hong Konger was allowed to read the draft law before it was imposed: Tam Yiu-chung, Hong Kong's sole delegate to China's National People's Congress, a veteran pro-Beijing figure so loyal that he publicly recommended China's government make the incoming law even tougher. He didn't reveal the details, though, making a mockery of the idea that delegates to China's parliament would represent the views of their constituencies.

In the dead of night one hour before the 23rd anniversary of the 1 July handover, China's newsagency Xinhua confirmed the imposition of the law.

Moments later, Carrie Lam essentially confirmed the farce of her 'executive' title when she said 'it wouldn't be appropriate' for her to respond to questions or comment on it. Activist Joshua Wong responded on Twitter: 'From now on, Hong Kong enters a new reign of terror, just like Taiwan's White Terror period in history, with arbitrary prosecutions, black jails, secret trials, forced confessions, media clampdowns and political censorship.'

Within months, Wong was in jail, sometimes shackled at court appearances. His colleague Agnes Chow was put in prison too. Their political organisation, Demosisto, which called for self-determination in the city, was disbanded. The group's other leader, Nathan Law, fled to the United Kingdom. Hong Kong authorities later issued an arrest warrant for him for supporting secession and collusion with foreign forces, despite being in exile.

The law had extra-territorial jurisdiction, meaning those who continued the fight for Hong Kong's cause from abroad could never return home. Jimmy Lai, the newspaper publisher, wasn't just in jail, he was in shackles—a 73-year-old humiliated in court like a violent criminal.

Slogans associated with the protest movement such as 'Revolution of Our Times' were banned, with authorities claiming they had separatist connotations. The minimum jail sentence was three years, the maximum life. And in a move seen by many as the death knell for 'One Country, Two Systems', Beijing deemed that only judges it approved could adjudicate national security cases.

If that wasn't enough, in some exceptional cases (with no clear definition of exceptional), Hong Kong suspects could be sent to the mainland for trial in Communist Party-controlled courts.

One year after the city erupted over plans to extradite sus-pects to the mainland, Xi Jinping had managed to not only get his way with extradition, but also a whole lot more. A national security hotline was set up for people to dob in their friends and neighbours. National security education was introduced to schools. Mocking of the national flag and anthem were criminalised, pro-democracy legislative councillors disqualified. China's government had gone from a 'little-by-little' strategy to a full-throttle offensive, with Beijing's biggest supporters in Hong Kong emboldened to keep pushing against perceived ene-mies, often with the backing of Chinese government media to foreshadow who was next.

'A chill is descending on Hong Kong and people need to take precautions,' wrote media outlet RTHK, one of the many targeted by pro-Beijing types as being biased in support of the protests. The online headline was referring to a weather forecast for an unusual cold snap, but the grim humour wasn't lost on anyone.

'We're seeing a remaking of the One Country, Two Systems idea away from what many overseas or Hong Kong democrats might have assumed it was to a model closer to what Beijing hopes it will be,' said Antony Dapiran, an Australian lawyer in Hong Kong who chronicled the protest movement so closely he wrote a book on it. He became one of the few voices in the city still willing to talk to me on record.

Others, who had regularly picked up the phone before the national security law, went mute. The lines had shifted, the boundaries were unclear and fear permeated society.

Those on the pro-government side felt more emboldened. One young ambitious member of the pro-Beijing DAB party smiled during an interview when I asked her about the prosecutions of Jimmy Lai and Joshua Wong.

'They're famous not because they're activists, but because if you ask anyone, "Who are the biggest traitors in Hong Kong?" they would give you those names,' said Nixie Lam—a former local district councillor swept from office by voters angry at pro-government figures. It wouldn't matter, though; the people in Hong Kong didn't hold the power.

From everything I'd seen, I doubted Lam's assessment that most people felt the top protest leaders were 'traitors'. But public opinion didn't count anymore. The promise of a high degree of autonomy for 50 years after the British handover only lasted 23.

17

CORONAVIRUS

Leaving Wuhan minutes before it went into a two-and-a-half-month lockdown to stem the spread of a relatively dangerous and poorly understood virus is the greatest journalistic regret I've ever had.

It was around 2 am on 23 January 2020 when the announcement from Wuhan's government came out. In what I still can't work out was good luck or bad, I was awake working at the desk in my hotel room at the Wuhan Westin when the announcement lit up my screen: the city was being literally locked down. It seemed extreme, unprecedented, unimaginable. But by the end of 2020, countries that didn't take such drastic measures seemed crazier.

Living the global pandemic in China is one of the luckiest experiences I've ever had. There was no greater contrast in organisational ability between China and the United States than the handling of the outbreak. Long term, despite the virus spreading from Wuhan to the world with government missteps and cover-ups contributing, the containment will likely be the greatest argument the Communist Party has in convincing Chinese people that life under the Party is superior to democracy. And like the tumult in Hong Kong, I had no idea in those early weeks of the outbreak that it too would contribute to the growing tensions with Australia that ultimately set the scene for my departure from China.

On the night when the lockdown was announced, Brant Cumming and I had only arrived a few hours earlier. Like much of the international media, we'd monitored developments from Beijing since state media reported on 1 January that a wholesale seafood and animal market had been shut down and disinfected. The state news agency reported that eight people had been reprimanded for 'spreading rumours', such a common offence in China that you heard it regularly reported.

This time, though, the punishment dished out to one of these rumour spreaders would come back to bite the police.

At the time, the most vital part of the Xinhua news agency dispatch was that 27 people were suffering from an unknown pneumonia. There had been online rumours about it in December, but I was in Australia for Christmas leave and was unaware of the story until the 1 January report. As the days went by, the reports of a mystery flu looked increasingly worrying but Chinese officials and Health Commission doctors kept making reassuring sounds in the state media. 'Preventable and controllable' was repeated, and with Wuhan officials frantically trying to suppress bad news during the next few weeks, the number of new cases, officially, stalled.

By the time I flew back into China, I was monitoring news on the virus but was preoccupied with a planned trip to Taipei to cover the Taiwanese presidential election.

The election was an anticlimactic thumping win for the incumbent, and that night I was glued to the increasingly worrying news coming out of Wuhan. There had been one fatality officially attributed to coronavirus, a 61-year-old man who had some other very serious ailments. But he shopped at the food market that had been closed.

Within days, cases began to pop up in Thailand and Japan, which made the repeated reassurances all the more suspicious.

At the time, disastrous bushfires were consuming the news in Australia, and so with 'only' 27 cases in such a big country, I held off heading to Wuhan. Few if anyone in Beijing believed the official figures, but it was hard to get a steer on how worrying the situation was. Only two months earlier, a husband and wife from Inner Mongolia had been diagnosed with the rare pneumonic plague, a more severe form of bubonic plague that ravaged Europe and Asia in the thirteenth century. After being diagnosed, the couple, both farmers, were flown to an infectious diseases section of Chaoyang Hospital in Beijing near the ABC.

It just so happened that on that same day, one of my colleagues was at the hospital. She had a foot injury and was visiting a different part of the large medical complex, but when the news broke the next day about the plague patients, it caused some serious consternation in the ABC bureau. Our office manager donned a mask and refused to go near the colleague, getting agitated to the point where she requested to work from home. I thought she was having a laugh but no, she was genuinely shit-scared.

In fairness, our office manager had what the Chinese called a 'small gallbladder', or 'small guts', and at the best of times was risk averse. But the commotion with the plague two months earlier made me wary of alarmism over the Wuhan breakout.

Over the following week in January, the number of confirmed cases climbed into the sixties, with eight people critical. It didn't sound good, and the talk from officials of a 'relatively small risk' of transmission fuelled deep suspicion among the population with vivid memories of the SARS cover-up in 2003.

I wondered if I should go to Wuhan. Many journalists in Beijing were unusually reluctant to chase the developing story at its source. Chinese New Year was coming up, and everyone had plans. The annual travel rush involving hundreds of millions of people crisscrossing the country made the situation all the more worrying if there was a virus on the loose.

A colleague told me about a Beijing media TV crew that went to Wuhan, came back and was now in a hospital. Authorities warned people to wear masks and, within days, most people in Beijing had heeded the warning. In a country where residents routinely wore masks when they had colds, it wasn't hard for authorities to encourage compliance.

The speculation about a SARS-like virus caused deep fear. People took it seriously, even when the Health Commission officials were telling barefaced lies in state-media interviews, trying to calm concerns.

'Our preliminary finding is that this new coronavirus is not very contagious,' said Li Gang, the head of Wuhan's Disease Control Centre at a press conference on 18 January. 'We can't rule out the risk of limited human-to-human transmission, but the ongoing risk of it spreading is relatively small,' he said, even as doctors in the city had become aware that fourteen of their colleagues in one hospital had tested positive.

As people began to cancel travel plans, I remained sceptical. Perhaps in a microcosm of the East–West divide that would later define the outbreak, I thought caution was excessive. I didn't believe the officials, but it seemed to me people were jumping to conclusions. The early indications were that the fatality rate was considerably lower than the 10 per cent seen in SARS.

Those that pressed on with their travel plans seemed confident. Traveller after traveller at Beijing railway station told me they had trust in their country's health system to handle the new virus. But what one says to a foreign reporter with a camera in China isn't a good guide to what they're really thinking. The mad rush by most to cancel travel plans spoke louder than words.

Soon the story started moving faster than I could anticipate. A modelling study from epidemiologists in the United Kingdom based on the odds of infected people in Wuhan travelling to Thailand and Japan concluded that the total number of people likely to be infected with the virus was around 1700. Japan, Singapore and the United States began to set up temperature screening at airports, while Australia demurred because the World Health Organization hadn't recommended it. Within months the WHO's advice would be viewed in a much more cynical light.

And then came the night that changed it all.

A team of visiting Chinese experts led by a widely respected octogenarian doctor, Zhong Nanshan, announced late in the evening of 20 January that human-to-human transmission was indeed happening. It was an absolute bombshell, delivered by a man hailed as a hero for defying authorities and sounding the alarm on SARS seventeen years earlier. Zhong Nanshan was admired and trusted, and here he was live on state television overturning twenty days of half-truths and flat-out lies in a nervous nation needing clarity.

He spoke of fourteen doctors who had been infected and confirmed that two cases in southern Guangdong province were human transmission. From there, the wheels were in motion. Brant Cumming would be heading into the danger zone with me at just the moment everyone else was avoiding it.

The other Chinese staff at the ABC were horrified that we'd have to travel there.

'If they can't cover it up anymore, it must be *really* bad,' one told me.

Everyone seemed to know someone who worked in hospitals in Wuhan or its wider province Hubei, and they were all hearing that the virus was spreading rapidly. Chinese experts were starting to theorise about a fourteen-day period needed to completely clear the virus.

When Brant and I hopped on a conference call with the ABC to discuss the assignment down to Wuhan, we raised the question: would we be quarantined in a Beijing hotel for fourteen days upon returning, as recommended?

This posed a thorny problem for the ABC, which liked to run assignments on the smell of an oily rag. It's taxpayer money after all, so adding fourteen nights in a hotel to what was supposed to be a three-day job received only lukewarm enthusiasm.

'Maybe one night in a cheap hotel, like a Hotel Ibis,' suggested a manager, perhaps tongue-in-cheek.

Once again the seriousness with which people treated the virus in China wasn't quite getting through. This new flu was dangerous enough to justify sending us to the epicentre to report on it, but not enough to abide by the recommended precautions to contain it.

Brant and I nonetheless packed our bags and boarded an evening flight to Wuhan, joining a few dozen people at the terminal gate, all wearing masks, all sitting quietly as they waited to fly into a city inspiring almost mythical levels of fear.

Dozens of passengers on the aircraft that had just arrived from Wuhan walked off through the airbridge, among them an older woman who appeared to be on the brink of collapse. Her adult daughter held her up while the woman struggled to walk, her illness so dramatically draining her of life that I wondered if she was a hypochondriac. She was stumbling up against the glass gate that siphoned arrivals from departures, moaning, shaking, crying, her daughter all the while looking less concerned than she should be.

In the departure lounge, everyone's eyes were glued to the woman. The knot in my stomach tightened.

A man in a flimsy plastic raincoat with a backpack liquid sprayer boarded the plane, tasked with disinfecting an entire passenger aircraft. He returned disconcertingly quickly, and then it was our turn to board.

―――

When Brant and I arrived at Wuhan's Tianhe International Airport, our driver stood out among the other chauffeurs waiting with handheld signs in the arrival hall. He was the only one not wearing a mask.

'*Ni hao, Ni hao, Ni hao,*' he repeatedly greeted us, racing over to take our trolley and lead us towards the airport carpark. Brant flashed me a look, almost chuckling at the contrast between the panic in Beijing and our relaxed driver.

Mr Liu was in his fifties, wore the standard-issue driver's uniform of a polo shirt and Bluetooth hands-free receiver in his ear, and was otherwise unremarkable. But he was chatty and told us he didn't wear a mask because he didn't need one. I'd seen a traveller at Beijing airport run a mile when another passenger sneezed near him, but Mr Liu had a breezy air and seemed happy that the virus had brought him work. Only a week earlier he'd driven a German TV crew for a few days, so he knew all the places that the foreigners wanted to go.

Given the multiple safety briefings Brant and I had gone through to make the trip, I insisted Mr Liu wear a mask in the car. He cheerily obliged, aware from his German encounter a week earlier that 'you foreigners are very concerned'.

As we drove into the quiet megacity at night, we passed through a live animal checkpoint. Ever since the seafood whole-sale market was shut down on New Year's Day, investigators were working off the assumption that the virus may have been transferred from a live animal that was sold there.

Despite its name, the Huanan Seafood Wholesale Market didn't just restrict its trade to marine life. It was a meat market too and some stallholders peddled exotic game meat. Media reports showed a sign from one vendor that would have looked more familiar in a zoo: peacocks, reptiles and hedgehogs were among the 'delicacies' adventurous diners could buy. Chinese internet reports purported to show photos of some of those animals being kept alive in cages.

So while it was a bit late, police now guarded toll checkpoints leading into the city and checked the boot of our car for anything that might be wriggling around.

The seafood market was an important part of the story. An early cluster of vendors and customers emerged among the first hospital patients in December, and the suggestion that lax controls on the live animal trade were to blame made it politically explosive.

As we continued our late-night drive past the sleeping city of new buildings and highways lit up in colourful fluorescent lights, the driver chatted away, telling me he had a friend in hospital with the virus.

'He's recovering, he's doing well,' said Mr Liu. 'He says it's not too bad.'

This was rather lucky, I thought. What are the odds that you fly in and are immediately one person away from a patient in hospital? With no time to find anyone before the morning, I asked if I could record an interview with our driver, breaking an unspoken rule of lazy journalism—'never interview the cab driver'.

But it was 11 pm and I needed something for the morning.

'How did your friend contract the virus?' I asked Mr Liu.

'He thinks it happened one night when he was playing mahjong. There were a lot of people there and the air in the room wasn't good.'

'So he doesn't think it was linked to that seafood market?'

'No, no, it was the mahjong room, he reckons.'

I then asked Mr Liu what his friend did for a crust.

'He works at the seafood market, he runs a stall there,' he said.

You couldn't make this stuff up.

His friend must have recovered well, because two days later I messaged Mr Liu to ask if his friend could accept an interview over the phone. The answer was yes, but only if I sent 500 yuan (about 100 dollars) to him first via WeChat. The virus clearly didn't sap his entrepreneurial spirit.

The drive into Wuhan extended for another half hour because Mr Liu mistakenly assumed we had booked the same hotel as the German crew a week earlier. I think he believed we were German.

'This is where your colleagues stayed,' he told us as he pulled into a Marriott Hotel right near one of the major hospitals treating coronavirus patients. 'It's so convenient,' he told us, but it wasn't where I'd booked, and instead we drove to the other side of the Yangtze River to the Wuhan Westin, where a few other journalists including CNN were staying.

The British study estimating a widespread breakout and the Chinese admission of human-to-human transmission had prompted a media scramble to Wuhan, but there was still plenty of caution. The BBC wasn't letting any of its people go down there, and the big British newsagency Reuters wouldn't allow its reporter to spend a night on the ground. He was planning to fly in and fly out in one day to lessen the risk of infection. Others, though, were like us—gloves, masks, hand sanitiser and social distance the only shields we had.

By the time we arrived at the right hotel, it was beyond midnight. Brant and I hauled our bags up to the rooms and plotted an early start the next morning. We desperately needed to grab a few hours' sleep, but I felt I should file a radio story for the *AM* program. I only had our talkative driver and a couple of travellers at the airport to draw on, hardly an adequate scene-setter for the mood in Wuhan, but enough to sew together a couple of minutes.

Things were moving fast. The death toll had gone from two to seventeen while we were in transit. So as Brant went to sleep in the room next door, I tapped away at the laptop, writing and editing audio in a mad rush to get it done and get some shut-eye.

I'd pretty much finished by 2 am and was sending it off to Sydney when notifications started appearing on my phone that Wuhan's government would be shutting down transport. Flights, trains and buses leaving Wuhan would be cancelled from 10 am, while public transport within the city would also be suspended. In Chinese, it was called 'closing the city'. In English, it was a 'lockdown'.

Either way, it posed an immediate dilemma for Brant and me. We were just a few days short of the Chinese New Year, when train and flight tickets were scarce. The annual 'biggest migration on the planet' was notorious for pushing up ticket prices, and my first thought was we wouldn't be able to get out.

But did we want to get out? This story was huge. Lockdowns were unprecedented. It was an epic step to take, and that unsettled me. So many people were in my ear in Beijing telling me it's 'worse than they say', 'don't trust the figures' and 'remember SARS'. Locking down a city of 11 million people three days out from the Chinese New Year made me think the situation must be extraordinarily bad. I thought of our flimsy protective gear, a few pairs of gloves each and a box of masks. I thought of the Reuters policy about one night on the ground being too risky. How many nights would we stay? Was the virus everywhere in Wuhan by now?

My head was racing.

I checked booking sites and found tickets on one flight to Shanghai, half an hour before the 10 am closure. Everything else was booked out.

I messaged my mate from CNN to alert him, assuming he'd be asleep.

'We're pulling out,' he texted back. 'Head office woke us up and told us to go.' Another crew from Sky News had been ordered to leave.

I rang an ABC manager in Sydney, who asked if I was sure we should be leaving such a big story so soon after we'd arrived. I insisted it made sense to pull out.

Then I woke Brant, who was just embarking on the deepest hours of an exhausted sleep. He sounded pretty grumpy that I'd woken him up, frantically squawking.

'They're locking down the city! All the planes and trains are cancelled! But there's a flight to Shanghai we can get that goes before 10 am! But we have to book it now and call back the driver!'

It took a moment for Brant to work out what the hell I was going on about. We'd only just arrived. He spoke words I'll never forget.

'Why are we leaving the biggest story in the world?'

It was a pearl of experienced wisdom that stopped me and almost changed our course. A similar sentiment had been expressed by the manager in Sydney. It made the decision to get out very difficult.

I'd rarely erred on the side of excessive caution for assignments, but this time, the worries of those around me and back in Beijing got to me. I decided we had better leave.

In fairness, Brant guessed that the lockdown would only last a few days, aimed at stemming travel for the Chinese New Year. In those early hours of the morning, we never could have guessed it would last for 76 days, or that, within weeks, other countries would be conducting evacuation flights to extricate their nationals. We never could have guessed that there were hundreds of Australians in the city, many of whom would end up spending two weeks in a former refugee-processing centre on Christmas Island for quarantine.

Had we known, I would have stayed. We would have been on that first Australian evacuation flight in early February, part of the 'last in, first out' policy that Prime Minister Scott Morrison promised. We would have had the inside story of the lockdown in Wuhan, of the Australian families desperate to flee and of the bizarre quarantine experience behind bars on an Indian Ocean outpost. By the time we would have travelled with them to tearfully reunite with loved ones in Sydney and Melbourne, we'd have had a documentary. And we would have likely been able to fly back into China before the country shut its borders to all foreigners in late March.

In the months that followed that fateful flight from Wuhan, I often pondered all of this.

But it's better not to be tortured by hindsight. In those early hours of the morning, it was all about getting out.

———

At Wuhan's airport, in the chilly fog of pre-dawn darkness, we gathered what interviews we could. No one appeared to be panicking but there was a random cruelty to the cut-off. I'd managed to get us seats on the 9.30 am flight, but at the departure terminal, I found a middle-aged couple staring wistfully at the board, watching as flight after flight turned red, placed into the 'cancelled' category.

Their flight was a 10.15 am long haul to Paris. They were going to spend Chinese New Year travelling around Europe, not the sort of trip you plan lightly. Their flight still said 'Scheduled', but they knew it couldn't stay that way.

I asked them, with Brant's camera rolling, how they felt.

'It's no problem, our country has to take measures, it's the right thing to do,' they told me, their words unable to convey the deep disappointment on their faces.

A few others we met chose to turn back, forgoing flights out of Wuhan to stay in the city with family.

Given the circumstances, it was an orderly scene. There wasn't the yelling at staff and anger you sometimes see at airports when the pressure's on. People seemed to be in a quiet state of shock and resignation.

At Wuhan's high-speed rail station, it was reportedly a bit of a different story, with armed military police deployed to block entrances at the cut-off time.

But the dominant theme was uncertainty. Three days? One week? Seventy-six days? Evacuation flights? Borders shut? A global pandemic? No one we spoke to on the ground could predict any of it.

From Wuhan we arrived in Shanghai to teams in full hazmat suits taking our temperatures. We checked into an airport hotel and decided it was best not to say we'd arrived from Wuhan, in case they didn't let us stay. As I arrived, news broke that Shanghai Disneyland was shutting, days before its busiest period of the year. Cinemas across the country were closing just as they would have unleashed a swag of blockbusters for the Chinese New Year box-office season.

The pace with which the closures were spreading genuinely shocked me. It was not just Wuhan, but everywhere. After weeks of officials hesitating, censoring information, playing down the severity and then flat-out lying when human transmission was blatantly clear, China's government was making up for lost time.

Xi Jinping would later use state media to claim he first personally gave instructions about the pandemic response in a meeting on 7 January. By then, doctors in Wuhan, Health Commission officials and everybody higher up the chain knew they had a crisis worthy of the national leader's attention, even though there was much uncertainty about the virus.

But Xi's involvement from early January was kept from the Chinese public, even as other items from that day's meeting were reported in government media. It took another thirteen days and the pressure of the international modelling study from the United Kingdom for Xi to flick the switch, and in a way only imaginable in China, the country was taking unprecedented action at rapid speed.

While people were still out strolling the streets of Shanghai over the Chinese New Year, the city of 25 million was subdued. Caution was setting in and people were beginning to stay home.

By the time Brant and I flew back to Beijing a few days later on a near-empty passenger jet, officials were urging everyone to stay in their apartments, and for the most part, the masses obliged.

Beijing during Chinese New Year rarely resembles itself. Many of the capital's population are migrants from other parts of China who flow out like a tide, coming back gradually over the following fortnight, so it was hard to gauge how much of the quietness was related to the annual holiday and how much to the outbreak.

But strange things were starting to happen. The security guards at my compound blocked the entry gates with whatever barricades they could find. As Beijing had a constant proliferation of dockless share bikes scattered over the streets, the guards grabbed a dozen or so and piled them on top of each other to obstruct the gates. The tangle of metal and rubber, unsightly but effective, forced all residents of the twelve-building compound to funnel through one entrance where some newly employed young men with handheld thermometers would take your temperature and check you had a residency pass.

During this period, the numbers of confirmed infections in Wuhan were shooting up by a few thousand a day. Other Chinese cities reporting dozens of daily cases included Beijing, although the capital was never badly affected. Plans to revive a SARS-era emergency hospital on the outskirts to isolate patients were drawn up but it wasn't ultimately used, such was the effectiveness of containment measures.

But the fear of the outsider gripped the city and many other parts of China. Residential compounds across the country restricted who could enter, mobilising a combination of volunteers from the residential community and paid security guards. Farmers blocked roads leading to villages, piling dirt or debris to ward off outsiders. Videos flew around the internet of men dressed in ancient battle attire theatrically perched upon makeshift thrones to guard villages. It was amazing how quickly it all turned.

The central government under Xi Jinping had initially played down the virus as it was rapidly spreading through Wuhan, ordering state media to devote minimal attention to what was unfolding. But once he flicked the switch, the state propaganda campaign put emotion and patriotism first. 'ZhanYi', or 'battle the pandemic', became the official slogan and it was everywhere, signifying a warlike effort to mobilise the entire nation against an enemy. State TV, state-media headlines and propaganda banners highlighted the 'battle', while military medics were filmed flying into Wuhan and racing from their transport planes like they were heading into war. Heroic murals of hazmat-clad doctors and nurses started to appear on walls along with the 'battle' slogan.

Thousands of doctors and nurses were deployed to Wuhan along with 300 state 'news workers'. The media was given the task of spreading 'positive energy' about the containment efforts, contrasting with the groundbreaking early reports that only the more freewheeling elements of China's media were producing.

Magazines and websites such as the state-run 'Renwu' and the privately run 'Caixin' had journalists in full hazmat gear entering Wuhan's hospitals and bringing stories of patients, desperate relatives and overworked doctors to both the nation and the world. Their journalism helped piece together a picture of a city well and truly ravaged by a virus that doctors were scrambling to contain. Their reporting also made it clear the early official numbers were not to be believed. They carried comments from outspoken doctors such as Ai Fen, the head of the Emergency Department at the Central Hospital of Wuhan, who criticised authorities for suppressing information about the virus. She faced disciplinary action.

But the window of relative openness only lasted so long.

When another Wuhan doctor reprimanded by police for 'spreading rumours' about the virus later died from it, Chinese journalists were at the front line of a propaganda battle over control of the narrative.

Li Wenliang, only 34, a father with a second child on the way, had originally posted news about a 'SARS-like virus' to a medical alumni WeChat group, warning others to wear masks and avoid the Huanan seafood market. He also warned members of the group not to share the news further, fearing repercussions. But his message spread like wildfire, ultimately culminating in police forcing him to sign a document admitting his wrongdoing.

In a stain on the Chinese government's efforts to portray itself as strong and effective in its response to the outbreak, Xinhua reported on New Year's Day that eight people had been detained for spreading rumours. Li Wenliang was one of them. The report also confirmed the closure of the seafood market.

Other state-media reports at the time urged people not to panic, saying China had a 'mature prevention and treatment system'. Given what transpired over the following weeks, people were horrified that this doctor punished by police for alerting others to a dangerous new virus had himself contracted it. His hospitalisation was well publicised, partly because Dr Li posted pictures of his reprimand letter online as he lay in hospital.

He posted that he wanted to return to work once he recovered. When news broke of his death less than a week later, the anger across China was at boiling point.

Yinan and her friends were devastated by Dr Li's fate. Conflicting reports came out about his death, and then about the last-ditch efforts to save him, further infuriating many who believed that even the information about his passing was being manipulated for public opinion purposes.

Yinan and her friends were part of a liberal big-city elite, many working in foreign media or creative fields. They were mired in sadness for someone they'd never met. The shock at Li Wenliang's death was widespread. Neighbours were writing his name in the snow on my street. People I interviewed in the following days wanted to talk about him on camera, though they were cautious about who was to blame for his treatment.

In my five years on the ground, no single moment had galvanised public anger and grief like the death of Dr Li. It seemed like the sort of moment that could spark social change or reform in any other country. Writers abroad with seemingly little understanding of the Communist Party's controls questioned whether the early weeks of the outbreak were China's 'Chernobyl moment', comparing its politically destructive force to the nuclear meltdown that exposed the fragility of the Soviet Union's final years.

But part of what generated more sadness than anger, at least among the well-educated, international-minded types I worked with and hung out with in Beijing, was a sense of resignation that Li's death wouldn't change anything. They'd seen time and time again the Communist Party's masterful ability to nullify threats and use them to its advantage.

Li Wenliang would be yet another. Initially, censorship and content moderation were used to reduce the online spread of anger and discontent about his death. The news stories about him remained, but slowly faded from the trending hashtags. Unlike, say the death of George Floyd at the hands of police a few months later in the United States—which triggered nationwide anti-racism protests—China's state-controlled media weren't able to go and interview Dr Li's pregnant widow at first. It was not as though family members could freely speak to the Chinese media. Other doctors and colleagues expressed grief through touching gestures, and images of Wuhan residents laying flowers outside his hospital flew around smaller media platforms, but these stories were ignored by the mainstream state outlets.

China did not allow independent unions or associations where fellow doctors could publicly come out and talk about the workplace danger that Dr Li and others had to face, so the momentum that usually propels stories in the media, inspires opposition parties to ask questions of government, gives voice to critical civil society groups and ultimately puts pressure on those in power to respond to an issue, was nowhere to be seen in China.

But occasionally, online discussion could grow so heated and widespread that censoring it would exacerbate the anger. I'd witnessed this in 2011 when photos of the fatal high-speed train crash in the eastern city of Wenzhou spread rapidly and generated anger about a local official's order to cover it up.

Li Wenliang's case was more vivid, and a stark display of what was rotten in China's political system. People across China were seeing this mild-mannered young doctor as a whistleblower, a hero and now a martyr.

So those at the highest levels of China's government decided to portray Li Wenliang as one of their own. A Communist Party member first and foremost. A diligent and committed doctor who bravely kept working as the virus threat increased. A man who was unjustly reprimanded by local police (and not the broader system those police worked in).

In an extraordinarily rare move, Li's death was reported on the flagship evening television news bulletin, a program observing such a rigid political hierarchy that obituary reports were normally reserved for Party luminaries. Then, an official inquiry was launched by a national body that usually probed corruption. Officials reported back that police were acting 'in line with the spirit' of Wuhan's prevention and control arrangements and that Dr Li's WeChat messages warning of 'SARS' were not factually correct. But it ultimately vindicated him, finding that by forwarding the messages he helped spur action to combat the virus.

The two police officers who had reprimanded Dr Li and forced him to sign that document were punished. The report promised action against officials who were slow to respond to the pandemic or loose in their prevention and control measures.

But then authorities revealed their true colours. As with many things that affect the Communist Party's grip on China, the blame was placed on 'hostile forces', implying that these nameless enemies, rather than the popular opinion of the masses, were driving public concern.

The government news agency Xinhua ended its statement on the report's findings:

The [government] official added that 'some hostile forces, aiming to attack the CPC and the Chinese government, have given Li labels including an anti-establishment "champion"— which is completely untrue'.

Li, a Party member, was not an 'anti-establishment figure', the official said.

'Those hostile forces with ulterior motives, who tried to stir up trouble, delude people and instigate public emotions, are doomed to fail,' the official added.

Among other doctors, Li Wenliang was later awarded a posthumous May 4th Medal for the sacrifices he made fighting the pandemic. His widow initially kept quiet except for setting up a new Weibo account to post a picture of a rather formally worded statement refuting online claims that she was trying to solicit donations. Curiously, she released one more statement online three months later, in response to some US politicians proposing to rename the street in Washington that hosts the Chinese embassy after her husband.

Upon hearing this news, I felt very sad. Wenliang was a Communist Party member, and he deeply loved his motherland.

If he knew, he would not allow other people to use his name to hurt his motherland.

As far as our whole family is concerned, Wenliang is a precious memory and our greatest heartbreak, we really don't want anyone to use Wenliang to stir things up.

We really hope this pain isn't induced again for no reason.

Whether Li Wenliang's wife really wrote those words or if it was her decision to post them, we'll likely never know. Given that she didn't use her account to post anything other than those two typed-up statements, it's difficult to believe that the heavy hand of the state wasn't involved in shaping this message that so perfectly aligned with the Party's information agenda:

Li Wenliang the Party member, the patriot and his wife being dragged through hell by those hostile foreign forces seeking to 'stir up' trouble. It placed them, not the Chinese government's system of top-down censorship and control, in focus.

Within the Party, there may be lessons learnt the next time something goes horribly wrong. Perhaps local officials will remember those police who rushed to censure the heroic doctor as he tried to warn others about the virus that ultimately killed him.

But it's doubtful the political culture of control will weaken. The Party has found it doesn't need to relax any rules when it can divert anger so effectively.

One day before Dr Li's death, when he'd already received considerable attention in China for publicising the police reprimand letter from his sick bed, a headline popped up from China's south-west province Yunnan.

'Five hospital staff who secretly photographed and disseminated information about pandemic control and prevention have been detained or fined,' it read.

Within a day, the story was deleted. Authorities have learnt one lesson—don't publicise the repression.

18

PANDEMIC

In the early months of the global pandemic, the world viewed China's response through a particularly harsh lens. The similarities to the SARS cover-up seventeen years earlier influenced much of the reporting, including my own. It would be poor journalism not to include the SARS context when viewing the Chinese response to the new virus, but the cover-up narrative distracted attention from how incredibly effective China's containment measures were.

Take the example of masks, which became a political lightning rod in much of the West before widespread consensus formed that they are generally quite effective. Just over a month after Wuhan was locked down, *The New York Times* published an article questioning the effectiveness of masks, concluding, 'They may help, but it's more important to wash your hands.' The confusing article pointed out that no study to date had proven masks were completely effective in preventing droplet transmission and highlighted the comments of virologists who lamented the lack of a complete seal around the face. In a particularly regrettable comment, one expert said the risk of being infected in the United States was 'way too low' for people to start wearing masks; officially there was only one confirmed case in the United States at the time.

No study had ever proven that masks weren't effective, but perhaps because China's government was pushing for mask use, the journalistic instinct was to question the grounds that advice was based on.

Other articles questioned the massive quarantine field hospitals that health officials hastily set up in Wuhan, or the heavy-handed enforcement of stay-at-home orders, which in some cases involved sealing apartment doors to keep people inside. The arrests and disappearances of several independent bloggers and journalists in Wuhan didn't help overseas perceptions of what Chinese authorities were doing, but the actual control and prevention measures were routinely referred to as 'draconian'.

Having made a mad dash to the airport to escape Wuhan before the lockdown, the measures certainly felt draconian to me. Subsequent interviews I did with residents of Wuhan and Australians who were trapped there made it sound pretty grim. As the days and weeks went by, they were largely confined to their apartments with deliveries of food and essential supplies organised by neighbourhood residential communities. They were bored and frustrated yet still anxious about the invisible virus outside. By the second month of lockdown, with the case numbers dwindling, some residents were extremely pissed off and were willing to say so down the phone to a foreign journalist.

Little could I imagine that residents of Melbourne would later be subject to similar conditions.

Some of the media focus shifted to privacy as China's tech giants created location-tracking programs through WeChat that could show whether a person had been near an outbreak zone. These programs were rapidly rolled out across China; it became impossible to travel between cities or even enter shops without first scanning a QR code and showing a security guard your status. The app trackers soon became a normal part of life.

At the time, it all felt like such a 'China' story—live animals at markets, cover-ups, draconian measures, Big Brother-style tracing of individuals and mass propaganda. There was genuine suffering among the families of victims in Wuhan, but it felt to me like this wasn't cutting through. Fear and judgement characterised the response to the outbreak abroad, compassion less so.

The Chinese government's constant attempts domestically to portray itself as strong, exceptional and *lihai*, meaning 'impressive', made it hard to mentally adjust and suddenly see the country's citizens needing empathy and help. Initially Chinese communities overseas, including people in Australia, organised the mass buying of masks to send to Wuhan. It was a practical gesture that no one had a problem with at the time, but it later became politically loaded when some blamed them for hoarding protective equipment and sending it to China as the outbreak reached foreign shores. A rise in racist incidents towards Asians in Australia was also a nasty development.

In the initial weeks, I joined a WeChat group of Australian citizens and residents in Wuhan who were pondering an Australian government evacuation plan. There were about 200 members of the group, some of them young students who had flown to Wuhan to visit family ahead of the Chinese New Year, while others were older Australian permanent-residency holders who lived in China and didn't speak much English.

Many wanted to leave and get back to Australia, but there was great consternation over the Morrison government's plan to quarantine them on Christmas Island. Further fuelling anxiety was the accommodation, a disused asylum-seeker processing centre that would house families with small children behind wire fences. Many questioned whether the choice of location was due to their ethnicity. It was rather hard to imagine a planeload of white Australians receiving the same treatment; subsequent evacuees were quarantined at a disused mining camp near Darwin instead.

The publicity around the evacuation was hampered by misunderstandings too, with one particularly upset mother complaining to a journalist about finding a cockroach in her room on Christmas Island. 'It's thousands of times worse than I imagined,' she was quoted as saying, with a picture of said roach. Australian diplomats, airline crews, customs officers, defence personnel and medical staff had moved heaven and earth to organise the evacuation flight safely and negotiate with China's government to make it happen, so the complaints looked a tad ungrateful.

Others tried to make the best of it. A mother of two young boys from Melbourne, Gloria Zeng, sent me a photo from their modest accommodation, the boys with a snack at the end of an arduous evacuation effort that took them from their family's apartment in Wuhan at three in the morning to a nine-hour flight to Western Australia, and then a transfer flight back in the other direction to Christmas Island, landing late at night.

'I try to make this experience as much an adventure as possible for them,' she told me.

With cameraman Steve Wang in Shenzhen, just across the water from Hong Kong, August 2019. We had often hopped across the border between the two cities but this time, as Chinese paramilitary troops gathered in a nearby stadium, I was stopped at the border. After lengthy questioning I was ultimately allowed to cross.

Back in Beijing, on 1 October 2019 I attended a massive military and civilian parade for the 70th anniversary of The People's Republic of China at Tiananmen Square. In front of me, members of a youth choir took a rest between singing patriotic songs.

People prepare to bow to a statue of Mao Zedong, founder of the People's Republic of China, at his hometown in Shaoshan, Hunan province, October 2019. We were visiting to prepare a story on the anniversary of Mao's Communist Party taking power.

Thousands protest on Hennessy Road, Hong Kong island, 15 September 2019. While the numbers of people attending street marches couldn't match the initial month of the protests, a broad cross-section of Hong Kong society continued to demonstrate.

We returned to Hong Kong again in November 2019. The protests had become more and more violent. Cameraman Steve Wang and I wore protective gear to avoid tear gas during the biggest stand-off—the siege of Polytechnic University.

Using a slingshot, student protestors propel rocks at police during the siege, 17 November 2019.

University students set fire to a bridge to prevent police entering the Poly U campus, November 2019. (Alamy)

Student protestors held out for several days at Poly U but ultimately gave themselves up to police. It was the last major protest of the movement before coronavirus hit and later a national security law put an end to the mass gatherings. (Alamy)

One of the lucky travellers at the airport able to leave Wuhan before a lockdown was imposed on 23 January 2020. It was the first lockdown anywhere in the world for the pandemic and lasted 76 days.

The empty streets of Wuhan during lockdown. The measures were depicted as extreme and draconian in many Western news reports, only for countries such as Australia to adopt similar measures later when the outbreak expanded. (Getty)

With cameraman Brant Cumming covering the early weeks of the global pandemic in Seoul, South Korea, February 2020. South Korea was less rigid in its response than China and showed there were different ways to approach virus containment.

Meeting locals at the Qingdao beer festival in August 2020 on what turned out to be my final assignment in China. The festival only went ahead because of effective coronavirus containment and it was a rare moment to drink, eat seafood and forget about all the tensions of recent years.

Hosting an Australian business event with CGTN presenter Cheng Lei in 2019. Cheng Lei was well known and respected in the Australian community in Beijing and everyone was shocked by her secretive arrest in mid-2020. Her arrest and subsequent investigation for leaking state secrets triggered a series of events that led to me leaving China.

With my ABC Beijing colleagues prior to my abrupt departure. *From left:* Steve Wang, Cecily Huang, Lina Qiao and Charles Li.

With *Australian Financial Review* correspondent Michael Smith at Shanghai Pudong International Airport before Yinan and I boarded a flight to leave China for the final time, in September 2020.

Back in Sydney with Yinan in December 2020.

As the virus spread beyond China's borders, Brant Cumming and I flew to South Korea in late February 2020 to chase the outbreak to the southern city of Daegu, where members of a quasi-Christian sect were being blamed for spreading the illness.

Having covered the outbreak so intensely in China, I was taken aback by how lax South Korean authorities seemed. We drove three hours to Daegu from Seoul with our fixer Soo, and as we neared the outbreak zone, emergency messages buzzed on our phones telling us someone with Covid had been in the area. More than a thousand cases had been diagnosed and I assumed an announcement to lock down Daegu was imminent, but it never came. Restaurants and businesses were quiet but open, and we spent an evening in a bustling Korean barbecue restaurant where few people bothered with masks. The warlike intensity of China's efforts was nowhere to be seen.

Returning to Seoul, I reported that South Korea's more casual approach to the virus compared to China would surely result in a surge of cases, but I was proven wrong. The case numbers there crept up but never exploded. There was clearly more than one way to manage the outbreak.

China was only gaining confidence in its authoritarian measures. Back in Beijing, I received several frantic phone calls from my building residency committee and someone from my office compound asking if I'd come back from abroad. A colleague texted me to ask if I'd just arrived home, and then a policeman knocked on my door. Clearly a 'ping' had gone off in the system and, with great efficiency, multiple layers of people were hastily ordered to chase me up.

The officer informed me of a new rule that all residents returning to Beijing must quarantine for fourteen days in their homes. The head of the building's management company was deployed to make me sign a commitment to remain at home before she affixed a notice to the front door informing neighbours that I had returned from South Korea and would be staying in the apartment to monitor my health until a certain date. The notice thanked them for their support and encouragement and gave them a number to ring . . . in case . . . well, the notice didn't need to spell it out.

The middle-aged building manager was friendly and said she thought the notice on the door was a bit excessive, but these were the rules. It seemed like overkill, particularly given that South Korea didn't have that many cases, but the failure of people in other countries to adhere to home quarantine would vindicate China's hardline approach.

When Beijing introduced centralised quarantine in guarded hotels for people flying into China, it again caused panic abroad. The wife of a fellow Australian journalist scuttled her planned return to Beijing for fear of the quarantine conditions. Many foreigners delayed plans to come back to China to resume work. In its all-out 'war' against the virus, China was going harder than any other country and, even as the number of new infections began to plunge, heavy-handedness defined how I and many other foreign journalists viewed China's response. The country had gone into absolute overkill after bungling its early handling of the outbreak.

But then, the narrative shifted.

—

When the virus spread to South Korea, it didn't seem dissimilar to SARS, which started in southern China but claimed lives in multiple Asian countries. When it started to ravage Iran, it looked worrying, particularly when the country's Health Minister profusely sweated through his press conference about it. But when the virus started to brutalise Italian hospitals in March, it was clear a worldwide pandemic was afoot. The scenes of hospital chaos, deaths and family heartbreak no longer made this a China story.

As the world descended into its worst pandemic since the Spanish Flu a hundred years earlier, China's response was out in front. I was out of home quarantine and enjoying a city bouncing back from a winter of fear and uncertainty. Beijing's tough measures had worked. The capital had quashed the spread of the virus and was slowly allowing millions of migrant workers to return. Bars and restaurants had social-distancing measures but were open again. Beijing's breweries were buzzing, as the city took tentative but increasingly confident steps back towards normality. The curve of new infections had flattened; while Wuhan remained under lockdown, the rest of China was largely virus free.

Meanwhile, in Europe and then the United States, cases were rising with a ferocity not seen even at the peak of Wuhan's outbreak. China's state media had meticulously tallied new infections and suspected cases, and now daily headlines were coming thick and fast highlighting the accelerating number of cases abroad. The state coverage in China, like elsewhere, was utterly obsessed with numbers, and as cases rose in the West, China's outbreak started to look relatively mild. The National Health Commission even began to include asymptomatic people who tested positive in its daily tally of figures—it had previously not counted them—possibly as confidence grew that China's numbers would end up comparatively low. (Although in a quirk of Chinese exceptionalism, the government never counted asymptomatic cases as 'confirmed'.)

As the virus took off in Australia during a first wave, I was suddenly presented with a new set of network-wide regulations about doing interviews outdoors and meticulous plans for filming simple assignments. With Beijing buzzing along at zero daily cases, I was getting frustrated with a new requirement for detailed risk assessments to film at a meat and vegetable market where I routinely shopped. We'd all been working from home for two months by that point and were eager to return to the office, but Australians were only just adjusting to the new reality of Covid.

One of my ABC colleagues in the Washington bureau was diagnosed with coronavirus, which she caught while covering a Donald Trump rally. In Europe, the London correspondents and crews were being told not to leave the British capital. To top it off, colleagues of mine in Delhi, Port Moresby, Jakarta, Bangkok and Beirut were all being brought home on DFAT's advice.

I too would have been sent home had China not moved first.

Instead, for a few weeks, I felt like I was living in the post-Covid future, where location-tracking apps, masks and strict quarantine measures allowed life to go back to relative normality. The night-life was thriving again in early spring, domestic travel was resuming but at all times there was caution. At one point, all restaurant staff across Beijing were ordered to undertake testing. At other times, entire districts with hundreds of thousands of people were locked down to nip small outbreaks in the bud.

In a sign of confidence, the government convened its annual political congress in May, delayed from its regular kick-off in early March. Such is the political predictability of the annual congress, I thought Xi Jinping was trying to avoid the embarrassment of having to delay it for the first time in decades. But for all of its ideological rigidity, China's system has the ability to adapt, and a very unconventional congress went ahead with every delegate aside from the top leaders wearing masks.

The media and other guests were excluded from the Great Hall, but the usual heavily staged press conferences proceeded via video link, giving China's political leaders yet another layer of distance from those who could potentially hold them to account.

Xi Jinping used the congress to drop the draconian national security law on Hong Kong, putting limits on freedom of speech, criminalising certain forms of dissent and destroying the barrier of separation between Hong Kong's legal system and the mainland.

Dramatic early-summer storms lashed the capital on both the opening and closing days of the congress, a symbol of the authoritarian clouds descending on China's liberal outpost far to the south. But, save for a localised coronavirus flare-up at a wholesale market, there was little gloom in Beijing, with a general view forming domestically that China's coronavirus containment was superior to the rest of the world's.

———

It was around this time that a fairly nasty xenophobic streak infected public perceptions in China about the virus.

Having lived in China twice, I'd always been struck by how monocultural it is. For a government that routinely boasts a list of 55 ethnic minority groups, it doesn't feel multicultural in the slightest. Some 92 per cent of the population is ethnically Han and many of the 55 minority groups are concentrated in distinct regions of the country such as Yunnan or Xinjiang.

The lack of diversity is so striking that China's government encourages ethnic minority delegates to dress up in colourful traditional costumes for the annual political congress. It's a symbolic nod to a level of diversity that simply doesn't exist at the highest levels of China's political structure. All 25 members of the nation's top governing body, the Politburo, are Han. All 25 members of the previous politburo were Han. And the 25 before that, and so on. The top political leaders of the most diverse 'autonomous' regions such as Xinjiang and Tibet are also Han, despite minority politicians occupying lower-level roles that have more of a public face.

But the lack of diversity goes deeper. Given that China has a race-based immigration policy that only allows ethnic Chinese to obtain citizenship and a paltry number of foreigners to gain permanent residency, it's no surprise that foreigners are scarcely seen outside of certain parts of major cities. This results in an 'us and them' mentality, and China's increasingly nationalistic rhetoric is anathema to Western notions of multiculturalism and diversity.

Foreign citizens of Chinese ethnicity are referred to in ambiguous terms such as 'overseas Chinese' or 'sons and daughters of the Yellow River' that play up ethnic unity and play down the idea that these people are foreigners who have their own country, which isn't China. When three ethnically Chinese *Wall Street Journal* reporters were expelled for political reasons that year, I was appalled to see a prominent Beijing commentator, Victor

Gao, sharing an article on his WeChat describing them as *Erguizi*, meaning 'enemy collaborators'. The trio were two Americans and an Australian, but in the eyes of Chinese nationalists, their loyalty should have been to the motherland.

It's this divisive worldview that undermines Western attempts to better integrate Chinese migrant communities and stokes a racially and culturally based narrative that no matter what their passport, ethnic Chinese should have an emotional and political loyalty to China.

As a foreigner living there, you're constantly reminded that you don't belong, through the stock-standard small-talk greetings of 'Your Chinese isn't bad' and 'How long have you been here?' I always appreciated an icebreaker, but they came with such consistency that my racial otherness came to define me.

When the Covid infection numbers surged abroad and China shut its borders, attitudes to foreigners hardened. The Chinese government's efforts to showcase how poorly the United States and Europe were handling the virus fuelled irrational fears that foreigners in China were infectious. Many people would have been unaware that China had already shut its borders and was quarantining arrivals in well-guarded hotels, so it was understandable that when people unexpectedly saw a foreigner, the first thing they thought of was the appalling stories of infections and deaths abroad.

One night while Yinan and I were dining with the Australian newspaper correspondent Will Glasgow, a group of men walked past our table and, perhaps assuming we didn't speak Chinese, exclaimed, 'Shit, there are foreigners here! It should be okay, it looks like they live here.' Yinan was appalled, but it showed how little contact most people in China had with non-Chinese.

A hairdresser across the road put a sign on the door saying foreigners weren't welcome. Similar signs popped up across Beijing, many on shops that the city's small foreigner community wouldn't frequent anyway.

But being white in China still carried considerable social privilege that wasn't afforded to others. Down in southern Guangzhou, the city's African community was caught in the crosshairs of an irrational panic. Despite African countries having nowhere near the pandemic numbers of the West, landlords started abruptly kicking out African tenants. A McDonald's in Guangzhou had a staff member hold a sign at the entrance saying, 'We've been informed that from now on black people are not allowed to enter the restaurant.'

Needless to say, it didn't go down well abroad.

Thousands of Africans in the city were targeted for coronavirus testing and some were forcibly isolated in a drive that looked very much like it was coming from the city government but had the usual plausible deniability. The episode caused a major stir in international media and prompted multiple African nations to call in their Chinese ambassadors, but in the Chinese government-censored media bubble, it barely raised a ripple.

Such blatant discrimination remained largely unknown to China's vast populace, with the only sign of it a state TV report showing nurses delivering flowers to Africans quarantining in Guangzhou. It didn't spell out why they were in quarantine, and, naturally, only their comments about how well they'd been treated made the cut.

—

Against this backdrop, a view formed about how well China had done in response to the pandemic. People were aghast at Donald Trump's dismissive statements about the virus; his initial disdain for wearing masks; his public disagreements with the chief medical adviser, Anthony Fauci; and the United States' general recklessness. Trump's constant attempts to blame China were viewed for what they were, a cynical attempt to shirk responsibility for appallingly bad political leadership.

When the Black Lives Matter protests broke out, many in China were shocked to see such large gatherings. This was a virus that, according to China's government, required an all-out war-like mobilisation, yet all of these Americans were running around protesting? For a human rights cause?! China's state media highlighted both the racism and the chaos, especially protests that involved clashes.

Never did the government media devote any such attention to the racism against Africans in Guangzhou or ethnic minorities in China's far west. Hundreds of thousands of ethnic Uighurs and Kazakhs were literally being locked up in 'vocational-skills training' detention camps due to Xi Jinping's belief that their race and religion potentially made them terrorists, but none of this made China's news in any critical way.

You could see the difference in the reporting on high-profile coronavirus cases at home and abroad. Europe's hapless efforts gained headlines, particularly UK Prime Minister Boris Johnson's brush with death in an intensive-care ward. If any national political leader in China ever came down with the virus, we'd likely never know. Censorship conditions people not to ask and to assume things didn't happen.

When the virus started to infect hundreds of thousands of people in India—China's only comparable population rival—it further strengthened the idea of Chinese exceptionalism. While countries such as Australia and New Zealand had very low numbers without the need for such strict measures, China's obsession with its superpower rival meant that the United States represented the Western world in the eyes of the masses.

As I sat down to a haircut in my compound, the hairdresser made the assumption.

'Gee, you Americans and the racism towards black people, all in the middle of a pandemic, what's going on?' she asked.

I told her I was Australian but she wasn't interested. The United States remained China's obsession, a rival to catch up to and surpass, an existential enemy always out to contain China, the country fuelling the hostile foreign forces, with a culture so worryingly appealing to young people that it needed constant resistance. For China, the world had become a two-horse race and its permanent 'struggle' with the United States the only foreign relationship that really counted.

On coronavirus, it wasn't just winning, it was lapping its great rival, which was bitterly divided along racial and political lines, had a president hospitalised with Covid, daily case numbers more than double China's total official tally and an economy bouncing back much slower than China's.

To top it off, the great asset Americans claim—democracy—was cast in a desperate light after the November 2020 election, with the defeated president launching divisive claims of widespread fraud without evidence.

All of this took place as China's state-backed vaccine makers jabbed hundreds of thousands of people in a sprint to prove their vaccine's efficacy and land contracts abroad. No matter how much anyone tried to focus on how it started, the greatest lessons of this extraordinary stretch of history would focus on how the pandemic ended. As 2020 came to a close, China's government had turned a 'Chernobyl moment' into something more akin to a Sputnik moment.

19

AN INDEPENDENT INQUIRY

When Australia's Foreign Affairs Minister Marise Payne made what has come to be widely viewed as one of Australia's all-time great diplomatic missteps in calling for an independent inquiry into the origins of coronavirus, I rang an Australian analyst who dismissed it as a 'thought bubble'.

It was a Sunday, Payne was appearing on the *Insiders* political program and, when I heard about it at a cafe in Sanlitun, I thought I could cobble together a quick reaction story and be done with it.

How wrong I was.

In the great downward spiral of Australia–China relations, Marise Payne's suggestion that an independent team of investigators probe both the origins of and the global response to the virus is often singled out as a mistake. Farmers, grape growers, cray fishermen and others from all of the Australian export industries that China targeted with trade bans and restrictions in blatant political retaliation cite it as the poke that woke the dragon.

But after five years on the ground, the call for an inquiry seemed like a minor development in the broader unravelling of Australia–China ties. Beijing likely leapt on it to settle some scores, but the relationship had been deteriorating over a five-year period that saw a global pandemic begin in China, a last-ditch political uprising in Hong Kong, a massive re-education internment program that literally locked up ethnic minorities in China's far west, plus a trade war with the United States.

Many journalists in Beijing asked me what exactly the dispute between China and Australia was about, but it was hard to pinpoint. It wasn't obvious. Chinese friends too would ask me what Australia and China were fighting over. I had to be careful not to bore them with my answer because it was never straightforward.

Prior to my return to Beijing in 2015, Australia's relationship with China was like a stockmarket soaring from a very low base. Prime Minister Gough Whitlam's trip to China in 1973 to establish diplomatic ties remained immortalised on the walls of the ABC's Beijing bureau. Large, framed, black-and-white photos of Whitlam towering over Deng Xiaoping and standing among Chinese leaders wearing Mao suits were a constant reminder of how historically shallow the ties between the two countries actually are.

The fact that foreigners were locked out of Communist China after Mao seized power in 1949, that ordinary Chinese weren't allowed to travel and that China's opening-up was still moving at a glacial pace in the subsequent decades meant that aside from trade, the two countries didn't have much to do with each other.

There were some deep historical links from the Chinese gold-miners who flocked to the goldfields in the 1850s, and some intrepid Australian journalists such as William Henry Donald and George Morrison forged extraordinary careers in China in the first half of the twentieth century, but compared to the bonds tying Australia to Europe, the United States or even the cricket pitches of India, there really wasn't much Australia and China had in common. There was no Bali equivalent drawing thousands of Australians to China each year, nor did common Chinese understandings of Australia go much beyond appreciation of good food, fresh air and nice beaches.

I'd been invited to so many awkward cultural events over the years in both countries that sought to emphasise common ties, I'd realised there just weren't many. Annual book events where the Australian embassy would bring prominent authors to China for small gatherings had little cut-through with China's wider audience. The state media, ever on guard against foreign influence, would give little if any attention to such attempts at cultural engagement. An art installation where an Australian sculptor hung a giant golden monkey from a Beijing hotel to celebrate the Year of the Monkey left Chinese onlookers with no lingering impression of anything particularly Australian. There was no shortage of monkey sculptures in Beijing that year.

In journalists' exchanges, Chinese reporters recycled Foreign Ministry talking points rather than taking any real interest in Australia's media environment. Even the Australian football games in Shanghai, which were well organised and a fun day out, attracted miniscule crowds in a city of 25 million. The Australian Football League and the Port Adelaide Football Club knew Australian rules football wasn't going to explode in China, but they saw the matches as a good way to court Chinese sponsorship. A couple of provincial TV networks and a secondary national sports channel agreed to broadcast the game, spurring on AFL officials to talk about the potential audience. 'The most-watched game in AFL history' became the mantra pushed by Port Adelaide's chairman David Koch, with talk of 160 million viewers across China.

When the first game took place in the blazing Shanghai summer of 2017, I was greeted by the sight of about 5000 Port Adelaide fans transplanted to the narrow and bustling streets of China's biggest city. These were diehard football fans, not Chinese-language students, businesspeople or wandering English teachers. Walking around in their Port Adelaide scarves and jerseys, they looked like fish out of water and the trip was a genuine eye-opener for most of them. There was an alcohol ban in the stadium but that didn't deter some fans, who loaded up on cold tinnies of Tsingtao at the 7-Eleven across the road.

'It's un-Australian,' one fan said to me, tongue-in-cheek, before his mate corrected him, conscious not to be denting the club's efforts to pull off the Shanghai experiment.

'It's fine, mate, no worries,' he said to the camera, beer in one hand, ciggie in the other.

Shanghai's scale, modernity and energy rarely fail to dazzle, helping to transform outdated perceptions. 'I thought the city would be shabbier,' one Gold Coast Suns player told me on the rooftop of the Ritz-Carlton.

Most of the fans seemed very impressed with their brief taste of Shanghai, although one Port Adelaide supporter told me, 'No one here seems to be aware of the game.'

Shanghai had a way of making you feel like small fry.

Most of the fans were travelling Australians, but among the Chinese spectators were employees of the main Chinese sponsor, property conglomerate Shanghai CRED, owned by the billionaire Gui Guojie, who was trying to purchase a parcel of Australian pastoral land bigger than some Chinese provinces.

Attempts in previous years by another Shanghai-based Chinese conglomerate to buy the S. Kidman & Co. properties had been blocked by the Australian government over national interest concerns. So Mr Gui's sudden embrace of Aussie Rules and a team from the city where the Kidman cattle empire was head-quartered was an attempt to build some public-relations clout that previous Chinese companies lacked. As one local man sitting in the stands and fanning himself in the sweltering heat laughingly told me, 'I'm only here because Mr Gui is my boss.'

Unlike Australia, China is a country with a fairly widespread aversion to sunbathing, particularly as white, untanned skin remained the common beauty standard. Watching the CRED employees sweat it out during one the most humid afternoons of the year made me think of the old Noel Coward refrain: 'Only mad dogs and Englishmen go out in the midday sun.' Australians too.

The game between Port Adelaide and the Gold Coast Suns was a one-sided fizzer but the Australian fans fired up when some of players started aggressively shirtfronting each other right in front of the Shanghai CRED employee section. Sitting among them, I couldn't think of a worse endorsement for a sport few Chinese parents would want their children, often their precious only child, playing.

The AFL's three-year run in China came when the diplo-matic relationship was beginning to deteriorate. Port Adelaide was embracing a Chinese future just as the Australian government and the wider populace was seeking to put the brakes on it. Gui Guojie eventually had to settle for a one-third stake in the Kidman property portfolio as the Turnbull government insisted on Australian ownership. Local mining billionaire Gina Rinehart ended up buying it, with Mr Gui as the minor partner.

Other Chinese-orientated Australian businesses that sponsored the game were not to reap the rewards they hoped for. Goldminer AusGold, run by eccentric businesswoman Sally Zou, later went into voluntary administration. Wine exporter Swan Wine Group prospered for a few years before copping a 107 per cent tariff when diplomatic relations soured, effectively ending its exports to China along with all other Australian wine exporters who copped even higher 'anti-dumping' duties.

When the second year of the AFL's Shanghai experiment rolled around in mid-2018, the political landscape had shifted dramatically. Australia was in the doghouse. The novelty had gone but there was a much better story about whether the Chinese would allow an Australian minister to attend the match. At the last minute, Trade Minister Steve Ciobo was permitted to visit on what was presented as a 'non-official' trip featuring no meetings with any national-level counterparts.

The heavens opened early on game day and never stopped. The game was a grey, soggy, one-sided spectacle in front of no more than a few thousand supporters.

By the third year, the sun was out but the stands remained half empty. China permitted Australia's low-level Minister for Sport to attend but with no meetings. A change of opponent for Port Adelaide did little to improve the spectacle, with the Power flogging a hapless St Kilda.

Plans for another game in 2020 were scuttled by the coronavirus before the diplomatic relationship soured further.

———

While political and diplomatic tensions had flared at times over the preceding two decades, the deterioration in the relationship could be pinpointed to a Monday three weeks after that inaugural AFL game in 2017, when the ABC aired a *Four Corners* documentary called 'Power and Influence'.

It was by no means the first media exposé of China's attempts to meddle in Australian democracy. Newspaper reports had zeroed in on the massive donations two Chinese billionaires were making to both major political parties. But *Four Corners* vividly drew the links, highlighting Australian-citizen donor Chau Chak Wing's background as a well-connected figure in his native Guangdong province, and the closeness of the other donor Huang Xiangmo to Australian politicians.

The program turned the heat up on Australian senator Sam Dastyari, who had stood next to Huang at a Chinese-language media press conference and stated a position on the contentious South China Sea dispute that aligned with China's interests. The program leaned heavily on security analysts and rammed home the point that Australia had to be vigilant about donations from wealthy Chinese business figures.

Behind the scenes, a lot more was happening. Two months earlier, a Sydney-based Chinese academic with Australian permanent residency, Feng Chongyi, was detained while on a research trip to China. He was studying human rights issues but he later revealed that interrogators who detained him in a Guangzhou hotel room for a week also pressed him about a former Australian journalist.

John Garnaut had gone from a China correspondent for *The Sydney Morning Herald* to China's number one person of interest in Australia when he was picked by Prime Minister Malcolm Turnbull to prepare a confidential report on Beijing's attempts to influence Australia. The report was never publicly released but the fact that Turnbull commissioned it must have rung alarm bells in Beijing.

It wasn't just Feng Chongyi who copped questions. Garnaut later revealed that another Chinese-Australian he knew, Yang Hengjun, had also been questioned about him while in Sydney. Yang, a one-time employee of China's state security ministry and a man described to me by multiple acquaintances in Beijing as a 'mysterious' guy, later flew into China to celebrate the Lunar New Year with his Chinese wife only to be met by state security agents at the arrivals hall in Guangzhou, put on a plane to Beijing and locked in a detention centre. His arrest in early 2019 came just days before the last Australian ministerial visit to Beijing, when then Defence Minister Christopher Pyne expressed his disappointment that Beijing broke an existing deal with Australia to notify the embassy within three days if authorities detained any citizens.

China's intense interest in Garnaut's advice to the Turnbull government and its intimidation of two of his Chinese-Australian acquaintances gave an insight into Beijing's deep concern about its interests in Australia.

China had been on the run of a century in Australia, turning from a Communist pariah that set tanks on student protestors in 1989 to a country so deeply embedded in Australia's economic and political fabric that a citizen who led Chinese government-aligned patriotic groups, Huang Xiangmo, was the biggest political donor in Canberra. The second biggest was a billionaire who, despite having an Australian passport, was so well-connected back in China that he was able to fly foreign dignitaries he hosted at a conference in Guangdong up to Beijing for a private meeting with President Xi Jinping. Chau Chak Wing's Kingold Group was also trusted by authorities to run a private media company in his home province, Guangdong, an extremely unusual situation for a foreigner.

As scrutiny in Australia increased, some sought to explain it away. A former Australian Foreign Minister visiting Beijing told me the two men's largesse could be explained by their rivalry for prestige in Australia's Chinese community. They were seeking to outdo each other, he surmised, each aiming to be the top local figure chosen by the Chinese embassy to greet Chinese leaders when they visited Australia.

It was Huang Xiangmo, as head of the Beijing-directed Australian Council for the Promotion of Peaceful Reunification of China, or ACPPRC, who had that honour when China's second-ranked leader Li Keqiang visited Australia in 2017. But Chau's meeting in Beijing with Xi Jinping in 2019 took the cake.

Whatever the motivation, the pair gave close to 7 million dollars to Australian political parties, opening doors and creating an ease of access absolutely unthinkable in China's tightly controlled political system.

It was inevitable that the media would start casting light on a political class that had become complacent and hooked on easy money, but Sam Dastyari's press conference with Huang in 2016 put the problem in full view. If the AFL match was the high point of Australia's public-relations push into China, that press conference could be viewed as the high point for China's inroads into Australian political life.

Standing side by side, Dastyari and Huang spoke about the South China Sea, the most pressing foreign-policy issue in Asia. China was building artificial islands and putting military bases with runways and missiles on them. A tribunal in The Hague ruled that much of what China was doing violated international law and had no legal basis.

Both the Australian government and the opposition Labor Party had called on China to respect the ruling. But that's not what the ALP's Senator Dastyari came to tell the Chinese-language media at the event organised by Huang. The influential up-and-coming politician later faced the mainstream Australian media cameras and tried to swivel out of it, claiming he couldn't be sure of what exactly he said while standing next to Huang. He said he supported his political party's stance on the South China Sea. But several months later, when one media outlet got hold of audio from the Chinese press conference, Dastyari's luck ran out.

Sharing the dais with a man who ran the Australian branch of China's top influence-peddling organisation, Dastyari made a statement that would have thrilled the officials in China's Foreign Ministry. His words were chock full of Chinese government talking points, telling Australia not to intervene in its 'internal' affairs, referencing the '5000 years of history' China constantly claimed, right through to equating Australian commentary on the South China Sea to an unfriendly act.

'The Chinese integrity of its borders is a matter for China, and the role that Australia should be playing as a friend is to know that within several thousand years of history, where it is and isn't our place to be involved,' Dastyari said. 'And as a supporter of China and a friend of China, the Australian Labor Party needs to play an important role in maintaining that relationship and the best way of maintaining that relationship is knowing when it is and isn't our place to be involved.'

Dastyari was no ordinary political opposition figure. He was young, but already a well-established Labor machine man, influential in fundraising and powerbroking, with a high media profile. He was a likely long-term future minister whenever Labor returned to power. And here he was accepting large donations for Labor from the head of the ACPPRC while publicly echoing Beijing's lines in defiance of his own Party.

Whether China's government deliberately had a hand in it or not, it was an incredible coup. Flip it around and imagine a Chinese Communist Party politician doing something similar. It's beyond comprehension. It highlighted just how vulnerable open democratic political systems are to influence and exploitation.

The saga came as John Garnaut's internal report and the security agencies were advising the Turnbull government to plug the holes in the system. New overdue anti-foreign interference laws were drawn up that were nowhere near as severe as China's, but Turnbull's government saw a need to get the laws through the parliament. Dastyari's dealings with Huang Xiangmo gave them the textbook example. When Australia's security agencies tipped off journalists that Dastyari had personally spoken to Huang to warn him his phone was likely being tapped, the government smelled blood. In late 2017, they turned up the heat on Dastyari, publicly piling on the pressure to force his resignation.

China's government appeared perplexed. Given its obsession with sovereignty, Beijing was in no position to criticise another country for combating external meddling, but the language around Chinese meddling—designed primarily for an Australian domestic audience—was unusually blunt. Turnbull went so far as to use Mandarin to quote Chairman Mao, saying the 'Australian people have stood up', a reference to Mao's 1949 speech in which he proclaimed 'The Chinese people have stood up' against foreign imperialists and reactionaries.

Were the Australian people standing up to China? That was how it sounded, and in the context of introducing anti-foreign interference laws because an opposition politician was taking donations and flipping his position to align with a Chinese businessman, how else could it be interpreted? Turnbull's statement drove the Chinese government media into a frenzy, with the normally mild-mannered *China Daily* declaring Turnbull Australia's 'China basher-in-chief'.

Watching from Beijing, it was clear the government was trying to force Dastyari's resignation and get the laws passed smoothly by wedging Labor into a corner where it would look unpatriotic to oppose it. On both fronts, Turnbull was successful.

But I got the sense that the saga genuinely took the Chinese government by surprise, because within China's patriotic, ethno-nationalistic political environment, there didn't seem to be anything unusual about what these donors were doing. Chinese (or any) businesspeople routinely donated money and tried to foster a favourable environment for their interests anywhere. Huang could be expected to make patriotic speeches supportive of Beijing's interests, as an 'overseas Chinese' contributing loyally to the 'great rejuvenation' of the nation. Australia is not adjacent to the South China Sea nor is it one of the claimant nations, so Beijing might wonder why Canberra would take such an interest in it. So a donor influencing an Australian politician to change his stance on a Chinese 'domestic' issue to one that is 'correct', in Beijing's eyes, seemed completely run-of-the-mill.

For the Australian leader to twist one of Chairman Mao's sayings in response to all of this must have felt like it came out of nowhere. Certainly that's how it felt in China, where in retaliation, the government started issuing safety warnings to Chinese students and tourists visiting Australia. A university student I'd met years earlier during a reporting trip to the city of Dalian messaged me. 'Was it true that Chinese were being beaten in the streets of Australia?' she asked.

For most people I spoke to, Australia remained a nice if not particularly interesting country in their imagination and the dispute received little widespread popular attention. Issues that had been bubbling away in Australia were out of sight, out of mind in China's domestic information environment. For example, the resignation of Australia's Trade Minister Andrew Robb, to immediately take up a role with a Chinese company that took a 99-year lease on the Port of Darwin in what remains a highly controversial deal, would barely have been noticed.

The proliferation on Australian university campuses of Confucius Institutes, which are funded and ultimately overseen by Hanban, an arm of China's government, was ordinary business (even if American efforts to establish similar US cultural centres in Chinese universities were thwarted by Beijing's obsession with foreign influence). Australian universities sought and accepted funding from China's government to host these centres, which created a major disincentive to rock the boat by hosting an event or guest speaker that the Chinese consulate wouldn't be happy about. The ever-expanding Confucius Institute footprint in Australia's top universities was starting to cause some unease, but viewed from China, as a commercial transaction on foreign soil, it didn't raise an eyebrow.

You might think that the Chinese community would be interested in one of its richest, most influential members, Huang Xiangmo, being caught in the crosshairs of foreign interference claims. Especially as discrimination was such a hot issue.

But the Huang narrative didn't appear to fit whatever 'opinion-guidance' norms Australian Chinese-language media outlets were abiding by. As WeChat news platforms became the primary news source for first-generation migrants, it was amazing to notice the lines they never crossed. While many catered to Chinese students in Australia, a considerable proportion of the readership comprised Australian citizens too, who, like the rest of us, vote in elections based on views formed in the information environment they're in.

Having the Chinese Communist Party ultimately confine that space through WeChat censorship on Chinese-language news sites based in Australia was and remains a huge problem. But perhaps that is just an Australian point of view. From China, where much of the Australian diaspora was regarded as 'overseas Chinese', it was expected that they would hold political views faithful to the motherland.

Around 2017, Australia's political class and government agencies were waking up to normalised practices that the Chinese state had been carrying out for many years. Insisting on loyalty among 'overseas Chinese' as they donated money to Australian politicians; fostering a censored news environment in

Chinese-language media; creating dependent relationships for universities through Confucius Institutes while blocking similar attempts at cultural engagement within China . . . none of this was new.

But another country realising it, calling it out and putting in place measures to guard against it was.

China's run of the century in Australia was over and Beijing wasn't happy about it.

—

From 2017 on, the state of the relationship came to dominate discussions I had with Australian diplomats in Beijing. The feedback they were getting from their Chinese counterparts was that Australian media coverage was a problem.

This wasn't exactly new. Eric Campbell, a former ABC China correspondent in the early 2000s, told me he was routinely called in by Foreign Ministry officials and cautioned about his stories. The officials assumed the ABC was Australia's state media and were puzzled and angered to see so many stories that were harmful to China's image and the diplomatic relationship.

By the time I was posted there, China's government had a far greater understanding of how foreign media worked. They didn't expect Australia's government could control the media, but they told diplomats the government needed to publicly push back against the increasingly critical tone of the coverage. The problem for Beijing was that the media, not the politicians, were setting the agenda, and stories such as Dastyari's saga with Huang Xiangmo were harming China's image and encouraging more journalists to dig and question how an authoritarian one-party state that was hostile to democracy, free speech and Australia's main ally could have made such successful inroads into Australian political life.

The business community was also losing its influence on Australia's policies. As journalists, researchers and the politicians themselves became more aware of China's strategy, the business lobby's appeals for a conciliatory approach were being drowned out. One Shanghai Australian Commerce Chamber leader expressed to me his dismay that then Australian Foreign Affairs Minister Julie Bishop was on text message terms with her US counterpart, but not with China's Foreign Minister. I pointed out that it would be the Chinese minister, not Julie Bishop, preventing a text message relationship from flourishing.

Many in the business community had a reflex to blame Australia for China's actions and non-transparency, always putting the onus on Canberra to modify its behaviour while giving 'complex' China a pass.

The debate in Australia about China developed in unexpected ways. Reading Australia's former ambassador to China, Geoff Raby, calling for the sacking of the serving Foreign Affairs Minister Julie Bishop in a newspaper op-ed was one such odd development. Could you imagine a retired Chinese ambassador taking to the media to put the blame on China's policies and call for Foreign Minister Wang Yi to resign? It was both a testament to Australia's free-speech environment and an unintentional propaganda gift to the Chinese government.

Calls to get the relationship 'back on track' for the sake of trade were, for the first time, coming up against stiff resistance. With some universities swelling their overseas student ranks with

Chinese applicants and some export industries overwhelmingly selling to China, questions about over-reliance began coming up. Australia's government was also becoming more forthright in calling out large-scale cyber attacks on government departments, all but naming China as the assumed culprit.

Perhaps most importantly, China itself was undergoing a political transformation that made close ties increasingly unpalatable. Around 2017, international media and human rights groups began reporting on the disappearance of ethnic minority Uighurs and Kazakhs in far-western China. By 2018, satellite imagery and Western media reporting revealed an elaborate program of buildings set up to intern thousands of mainly young Uighur men. Xi Jinping had ordered a program to round up young ethnic minority Muslims in Xinjiang, detain them behind heavily secured fences in dormitory-style buildings and re-educate them to love the Communist Party and the motherland.

Women weren't spared either, thousands disappearing into the program, which Chinese officials originally denied was happening but later confirmed with gusto, declaring them 'vocational skills training centres' and boasting that the program exemplified human rights by steering people away from terrorism and Islamic extremism.

Sporadic violence had been carried out by Uighur groups in Xinjiang and other parts of China, including a small but brazen car attack at Tiananmen in 2013. Xi Jinping had decided the best response would be to forcibly re-engineer the thinking of large sections of the Uighur population, whether they were Islamic extremists or not.

Human rights groups estimated up to a million people from China's ethnic minorities were at some point detained in these centres, while Xinjiang itself became a police state where digital surveillance and domestic security rendered the Uighur population second-class citizens subject to a level of scrutiny the Han residents didn't have to endure. There were horrific tales of families abroad losing contact for years with relatives back in Xinjiang. China's government convicted hundreds, including academics, for terrorism- or separatism-related offences.

While all of this had nothing to do with Australia, it spoke volumes about the values of the country Australia was economically hooked on. Combined with a state media that was more than willing to chide, mock and blame Australia while completely incapable of any critical self-reflection on China's actions, it contributed to a profound shift in Australian impressions of China.

The Hong Kong uprisings in 2019 and 2020, while a futile attempt to gain the same democratic rights that Australians enjoyed, sealed a major rethink among ordinary Australians. It had become abundantly clear that China was no longer a great power 'opening up', but an authoritarian state going in the opposite direction. Yet Australian wealth was dependent on this increasingly nationalist country, more than one-third of our export income deriving from this one customer.

When China began economically retaliating against Australia's pushback in 2020, however, it was a bit too late for Beijing. The massive market and power imbalance that allowed Beijing to get its way was no longer working so effectively. Through its actions at home and abroad, China had exhausted the goodwill it had built up in earlier years, so when Beijing began launching highly dubious anti-dumping and subsidy levies to block Australian barley and wine exports, it triggered anger but not capitulation.

Throughout 2020, Beijing cooked up all sorts of reasons to restrict, slow down or stop the imports of coal, timber, lobsters and beef, among other Australian products. China's government refused to admit it was doing any of this, instead claiming labelling irregularities, pests or even mercury contamination for seafood.

Yet officials would in the same breath say it was up to Australia to repair the relationship, blaming a 'Cold War mentality' for Australia's general hostility to the Communist giant.

As Beijing targeted more and more sections of Australia's export economy, Chinese diplomats posted to Australia became increasingly desperate. Two of them called up a journalist and slipped a fourteen-point list of grievances to him, casting a wide net on Australia's wrongdoing. The list contained everything from Australia's blocking Chinese company Huawei from the 5G network over national security concerns through to complaints about the Australian government funding a think tank that published critical research on China. Some more practical issues were raised, such as Australia blocking Chinese investment (even in agricultural projects) on security grounds and Beijing's anger with Australia for commenting on human rights issues that China regarded as foreign meddling.

But the Australian government wasn't for turning. Australians had become more sophisticated about China just as Beijing was moving in an unsettling direction. China remained economically indispensable to Australia's future, but there was a limit on how much Australians would compromise to maintain their standard of living.

Australia wasn't abandoning the Asian century, but drawing some lines in the sand about how to embrace it. The relationship had been reset.

20

HIGH SUMMER

In the months before my unexpected departure from China, I'd resigned myself to a new normal for reporting conditions. Whether it was business types and analysts or people on the street, it was getting harder and harder to get anyone to speak on camera.

When coronavirus dominated the global agenda, there was little demand for any other type of story. We interviewed one of the Chinese vaccine makers, Sinovac, and did multiple stories about relatives who lost loved ones in Wuhan and wanted answers from authorities. We did the wet-market angle, interviewing activists who had spent years campaigning for the closure of the live animal trade. And having left Wuhan at the outset, we made plans to return once it opened up, only to scuttle them due to ever-shifting quarantine regulations for travelling in and out of Beijing.

With Australia–China relations souring so sharply, we spent a lot of time at the Foreign Ministry, getting repetitive answers from the rotation of spokespeople sticking to their theme—the Australian side was wrong, influenced by 'Cold War thinking' and many people 'poisoning' the relationship. China was never ever wrong. Its government had an inability to critically self-reflect that left me quite worried for the long term.

Privately, though, there was a split within foreign-policy circles on Xi Jinping's new preferred style of diplomacy, dubbed 'Wolf Warrior', in reference to a wildly popular Chinese film where a Chinese mercenary kicked some American butt on behalf of friends in Africa, a Chinese version of *Rambo*.

One journalist for the international news agency Reuters who had some access to the Foreign Ministry told me there was genuine discontent among officials 'inside the building'. 'Not everyone's on board at all,' he told me, referring to older Chinese diplomats raised on the mantra of 'hide your weaknesses and bide your time' now having to adjust to the assertive and at times downright hostile rhetoric of the young wolf warriors.

Multiple foreign-policy analysts from Chinese universities expressed similar sentiments to me, believing the new, aggressive style that was so popular with China's patriotic youth was harming the country's efforts to win friends and influence abroad. But they'd rarely want to express that view on the record.

There were others, of course, who were more than happy to play to the Party's tune. Chen Hong, a Shanghai-based academic, enthusiastically courted media attention, writing columns in the jingoistic *Global Times* blaming Australia for the diplomatic woes, appearing on Chinese state TV and making himself accessible to foreign media. During a phone interview, I asked him if he thought it was all Australia's fault, to which he replied 'yes', confidently assuming that a reasonable Australian audience would agree with him.

Other Australia-focused Chinese analysts privately expressed their dismay that Chen was monopolising the 'Chinese voice' in Australia's media at the expense of more rational, moderate opinions. But by this point, the country was in such a tight political clamp that no one else in the small Australia studies sphere would dare talk to me. One academic fumbled a series of excuses over WeChat before telling me I'd have to get permission from his superiors to do an interview.

'Sure, who do I contact?' I texted.

'I don't know,' he replied.

Another, Li Jianjun, would send articles in WeChat groups full of Australian business types piling on the Morrison government. He was fairly active, so I contacted him to organise a beer near the Foreign Studies University in north-west Beijing where he taught.

I arrived to find a Communist flag hanging from the gates of the campus but I couldn't find the obscure whiskey den he'd chosen as a meeting place. Finally, after asking around, I went to the back of a compound next to the campus, up some stairs and into a massage parlour where a stern-looking receptionist pointed me to a door down the hall.

Inside I found a dark cocktail bar, empty save for one awkward-looking middle-aged man.

Professor Li—an Australian expert—was clearly nervous about meeting an Australian journalist. But over an expensive imported VB, he showed a very good understanding of Australia's China debate and also expressed reservations about the effect 'Wolf Warrior' diplomacy was having on China's image abroad.

He also made some solid points about the board of a national Australia–China foundation that the Morrison government had established. After years of slotting friendly business types into engagement roles, the Morrison government decided to assign a mixed group of Australians for this new initiative, including one who worked for a dissident media outlet linked to Falun Gong and others who had written critically about the Communist Party.

The group certainly had more balance and a more well-rounded grasp of China than previous boards, but Li pointed out that the Chinese side would never deal with them.

'Why would Morrison appoint them to a board which was purely set up to enhance diplomatic ties with China?' he asked.

Good point. It was nice to hear a rational voice, but Li rebuffed my suggestion that in future I occasionally call him for on-the-record comment.

'With Morrison in power, what's the point of doing interviews?' he said.

I suspected it wasn't Morrison who was spooking him. China had increasingly become a place where hawkish voices dominated the public domain, and the moderates knew to keep their heads down.

Later the Australian government cancelled both Chen's and Li's visas on national security grounds, ending their ability to travel to the country in which they specialised. They ridiculed the move as a sign of Australia's fervid paranoia about China, but a person involved in making the decision later told me Chen had a second job aside from being an academic. He seemed less like an intelligence operative to me and more of a blunt instrument, who only helped to harden Australian opinions towards China with his hawkish commentaries.

So with little to film for these continuous diplomatic stories and few people willing to speak, I was left to stand on footpaths in the middle of Beijing and beam in live to Australian bulletins giving my own version of the latest reaction from China, an inferior form of journalism to getting people speaking on the record.

In time, it became increasingly hard to even do that. Patrolling security guards, or even random pedestrians, would inform police, who would then turn up, demand press cards and disrupt the filming.

On one occasion a middle-aged man claiming to be plain-clothes police demanded we pull the plug then and there.

This sort of annoyance became a predictable part of the job.

———

With several fellow Australian journalists booted out earlier in 2020 and no new correspondents from any foreign media allowed to travel to China, Beijing was becoming quiet.

Brant had been made to wind up his posting once the coronavirus took hold, a whirlwind end to three months in which he chased the virus from Wuhan to the *Diamond Princess* cruise ship in Japan and then on to the earliest outbreak in South Korea. He was being hurried out by HQ before flights were cancelled, and the security guards wouldn't even allow us into his compound to help pack because of virus-control measures.

My colleagues and I were deflated about how difficult it was to do any meaningful journalism, but we pressed on. I used the time to do a bit of office decorating. The walls of the ABC bureau are covered in fading collages of photos showing correspondents, producers and cameramen at work. From Richard

Thwaites standing in the middle of an interested crowd in Mao suits in 1978, to Sally Neighbour in the 1980s, to Eric Campbell, Jane Hutcheon and Stephen McDonnell, the walls told a history of intrepid journalists, street-smart producers and epic adventures.

But the walls needed an update.

Multiple teams had rotated through since the ABC last commissioned new photo boards, so I asked Cecily Huang to help select a 'greatest hits' collection of photos and get them designed and printed on large cardboard posters. For most of the boards, there were no problems. But in one room, I wanted to complement a special board that documented the ABC's coverage of the Tiananmen Square crackdown in 1989. There was a blank space perfectly suited to a 'Hong Kong Protests 2019' board, featuring stunning photography that our camera teams captured of the demonstrations and the police clashes.

We designed one, but staff at two separate printing shops in Beijing, having examined the photos we wanted to use, told us they couldn't make the board. One print-shop boss told us he would have to report us to the police.

It was a small issue in the scheme of things, but it summed up the mood of the place.

The wall remained empty.

Even the history of the ABC bureau was subject to the whims of censorship.

With the Chinese Foreign Ministry indefinitely stalling a visa for the ABC's next Beijing bureau chief, Sarah Ferguson, and with Covid scuttling all new journalism work-visa applications, I clearly wasn't leaving Beijing anytime soon.

Yinan and I had spoken about trying for a baby. I'd always wanted to put off children until my late thirties, but that was easy for a man to say. It looked as though we would spend at least another year in Beijing as the world sorted itself out, so perhaps we could benefit from China's success against Covid.

As cases in the United States and Europe soared, China squeezed the virus down to negligible daily new numbers. Compulsory tracking apps that you couldn't opt out of became the key factor in stopping people from outbreak zones moving around. The economy largely bounced back and we travelled to China's Hawaii, Hainan island. I'd always avoided going there due to visions of oversized hotel developments and thousands of screaming kids running wild at the beach, but in the middle of the year it was empty, less because of the pandemic than because many Chinese regarded the June humidity as too stifling.

While the resorts did have a concrete colossus feel, the island had plenty of local fishing villages where, sitting beachside at sunset with fresh fish and a chilled bottle of Tsingtao, it really felt like bliss.

A baby on an adjacent table smiled at us. Yinan and I cooed back, making faces and waving as the baby girl's family laughed and greeted us.

Then the young-looking father got up, walked over, held out his hand and said, 'Bill, good to see you again.'

Astonished, I looked him in the eye but couldn't quite place him.

'We worked together in Xinhua,' he said, 'on the *World News* program.'

Like a lightning bolt from ten years earlier, I suddenly realised the face looking back at me was once a skinny kid in his early twenties called Zhong Xie. Back then, he and the other young guys in the office looked like teenagers who had snuck into a newsroom, shy, not particularly confident and very much learning the ropes.

Now here he was, at an obscure seaside village on an island 3000 kilometres south of Beijing with his wife, baby and parents.

Zhong Xie had left Xinhua years ago to pursue more fruitful endeavours. He now worked at China's Commerce Ministry, the very organisation involved in restricting and banning Australian imports due to political tensions. Just weeks earlier I was at a farcical press conference trying to question the Commerce Minister about why he wouldn't take a call from his Australian counterpart to discuss the bans.

Zhong Xie and I chatted a little and then returned to our seafood dinners without undertaking the one ritual standard in such situations.

He didn't ask me for my WeChat and I didn't ask him for his.

It went unspoken but we both knew it wasn't politically 'convenient' anymore for a Commerce Ministry employee to have an Australian journalist chatting to him online.

They were flying back to Beijing the next day. As Zhong and his family got up and put the baby in the pram, we waved them off.

'Maybe we'll run into each other again in Beijing,' he said, referring to a city of 20 million.

The golden sun disappeared behind the tropical water, the balmy air lingered and I ordered another cold Tsingtao.

After five years, it was nice to just stop and enjoy it.

A week later, back in Beijing, we attended birthday drinks for Stephen McDonnell at a small Beijing pub that once upon a time had an Australian owner called Louis. Well over 70, Louis had packed up his life as a furniture importer and moved with his wife to Beijing to open an Italian-style restaurant and pub called Godfather's. They never quite had the right visa and Louis had told me he would have to do border runs to South Korea every three months to go through customs, drink a coffee at Starbucks and then board an afternoon flight back to Beijing in time to reopen the business for evening trade.

Louis also had a problem with local partners doing him over and staff stealing money from the till. It sounded like an exhausting pursuit for a couple in their golden years and it was hard to understand why they kept going.

Eventually, Louis' restaurant was taken over by the Chinese partner.

Godfather's was gone. It was now named Master Feng's.

That night it was boisterous as journalists young and old gathered to wish Stephen a happy birthday. He was one of the great survivors of the Beijing foreign media scene. The *Global Times* or nationalistic WeChat accounts had often attacked him, and he'd had a few stints in visa exile. But here he was, fifteen years in Beijing, still going strong.

Steve Wang was there too, getting stuck into the beers. His wife was newly pregnant and he was enjoying the benefits of childlessness while he still could. With half a dozen lagers in him, he leaned on my shoulder and told me I should have a baby.

'It's time,' he joyfully slurred with that big Beijing smile. 'It's time to grow up.'

Cheng Lei was there too, engaging and humorous as always. Yinan had a longer chat with her in which Cheng Lei joked about a prominent CGTN colleague hogging all the closet space when they had to share a cruise-ship room together on a recent trip to Papua New Guinea to cover the G20 meeting. Hardly state secrets.

I briefly chatted to her about arranging a game of tennis sometime.

We never got around to it, though.

Coronavirus restrictions had closed half of the city's courts and I was soon preoccupied by Yinan's news that she had become pregnant. We chose a private hospital and had a very early scan, listening to the accelerated heartbeat of the fetus with a mix of joy and crippling anxiety. If it was time to grow up, I was glad I had nine months to mentally adjust.

Yinan went off to host a summer camp for children for her theatre company, taking naps between sessions as the early pregnancy fatigue set in.

Over in America, Black Lives Matter protests and Covid dominated the headlines, but I was not unhappy that things had gone quiet where I was. In those midsummer weeks, I was even able to organise my first assignment in months. Steve, Cecily and I were taking the train across Shandong province to Qingdao, the city of the famous beer. Somehow I'd convinced my bosses to send us to a beer festival—an idea that once would have seen me laughed at. Now, with the pandemic, it was a miracle they were holding the festival at all.

The annual celebration of malt, hops and yeast would be a showcase of China's virus containment, a boozy, rowdy tribute to a country that fumbled the outbreak early before setting an example for densely populated countries by taking it extremely seriously.

It was a dream assignment and, with new network-wide Covid risk-assessment processes to deal with, I was hastily organising the forms while stocking up on masks.

Then Zoe Daniel randomly sent me her text message inquiring about Cheng Lei's disappearance. I made some inquiries but didn't follow up as much as I should have. It all sounded a bit too extreme to be real.

I had an assignment to organise, and in order to get taxpayer bang for buck, we rolled in a second feature about cockroach farming. Shandong was known to have quite a few farms harvesting the dreaded pest for use in Chinese medicine and livestock feed. Cecily had managed to get us into one such farm on the way to the beer festival, and for an afternoon we filmed the type of story we used to do before everything became so political, a 'slice of life' curiosity piece involving a billion cockroaches scuttling around us in pitch-black darkness.

Wedged between narrow shelves with foul-smelling food waste dripping onto him, Steve filmed for hours in an intensely humid hangar that had been specially designed to encourage breeding. I headed in with him to film the piece to camera. Drenched in sweat, immersed in the stench and with the walls jumping around me, I delivered two takes and climbed back out.

But Steve is the quintessential professional. He insisted on shooting until he had the makings of something he was proud to put his name on.

Reeking of sweat and the foul smell of rotting food, we took the train on to Qingdao, lugging the gear up and down the giant stairs of China's high-speed rail stations. At each station, the lifts were either out of order or we couldn't find them.

'How do people in wheelchairs manage?' Steve pondered, sowing the seeds for a future feature story we never got to do.

The festival turned out to be busy and vibrant, despite locals saying it was subdued compared to normal years. We filmed boozy retired soldiers reuniting with their mates over jugs of the local drink, tourists who rarely imbibe tentatively sipping from large yard glasses for the sake of a selfie, and Qingdao locals who rarely abstain slamming down round after round. Chinese pop music blasted, young kids danced, elderly grandparents strolled up and down, and the locals chatted away, shirts rolled up over generous bellies, empty jugs of beer piling up on the tables.

In between shoots, I told Steve that he wouldn't be the only one expecting a baby.

He was stunned. We were both growing up. A jug was in order. We clinked glasses over fresh-cooked prawns and carried on working, filming revellers, families and anyone who would stumble in front of our camera.

Never had I seen people in China so happy to be interviewed. Some were rushing up to give us their thoughts, the amber liquid breaking down the barriers. Buskers would come around and offer to play three songs for 50 yuan, about ten bucks. After we'd finished filming, we forked out the money and sat at the outdoor tables singing Chinese rock ballads with jugs of fresh beer and steamed fish.

Locals nearby sang along. The late evening slid into the early hours of the morning. The outdoor tables remained busy, young men with sharp haircuts rushing in and out with plates of scallops and prawns and then sneaking down to the road to smoke cigarettes with local girls.

It was high summer in China, a golden window to take in the atmosphere and forget about the pandemic, the trade war, Hong Kong's woes and the ever-present shadow of politics.

I was lucky and thankful to be there.

The next day we headed back to Beijing and everything changed.

ACKNOWLEDGEMENTS

This book was only possible in the first place because of the faith Australian taxpayers (indirectly) placed in me to be the ABC's China correspondent, so I'm forever grateful for that opportunity. Thanks to Gaven Morris, Dee Porter, Gavin Fang and Matt Brown for your guidance from afar during my time in this role.

And on the ground in Beijing, thanks to former China bureau chief Matt Carney for his help and advice, to Brant Cumming for sharing some of the most extraordinary moments with humour and memorable observations, to Charles Li for always helping me to see the big picture, to Cecily Huang for pushing me to see the human side in all stories, and to Steve Wang for your great friendship.

Also to ABC colleagues Peng Ming and Lina Qiao for your help, particularly when the shit hit the fan at the end.

Outside the bureau, my thanks go to Phil Wen and Stephen

McDonell in particular for sharing the best of the Beijing journalistic days in the ever-shrinking Australian press corps.

To my mother, Penny, who always ensured we had the ABC 7 pm news on while I grew up. She sadly didn't live to see me go to China for the ABC (or get rushed out), but I'm sure she would have been proud.

Finally to Yinan, thanks for your overwhelming positivity, enthusiasm and sense of adventure, which I'm sure will shine through in our son.